*John Finerty Reports
the Sioux War*

John Frederick Finerty cut a wide swath on General Crook's summer expedition against the Sioux. Standing a willowy six foot, two, with auburn hair, an ever-present mustache and chin puff, and a gregarious personality, the fearless twenty-nine-year-old reporter was a determined newshound who wielded, as one fellow campaigner remembered, "pencil and carbine with equal facility." Elmo Scott Watson Papers, Newberry Library, Chicago.

John Finerty Reports the Sioux War

Edited by
PAUL L. HEDREN

University of Oklahoma Press   Norman

Publication of this book is made possible through the generosity of Edith Kinney Gaylord.

LIBRARY OF CONGRESS CATALOGING-IN-PUBLICATION DATA

Names: Finerty, John F. (John Frederick), 1846–1908, author. | Hedren, Paul L., editor.
Title: John Finerty Reports the Sioux War / edited by Paul L. Hedren.
Other titles: Chicago times (Chicago, Ill. : Weekly : 1861)
Description: Norman : University of Oklahoma Press, [2020] | Includes bibliograph-
  ical references and index. | Summary: "When writing his book 'War-Path and Bivouac,' John Finerty rewrote his war-time narrative almost entirely, adding matter here and deleting or ignoring details there. Appearing here are the original detailed 1876 Sioux War dispatches to the *Chicago Times* newspaper, all judiciously introduced and annotated"—Provided by publisher.
Identifiers: LCCN 2020004165 | ISBN 978-0-8061-6505-9 (hardcover)
ISBN 978-0-8061-9100-3 (paper)
Subjects: LCSH: Indians of North America—Wars—1866–1895. | Black Hills War,
  1876–1877. | Crook, George, 1829–1890. | Custer, George A. (George Armstrong), 1839–1876. | Finerty, John F. (John Frederick), 1846–1908. War-path and bivouac. | Indians of North America—Wars—1866–1895—Journalists. | Black Hills War, 1876–1877—Journalists. | Journalists—Great Plains—Biography.
Classification: LCC E83.866 .F495 2020 | DDC 973.8/2—dc23
LC record available at https://lccn.loc.gov/2020004165

The paper in this book meets the guidelines for permanence and durability of the Committee on Production Guidelines for Book Longevity of the Council on Library Resources, Inc. ∞

Copyright © 2020 by the University of Oklahoma Press, Norman, Publishing Division of the University. Paperback published 2022. Manufactured in the U.S.A.

All rights reserved. No part of this publication may be reproduced, stored in a retrieval system, or transmitted, in any form or by any means, electronic, mechanical, photocopying, recording, or otherwise—except as permitted under Section 107 or 108 of the United States Copyright Act—without the prior written permission of the University of Oklahoma Press. To request permission to reproduce sel ections from this book, write to Permissions, University of Oklahoma Press, 2800 Venture Drive, Norman OK 73069, or email rights.oupress@ou.edu.

To my grandchildren,
Gabriella, Sophia, Emma, Kate,
and Finn, who shares a birthday

Contents

Preface	ix
Acknowledgments	xvii
1. Finerty's World	1
2. Preparing for War	25
3. Life on the Trail	45
4. The Rosebud Battle	82
5. Loafing Hangs Heavily upon Us	100
6. The Trail Leads to Terry	142
7. Mud, Mules, and Blood	164
8. Deadwood Gold and the End of the Trail	200
Appendix: Finerty's Sioux War Dispatches Published in the *Chicago Times*	229
Notes	231
Bibliography	251
Index	257

Preface

I CONFESSED IN *Rosebud, June 17, 1876*, to my own shallow understanding of John Frederick Finerty's contribution to the historiography of Crook, the Rosebud Creek fight, and the Great Sioux War. Like the scholars and aficionados I chided there and here, myself among them, I knew well of Finerty's book, *War-Path and Bivouac*, an indispensable memoir of Crook's campaign against the Sioux and Northern Cheyenne Indians in 1876 (and Miles's brief campaign against Sitting Bull and many of those same Indians in 1879). I've used the book repeatedly in virtually every Sioux war history I've written. My confession in the *Rosebud* preface materialized in light of my discovery of Finerty's newspaper stories appearing summer-long in the *Chicago Times*. An early objective in the Rosebud project was to collect, digest, and fully utilize every newspaper account from that campaign and battle that I could lay my hands on. It was a massive undertaking and an incomparable body of material. Five full-time reporters accompanied Crook to the field, most of them writing for multiple papers. Another half dozen officers and scattered civilians penned additional occasional stories for hometown newspapers. The army column even welcomed a full-time illustrator, who sketched scenes from the campaign and also wrote letters to his paper. These various newspaper accounts comprised a veritable mountain of vibrant primary source material, with very little of it having been used by previous Rosebud scholars.

I met my objective, but as I handled this mass a revelation occurred when reading Finerty's telegrams and letters to the *Times*. As much as I thought I knew the book, in his news columns I kept encountering side notes, amplifications, and discourses original to the campaign that were nowhere in the published volume. It quickly dawned on me that I had at hand an entirely new body of material on Crook's summer operation, spanning the organization of his column in Cheyenne and at Fort Fetterman, the Tongue River Heights skirmish, the battles at Rosebud Creek and Slim Buttes, the Sibley scout, and the Black Hills gold rush and Deadwood. I grew ever more assured that those stories deserved proper assembly and availability to the community at large.

My exuberance notwithstanding, a fundamental question demanded an early answer. Just how different were Finerty's newspaper texts from his book? To explore the point I compared the two versions side by side, virtually paragraph by paragraph, a challenge slightly eased since both are relatively chronological. I presumed, of course, that Finerty's newspaper narratives formed the basis of the book and that I'd see substantial blocks of identical texts in each form. I presumed, as well, that his many telegrams from the field also informed the text in some apparent way. My presumptions were mostly incorrect.

First off, I was immediately struck by how little of Finerty's newspaper narrative was replicated straightforwardly in the book. More than the added connective texts where necessary, I discovered that Finerty almost wholly rewrote his newspaper columns when creating *War-Path and Bivouac*. The book is a gem, no doubt about that, but the newspaper stories comprise a jewel of another sort. What we have are two almost entirely separate renditions of the same story, each unique and important in its own right, one perceptively "in the moment" and the other delightfully reflective.

I was startled, as well, by the wealth of *Chicago Times* material that did not find its way into the book. Finerty seemingly purposely excised virtually all of the poetical asides that were commonplace in the newspaper copy. They may seem strange to modern readers, and perhaps seemed strange in 1890 to Finerty as he went about repurposing his news columns. I took them as unique reflections of a cultured Irishman on an American Indian war landscape, and a sense perhaps of conviviality on the trail or around an evening campfire. As well, virtually nothing in Finerty's telegrams from the field made their way into his book. In their immediacy, they represented headline news, variously reporting in brief the arrival of Crook's Indian auxiliaries, the Rosebud fight and its casualties, the Sibley scout, notice that Crook was safe after news of the Custer disaster devastated the nation, and the Slim Buttes fight. Many details were repeated in Finerty's letters, certainly, but not all, and not in the same manner.

More dramatically, I encountered other wholesale excisions of major segments of news copy. In his letters Finerty provided compelling descriptions of Cheyenne, Fort Laramie, and Fort Fetterman, but in the book those texts were abbreviated or largely eliminated. In a different manner, his descriptions of the Rosebud battle appearing in the newspaper focused largely on what he alone had experienced. For Finerty this was an exhilarating fight to be sure, and one senses that his adrenaline was still flowing as he scribbled his several reports of the action. The book version of the battle reads quite differently. There the immediate moment gave way to a graceful, reflective narrative that also respected major action occurring elsewhere on the field that he gained secondhand.

As with Finerty's newspaper descriptions of Cheyenne and Fort Laramie, in his letters he wrote extensively about Crook City, Deadwood, and Custer City, each a notable Black Hills gold rush community that in September 1876 was variously booming or in a noticeable wane. As well, in Deadwood Finerty opportunistically conducted lengthy interviews with three objective residents, Andrew R. Z. Dawson, William R. Keithly, and William H. Parenteau, inviting reflections from each on the general merits of gold in the Black Hills. Virtually none of this appeared in the book. Simply put, the gold rush was booming news in 1876 and all but passé in 1890.

Two other distinguishing features stand out in the newspaper columns alone. In his *Chicago Times* reports, Finerty described how Third Cavalry troopers at the Rosebud had trouble with their Springfield carbines, a weapon prone to jamming in combat. The troopers' problems with their guns represent an issue that has dogged the legacy of the Great Sioux War and its battles to the present day, and I was stunned to read Finerty's words, which were new to me. I immediately scoured *War-Path and Bivouac*, puzzled by how I could have somehow missed this, but Finerty's discussion of the problem, which appeared in his August 1 letter to the *Times*, did not make the book.

Likewise, one other important element common in Finerty's mid-to-late summer letters—his criticism of the army's effort and its leadership—was also nowhere in the book. Aside from his snivel over eating horse and mule flesh, Finerty offered virtually no criticism of Crook, Sheridan, or the army in *War-Path and Bivouac*, whether for their missed opportunities or their outright failings in the 1876 campaign. In the newspaper, one encounters quite a different story. In a reflective note written on June 28, for example, Finerty labeled the Rosebud fight "a barren victory, leaving the campaign as undecided as if no shot had been fired." In his July 11 published letter he concluded a segment with a puzzling quip. The ever-stoic Crook, on learning of Custer's death said little, but "kept up a big thinking." In light of the inactivity in Crook's sizeable camp at a time when others were dying in battle, one can see those simple words dished with cutting intent, especially in light of what followed in other letters. In Finerty's July 27 published letter he bristled over the weeks of inactivity in the Goose Creek camp. "Truly this is a nice little war for our newest brigadier general to have on hand. Let us hope for the best. It is the only thing we can do." Finerty messed with the Third Cavalry, first with Captain Alexander Sutorius and then with First Lieutenant Joseph Lawson. Officers in that regiment were not on warm terms with Crook, and Finerty's cynicism only worsened.

In Finerty's August 1 published letter he derides Crook, Sheridan, and the army over what by then was being viewed as a misguided campaign. Crook's inactivity pained the newsman and many in the Goose Creek camp. So did the manner in which Sheridan orchestrated this seemingly unwinnable war, with its questionably independent field commands, cavalry recruits who could not ride, infantry companies that were mere skeletons in size, and its widespread nonexistent marksmanship. The Indians, moreover, were not giving up the struggle. "This Sioux war will not be terminated this year," Finerty admonished. A month later the rhetoric sharpened even more. In Finerty's published letter of September 30, in a segment written in Dakota on August 31, he severely lambasted Crook, "a hard officer to serve under," with a "terrible disregard for shelter and other human necessities," who was "by no means popular with the rank and file . . . [while even many] officers do not seem to like him." In criticizing Crook, Finerty doubtless walked a fine line. He saw himself as a part of the military establishment. Soldiers were his friends and comrades. Their enemy was his enemy. Soon enough, others in Crook's Big Horn and Yellowstone Expedition also spoke unfavorably about the general, but Finerty never did again. His criticisms from the field in 1876 did not reappear in *War-Path and Bivouac*.

Before commencing this effort in earnest, I needed to confirm one other matter. Early on in the Rosebud project I sought out the *Chicago Times* in digital format and quickly learned that this newspaper is not available on any known online historical newspaper platform. This remains so. Moreover, these texts have not been collected and published by my newspaper friends, acknowledged elsewhere, who have otherwise so vigorously transcribed and made available so many other tabloid accounts of the Great Sioux War. Their work is a boon to researchers, as I trust this product also will be.

Preparing Finerty's newspaper texts proved rather straightforward. For the Rosebud project, I made oversize paper copies of Finerty's published dispatches from microfilms. Those I carefully transcribed and they appear here verbatim and chronologically complete. Finerty was a marvelous wordsmith. I did little to the stories themselves beyond what seemed conventional in preparing old texts for publication in a new guise. Occasionally Finerty presented individuals by surname only. In those instances I introduce them more formally. Such insertions are consistently in brackets. I did not alter the officer ranks given by Finerty, which ran the gamut and mostly reflected the honorific brevet system then in vogue. I corrected spellings occasionally, but not always, and I also noted most of those changes in the notes. I silently corrected words that seemed mishandled by the newspaper's compositors, in those instances believing that Finerty would have known the difference. And I often broke apart lengthy newspaper columns into coherent paragraphs. Finerty plainly understood such a simple rule of composition, but for the sake of efficiencies and space management his typesetters often ignored him or inserted simple clues in their own work—perceptible triple spaces and such—that respected, if almost imperceptibly, Finerty's original handiwork.

In ordering the texts I chose to present them chronologically, as noted by the initial date-line of each new published entry. This is not necessarily the way they appeared in the *Chicago Times*, where telegrams usually took timely precedence over letters. Finerty's letters often ran consecutively day by day. In the field, he obviously interrupted his daily narrative to provide immediate news. News by telegram was invariably repeated and amplified in the letters. The appendix provides a full newspaper chronology of it all, with a listing of headlines therein consistent with the narrative texts as presented here. Headlines, it should be noted, were invariably provided by Finerty's editors, and most particularly Wilbur Storey, who loved alliterative, epigrammatic headers sure to catch his readership's attention. Storey is most famously remembered in Chicago for a bold black headline in 1875 covering the story of a heinous murderer who, with noose around his neck and about to be hanged, was "JERKED TO JESUS." Finerty's headlines were not nearly so outlandish but were effective all the same, with "Gold and Gore," "Bound for Blood," "Fighting Folks," "Crook and the Crows," "Braving the Braves," "The Hunt for Hair," "A Siouxprise," and "Mule-Masticators" among the lot.

To round out Finerty's texts, I sparingly added annotations. My additions were guided by a premise that the essential story of Crook's campaign, his personnel, and their encounters with the Sioux are well known to most readers, making no need to expound on the obvious while appreciating Finerty's detail. I tended instead to address Finerty's literary and historical asides that undoubtedly were better understood in his own day but may seem strange to all but the rarest reader today. Modern-day Sioux war scholars are not known to read Byron, argue the strategies of Napoleon and his marshals, or rally to the Irish flag.

My opening introduction places Finerty in his day. Two brief but noteworthy and accessible biographical sketches have been the standards before this, Milo Milton Quaife's and Oliver Knight's respective 1955 and 1961 introductions to reprint editions of *War-Path and Bivouac*. Both are generally sound, and both utilized the logical sources available in the day. I accessed and examined again all of their sources and other materials pertinent to Finerty's exploits. The Internet has greatly expanded the spectrum of biographical source matter easily available to researchers, particularly at such sites as HathiTrust that make accessible rare and obscure books. I utilized the Internet to its fullest. Wilbert H. Timmons's introduction to Finerty's stories from Mexico in 1879 and Timmons's preserved papers at the University of Texas at El Paso also informed the project. While Timmons's introduction played heavily on Quaife's and Knight's biographical sketches, he uniquely also connected with Catherine P. Finerty, second wife of Finerty's son, John Jr. Catherine, a literary virtuoso in her own right and author of a delightful memoir, *In a Village Far from Home*, was a font of useful information on JFF Sr., as she called him, and I plumbed that entire informative exchange.

Finerty has yet to receive a full biographical treatment. His was a complicated life lived in multiple universes. Service as a reporter in the American Indian wars dominated his existence in his late twenties and early thirties. Firebrand Irish politics and nationalism dominated his life before and after his work in the West. Through it all ran a career in journalism and American politics. Today the lens is clearer. It seems safe to suggest that his most memorable accomplishments occurred in the American West. I hope that my introductory words here and throughout add additional luster to the story of an extraordinary individual in a compelling time. Hopefully, as well, Finerty's newspaper dispatches from the Sioux war find the same welcome embrace that I've given them and that they deserve.

Acknowledgments

I AM GRATEFUL always to those who assist me in chasing details, large and small, provide copy materials from archival collections, comment on chapters, or simply bear with me as I prattle on about the wonders of the latest historical character or story line in my life, here John Finerty, and I accordingly extend warm thanks to Thomas Heski, Cannon Falls, Minnesota; Jim Dunphy, editor, *Little Big Horn Associates Newsletter*; Bill Butler, Indian Land, South Carolina; Bruce Liddic, Lancaster, Pennsylvania; Mike O'Keefe, Albuquerque, New Mexico; David Wolff, Spearfish, South Dakota; Paul Hutton, Albuquerque, New Mexico; Randy Kane, Crawford, Nebraska; Shelly Dudley, Guidon Books, Scottsdale, Arizona; Marvin Kaiser, Prescott, Arizona; Abbie Weiser, Special Collections, University of Texas at El Paso; Lisa Schoblasky, Special Collections, Newberry Library, Chicago, Illinois; Jerome Greene, Arvada, Colorado; Sandy Barnard, Wake Forest, North Carolina; Harl and Kay Dahlstrom, Omaha, Nebraska; William Lass, Mankato, Minnesota; Karen Raber, University of Mississippi, Oxford; and Eli Paul, Kansas City, Missouri. The artful map appearing here was produced by Robert Pilk of Lakewood, Colorado, whose clean-cut graphics have graced so many of my works.

Once again, my longtime friend and editor, Charles Rankin of Helena, Montana, deserves special thanks for so willingly shepherding another Hedren book, this one so quickly on the heels of *Rosebud, June 17, 1876*. I have long appreciated Chuck's keen sense of an evolving narrative and his artful, persuasive direction, but this time I knew I was also treading into his own realm of expertise in American journalism and western journalists. I stepped lightly at first but soon came to relish our exchanges. It was Chuck who encouraged me to look at Finerty in broader contexts, confident, for instance, that I'd discover—and enjoy—such matters as the greater world of contemporary battlefield journalism. I followed Chuck's suggestions to a T, expanding my introduction of Finerty and along the way encountering characters like Wilbur Storey and Junius Henri Browne, contemporaries whose imprints on JFF Sr. were unmistakable.

My able friends at the University of Oklahoma Press again gracefully handled another of the author's works and I am ever pleased with the efforts of Adam Kane, editor-in-chief, Steven Baker, managing editor, and Amy Hernandez, marketing assistant, who tended me well. This time, Steven connected me with Tim Bryant, copyeditor, who proved a perfect partner.

The long-suffering women of my life, wife Connie, daughters Ethne and Whitney, and stepdaughter Alicia are ever encouraging. They, too, have traveled literally and figuratively most of Finerty's Sioux war trail.

Thank you all.

CHAPTER I

Finerty's World

AMONG HISTORIANS AND STUDENTS of Custer, Crook, and the Great Sioux War, the name John Frederick Finerty is instantly recognized. The twenty-nine-year-old reporter for the *Chicago Times* rode with Brigadier General George Crook's Big Horn and Yellowstone Expedition in one of the three summer movements of the 1876 war, chronicling its day-to-day activities, its rich array of characters, the heady battles of Rosebud Creek and Slim Buttes, and the hairbreadth escape of the Sibley scout. Finerty remembered it again in an erudite memoir, *War-Path and Bivouac, Or, The Conquest of the Sioux*, published in 1890. Fearless in the hottest of action, Finerty seemed especially to enjoy the danger. Contemporaries assumed that fighting was in his Irish blood.

For all of *War-Path and Bivouac*'s lasting acclaim, those same astute historians and students of this war have universally ignored that narrative's remarkable roots.[1] In 1876 Finerty penned twenty-seven telegrams and letters from the field for his employer, the *Chicago Times* newspaper, where they appeared from mid-May through early October. In that span, rarely a week passed without news from Crook's camp. Often Finerty's stories appeared two and three times a week. Sioux war enthusiasts seem to have assumed that Finerty fully exhausted his newspaper file copy when preparing his book. To a degree he did, certainly, but as readers will quickly discern here, considerably more remains in those many dispatches from the field, enough to warrant their republication now. A parallel, suggesting the incongruity, might be drawn with having at hand John G. Bourke's compelling memoir, *On the Border with Crook*, and finding no need for his diaries, from which, of course, his book was largely drawn. And yet all along, Bourke's meticulously tended and now well-published daily journals have proved their enormous worth, even if one dealt in an earlier era with the manuscripts themselves preserved at the U.S. Military Academy or their microfilm versions. And so it is that we should have both John Finerty's *War-Path and Bivouac* and his war-time dispatches that appeared in the *Chicago Times*.

John Finerty was never a quiet man. Bits and pieces of his life are revealed quietly in his Sioux war dispatches and other writings. He was born in Galway City, Ireland, on September 10, 1846, to Michael J. Finerty and Margaret J. Flynn. His father, longtime editor of the *Galway Vindicator* and a devotee of the Young Ireland nationalism movement, died when the boy was two. Not much later his mother abandoned him when she and her family emigrated to the Southern States of America. John was brought up by an uncle, who provided an excellent classical education in the national schools and augmented the boy's studies with a private tutor. Finerty excelled in history and literature, to such a degree in fact that years later one of his colleagues at the *Times* remembered that "he possessed the widest sweep of classical and mediaeval lore and history of all the men of that remarkable news force." References to classical literature and continental lore and history abound in Finerty's Sioux war dispatches.[2]

That same fostering uncle, a pro-British estate manager, attempted to shield young Finerty from the roil of mid-century Ireland, an impoverished nation subsumed by the Great Famine and issues of accommodation as a subordinate element of the British Empire, but the opposite effect took hold. At age eleven Finerty relocated to Tipperary and was radicalized under the influence of Father John Kenyon, a firebrand Catholic priest and nationalist involved in the Young Ireland movement and the Irish Confederation. By age fifteen Finerty had joined the National Brotherhood of St. Patrick, a social and political organization embracing socioeconomic change and Irish independence. Finerty fled Ireland for America in 1864, barely ahead of arrest and prosecution for his rebellious activities. In America that same Irish nationalism was espoused by the Fenian

Brotherhood, and Finerty aligned with that movement almost immediately.[3]

In America, eighteen-year-old Finerty could hardly avoid getting enmeshed in the Civil War, and in August 1864 he enlisted in the Ninety-Ninth New York Infantry National Guard. Whether his service was driven by the "greatest desire for military knowledge," as one contemporary proclaimed, patriotic duty in a newly adopted nation, or simple economic survival is unclear. The Ninety-Ninth New York was a 100-day outfit detailed for duty at the Elmira Military Depot in western New York, an enlistment center early in the war now turned hellish prisoner-of-war camp for Confederate enlisted men. Finerty's service during the war appears limited to duty as a prison guard, unremarkable in itself although he entered the army as a private and was discharged one hundred days later as a second sergeant.[4]

Following his discharge in the winter of 1864–65, Finerty settled permanently in Chicago, a mecca for emigrating Irish. From there he remained active with the American Fenian movement and also connected with the Chicago daily press, where in coming years he was successively employed as a reporter and then city editor of the *Chicago Republican* (succeeded in name by the *Chicago Inter-Ocean* in 1872), the *Chicago Evening Post*, and the *Chicago Tribune*. In 1875 he joined Wilbur Storey's *Chicago Times* as a city reporter, in all likelihood drawn by Storey's open courtship in his news coverage and editorial page leanings of the laboring classes and Irish Catholics. It was an auspicious move. The *Times* enjoyed the largest daily circulation in Chicago, equaling the circulation of all other Chicago newspapers combined.[5]

The crotchety, eccentric Democrat Wilbur F. Storey acquired the *Times* in 1861 and built it into one of the nation's premier newssheets. Although supporting the preservation of the Union, Storey stridently opposed Lincoln and a war, as he saw it, "solely for the freedom of Southern blacks." But campaigns and battles sold newspapers and he favored having his own reporters in the Union camps and on Union battlefields. He instructed his newsmen to use the telegraph lines often, regardless of tolls. The paper's business manager remembered that it often took all the ready cash the paper could raise to pay those charges. In 1870 Storey sent one of his own men to Europe to cover the Franco-Prussian War. He established a London bureau to forward cable news, an innovation well ahead of its time. And he staffed his newspaper with keen-eyed opportunists ever intent on securing bold news. One of Storey's long-time associates, Franc B. Wilkie, remembered instances where colleagues would enter the Old Man's office and say, "Mr. Storey, such and such a thing has happened in Southwestern Texas. Shall we send a man down to work it up?" Storey's response was an invariable, "Yes, if you like."[6]

And so it was that Storey dispatched Finerty to Crook's campaign early in the Sioux war. Finerty related the invitation in the opening pages of *War-Path and Bivouac*. Clinton Snowden, the paper's city editor and Finerty's boss, cornered his underling one day and told him that Storey wanted a man out with the Big Horn and Yellowstone Expedition, then forming in the Department of the Platte. "If you don't care to go, you needn't see Mr. Storey," Snowden added. The legacy of such assignments ran deep at the *Times* (as did the writing of memoirs later on) and Finerty agreed in an instant, though when subsequently meeting with Storey he expressed some confusion over whether he was joining Custer or Crook. Storey brusquely set the matter straight. He would accompany Crook, "who knows more about Indians, [and] is likely to do the hard work." That the gray-haired senior directed Finerty to Crook's camp doubtless saved the eager reporter's life, appreciating as history so plainly tells of Finerty's own fondness for riding at the front, and the horrendous end for all who rode with Custer at the Little Big Horn. Storey likewise advised Finerty to "spare no expense and use the wires freely, whenever practicable," and indeed he did.[7]

Storey had no intention of ignoring Custer, however, and separately engaged Mark Kellogg of Bismarck to report on Terry's and Custer's movements. Kellogg primarily reported for the *Bismarck Tribune*, but, like many newsmen of the day, including others who rode with Crook's column, he provided separate original copy to other newspapers caring to engage him. When Kellogg was killed with Custer, Storey promptly dispatched another of his Chicago men, Charles Diehl, to the Yellowstone River to carry on the work. For a short while, Diehl and Finerty consorted in the same camp while carefully avoiding each other's prime reporting assignments.[8]

Of Storey's wartime reporters, Diehl and Wilkie among them, Finerty was clearly the Old Man's favorite. Diehl acknowledged that the *Times* recognized Finerty as the dean of their war correspondents and that he, like Storey, held his colleague in high esteem as both a brilliant writer and a gallant campaigner. Wilkie, who had covered Civil War battles and the Franco-Prussian War for Storey, likewise recognized Finerty as one of the most valuable men on the paper, and a "species of factotum," adding in his own memoir, "His greatest work was his correspondence from the front during the Indian war in the seventies. He showed himself to be the possessor of undaunted courage, and of an endurance which no hardship could impair." The bullets, rain, snow, dust, mud, and horsemeat permeating Finerty's news copy and subsequent book clearly made lasting impressions, as colleagues and readers, then and now, so plainly comprehended and admired.[9]

Finerty returned to Chicago from the Sioux war in early October, and on the sixth penned a final note to his *Times* readers. After a tease at his own expense about a sunburned nose and a distaste for horsemeat, he allowed that he did his best to report the Sioux expedition without exaggeration or malice. Moreover, he could hardly conceive of anything more exciting or distressing than that which occurred in the summer and fall of the centennial year on the lands between the Big Horns and the Belle Fourche. Storey, who as Finerty remembered, "was by no means liberal of praise, gave me his best congratulations, and I settled down again, for a while, to the routine of journalism and city life." Campaigning with Crook had provided the adventure of a lifetime. But then again, Finerty lived a life of adventure.[10]

Finerty never penned any semblance of an autobiography and no body of personal papers or letters is known to exist. In 1941 his son, John Jr., a Washington, D.C., attorney of considerable repute, remembered once having manuscripts and letters belonging to his father, including a notebook containing, among other things, entries made during the Sibley scout and the Battle of Slim Buttes, "but they have entirely disappeared." [11] Historians today are bequeathed only his official writings, of which fortunately there is much, and sketchy biographical essays by contemporaries, usually for various forms of encyclopedia. As the reader pores through the disparate body of newsprint matter, it is often difficult to distinguish between Storey's pushing Finerty to his next dramatic assignment and Finerty's own gravitation toward it. Regardless of the push or pull, a succession of major field assignments came Finerty's way for the duration of his employment with the *Times*.

Three notable back-to-back but shorter assignments took Finerty from Chicago in 1877. He first visited and reported on the so-called Nicholls-Packard dispute in Louisiana. Former Confederate general and Democrat Francis T. Nicholls and Republican Stephen B. Packard disputed the Louisiana gubernatorial election in 1876, each claiming the office. President Grant sided with Packard, but a commission eventually awarded the office to Nicholls, a turn effectively ending the era of Radical Republicanism in the state and inaugurating a century of Democratic rule. Then in July Finerty ventured to Pittsburgh to report on the railroad strife engulfing the city, where a wave of labor unrest and violence as part of the Great Railroad Strike of 1877 claimed the deaths of forty individuals and the burning of the city's Union Depot and thirty-eight other structures in its rail yard. After a week of rioting, federal troops intervened and quelled the unrest.[12]

Later in 1877 Storey sent Finerty to Texas to report on the border troubles plaguing the Rio Grande. For nearly two months he explored the difficulties and challenges of a boundary area beset with Indian raiding, horse and cattle thieving, Mexican renegades, American border ruffians, and transborder retaliations by American troops. At one point he ventured into Mexico as far south as the Cedral mines in the northern Mexican state of Coahuila, a place of intrigue and substantial American investment.[13]

This eye-opening initial visit to Mexico was followed fifteen months later by an extended tour partly organized by Chicago-area businessmen and branded the American Industrial Deputation, intent on promoting commercial relations between the countries. Finerty and eighty merchants, politicians, and newsmen sailed from New Orleans on January 9, 1879, bound for Vera Cruz on the Gulf of Mexico, due east of Mexico City. There the excursionists entrained for the capital and spent nearly three weeks touring the city and its environs as well as several battlefields of 1847, including Molino del Ray and Chapultepec. Among highlights were a reception hosted by President Porfirio Diaz and a bullfight. During the stay, Finerty succeeded in interviewing Diaz, which he proudly heralded as "the first obtained by any American correspondent." He traveled in the company of seven other newsmen, so the occasion was indeed a coup.[14]

When the deputation embarked Vera Cruz for New Orleans on February 9, Finerty stayed on, intent on exploring and reporting from Mexico "on his own hook." For two additional months he made his way alone by train, stagecoach, wagon, and horseback from the Mexican capital northwest by way of Querétaro, Aguas Calientes, Zacatecas, Durango, Parral, and Chihuahua, to Fort Bliss, Texas. From there he continued to Chicago by way of Albuquerque, Santa Fe, Colorado Springs, and Denver. In Denver he chanced onto an old friend, fellow reporter from the 1876 campaign, Robert E. Strahorn. Finerty chronicled the trip in fourteen lengthy letters to the *Times* that appeared in the first four months of 1879. He liked much about Mexico, especially its hospitality, scenery, architecture, women, and upper classes, but his general impression was unfavorable, and in his final letter he emphasized the insecurity, instability, banditry, and lack of sanitation he encountered across the country.[15]

Finerty's Mexican travels had been another high adventure. He loved placing himself in his own stories, and when he did so readers then, as now, caught glimpses of the personality that so many friends and colleagues found endearing. Barely having crossed the border into Texas, dressed in a Mexican serape and wide-brimmed hat, with a battered face, and a Colt revolver hanging from a thimble belt around his waist, his driver, puzzled by the unkempt character needing a ride, flat-out confronted him.

"Do you know, stranger, I have a curiosity to find out who and what the h— you are anyway?"

"I'm not a fugitive from justice," was Finerty's surprised reply.

"By G-d," said he, "that 'ere d——d blanket shows you came from the other side, and you must be either a highwayman or a detective."

"I'm neither," Finerty spurted. "You'll have to guess again."

Finerty finally revealed his identity, and much to his inquisitor's astonishment. "You're the most dustiest and roughest lookin' newspaper man I ever seed."

"By this time the sun was above the horizon," Finerty recalled, "and I took a long survey of my countenance in a small pocket mirror. What I saw did not make me feel like Narcissus when he plunged into the water, attracted by his own beauty."

Finerty was a man of delightful prose, and succeeded again in serving up a captivating snapshot of a unique scene in the American West. His writings were full of them.[16]

The perpetually mobile and willing newsman was barely home when Storey dispatched him to the Indian Territory and Dakota for stories, and then to Montana to investigate border troubles of another sort. Many Sioux, including Sitting Bull and most of his followers, fled to Canada early in 1877, evading the U.S. Army only to encounter an indifferent British government and the country's own native inhabitants caught in their own struggles. For the Sioux this hegira was a time of great privation and hunger. Those were the days, however, when buffalo still roamed the Yellowstone and Missouri River countryside in dramatic numbers, and served as a powerful lure for transborder hunting by the American refugees. The U.S. Army and the American government viewed the matter as unfinished business from the 1876 war and repeatedly intervened when word came of Sioux incursions south of the border. On the present outing, Finerty hurried by rail from Chicago to Saint Paul to Bismarck, and by steamboat to Fort Peck, Montana.[17]

Finerty's travel occurred in early July, when the Upper Missouri country was yet a lush green. A plainspoken adherent of the notion of Manifest Destiny, that being the righteous redemption and remaking of the West in the image of agrarian America, he saw a land having significant grazing and agricultural potential, were it not for the lingering threat of Indian resistance. Soon enough Colonel Nelson Miles and a contingent of infantry, cavalry, and Indian scouts from Fort Keogh reached Fort Peck, where they were joined by troops from Fort Buford, Dakota. The deployment resembled an orchestration from the 1876 campaign, though on a modest scale. Finerty quickly recognized old friends from Crook's campaign, particularly among the Second Cavalry, the bulk of that regiment having transferred to Montana after the war. It was supposed now that Sitting Bull and his followers were hunting buffalo on the Milk River or a north-reaching tributary, Frenchman's Creek, both drainages sandwiched between the Missouri and the Medicine Line. In an interview with Miles, Finerty asked whether he would lead troops across the international border if an engagement with Sitting Bull led him there. Finerty easily remembered similar instances along the Rio Grande, where cross-border incursions by American troops stirred the ire of Mexican and American authorities. The colonel's response was perfectly coy. "That must be an after consideration," said Miles. "I can hardly give a specific answer at this stage of the proceedings."[18]

The quick campaign was spirited and succeeded in driving Sitting Bull and his people across the border. At its climax, Major James Walsh of the North-West Mounted Police crossed the line and conferred with Miles. Their political viewpoints were diametrically opposite. Sitting Bull's people had gone south to hunt buffalo, and Walsh was not certain that that constituted a hostile act. "The people were hungry," he plainly observed. Miles allowed that he was following orders, explaining that hunters did not always confine themselves to game, but also killed settlers and stole horses. Walsh obviously admired Sitting Bull. Finerty thought that were it not for his Irish accent, he might actually be conspiring with the Indians.[19]

The highlight of Finerty's second campaign against the Sioux came when Walsh invited him to cross the border and visit Sitting Bull's camp. "I had a not unnatural desire to represent the American press before the Teton chiefs in their war paint, especially as the famous red marauders were making themselves quite at home, and supposedly comfortable, on British soil." The American Sioux were then encamped on Mushroom Creek at Wood Mountain, a distinctive highland region with an abundance of poplar trees surrounded by an otherwise barren prairieland. A council of sorts occurred on July 30 near Walsh's police post. Sitting Bull was present and listened intently as Walsh admonished the American Indians to stay north of the Medicine Line. Wait for the buffalo to come to you, he charged.[20]

One of the Sioux chiefs inquired about the individual sitting with Walsh. "This man is a friend of mine," he responded. "He writes for the white men's newspapers and will tell the straight truth about you." Several of the chiefs sprang forward and shook Walsh's and Finerty's hands, and the reporter quickly became an object of curiosity. One of them said, "The chiefs would like to hear the stranger talk." With Walsh's encouragement, Finerty stood and delivered a simple statement through an interpreter, assuring the chiefs that he was not a soldier, and that he had not come to spy on them. They knew, he said, why the soldiers had fired on them beyond the stone heaps (the distinctive boundary markers scoring the international line across the plains) but the "Americans do not desire to starve your families or yourselves if you cease to make war on them." It was an inspiring, self-satisfying moment. Irishman Finerty had turned diplomat.[21]

Although Finerty chanced onto a distinctive Sioux warrior whom he actually recognized—one of Crook's prisoners from the Slim Buttes fight in 1876—he never succeeded in interviewing Sitting Bull. The famous chief was plainly present in Walsh's and Finerty's meeting with the chiefs and broke a smile from time to time, but when the conversation tailed off he abruptly gathered his blanket and rode away. Walsh and Finerty explored the sprawling Sioux camp on Mushroom Creek the next day, and again Finerty spotted the chief, who seemed all the more unapproachable. "Tell Sitting Bull," Finerty told the interpreter, "that if he does not seek me, neither do I him." The interpreter laughed. "It is just as well not to take any notice." Finerty could finagle an interview with the Mexican president but not with the greatest of all Sioux chiefs.[22]

Finerty's Montana adventure ended in early August. Returned to Chicago, he had barely recovered before Storey dispatched him to the West again on what was his fifth field assignment in 1879. This time he journeyed by rail to Rawlins, Wyoming, and connected with Captain Guy V. Henry's battalion of the Third Cavalry, mustering against the Ute Indians in northern Colorado. The normally complacent Utes had revolted against their tyrannical agent, Nathan Meeker, killing him and others and the officer leading the initial relief, Major Thomas Thornburgh of the Fourth Infantry, plus ten of his soldiers. In Finerty's instance, this was the same Guy Henry who was memorably shot in the face in the Rosebud Battle in 1876. As in Montana, a host of Finerty's friends from that campaign were in this battalion as well. One veteran trooper who Finerty remembered as a model soldier, likewise recalled the newsman immediately. "You've been under fire with the regiment," he exclaimed boisterously. Henry similarly embraced the scribe, calling him "Finerty of Ours." Crook's aide, John Bourke, encountered Finerty then, too, remembering him as "an old campaign friend and one of the most gallant fellows on earth." But by the time Finerty arrived in southern Wyoming and advanced into Colorado the trouble had been quelled. Concluded one chronicler, at this late stage "it was a dead story from the standpoint of war coverage."[23]

Over the next several years Storey continued to utilize Finerty's keen eye and aptitude on an array of field assignments, engaging him on an extended tour of the southern states in 1880 and a summer tour in 1881 on the Canadian Pacific and Northern Pacific Railroads, both lines then unfinished but inching westward across respective prairielands. John Bourke, Crook's longtime aide-de-camp, recalled reading one of Finerty's letters to the *Times* reporting on the Canadian leg. Finerty noted that the music of the Ojibwa Indians of British America sounded to him just the same as that of the Sioux, Cheyennes, Crows, and Shoshones he had heard on his first Indian campaign. The note was important to Bourke, who had taken a special interest in such anthropological matters.

Finerty, when not afield, then mostly bided his time in Washington, D.C., as a *Times* correspondent in the nation's capital. There he and Bourke crossed paths often and always enjoyed, the aide remembered, "long and interesting chats about old times." Bourke was a devoted diarist and in his jottings invariably recalled Finerty's heroics and cool courage in the action on the Rosebud. He's an "old friend . . . holding a prominent place in these note-books," he penned on one occasion.[24]

Storey finessed one final Indian wars assignment from his favorite war correspondent. Finerty was in San Francisco when Storey hurriedly redirected him to Arizona in September 1881 in the wake of the so-called Cibecue Massacre, a treacherous killing of soldiers and Apaches that had gained national attention. Finerty made his way to Fort Thomas on the San Carlos Reservation in eastern Arizona and attached himself to the command of Captain Tullius C. Tupper of the Sixth Cavalry. Tupper trailed his company to Fort Apache, where they rendezvoused with Colonel Eugene A. Carr's column, and the larger command then revisited the Cibecue site. Carr commanded the Sixth Cavalry Regiment. As a lieutenant colonel of the Fifth Cavalry five years earlier, he was prominent in Crook's Sioux campaign and the fight at Slim Buttes. The veteran trooper recognized and welcomed Finerty immediately. The outing at this late stage proved to be another dead story, but Finerty made the most of it, remaining in the field until mid-October. In typical fashion, his dispatches to the *Times* carefully described the day-to-day movement of the column, a parched uninviting desert landscape, and the odd and interesting personalities encountered along the way. It was Finerty's final Indian campaign.[25]

In November 1881 John Finerty severed his ties with Wilbur Storey and the *Chicago Times*. Extended assignments in the preceding six years had taken him to Mexico, Canada, and coast to coast in America. He was Storey's favorite Indian war correspondent and had chased tribesmen in Wyoming, Montana, Dakota, Colorado, and Arizona, oft-times more literally than figuratively. One might suppose that Finerty had grown tired of such duty and wished to settle down. He was now thirty-five years old. He had been married briefly in 1877, but spouse Alice Radin died less than a year later. Importantly, Irish political matters beckoned again. That ceaseless spark had been an undercurrent in his life all along.[26]

Historians remember Finerty as a remarkable field reporter on repetitive Indian campaigns in the American West. Chicagoans remember him primarily as an Irish nationalist firebrand. Almost immediately upon severing his connection with the *Chicago Times*, Finerty organized the first Irish National Land League convention in Chicago. This was a local manifestation of a movement in Ireland aimed at helping poor tenant farmers by abolishing landlordism and enabling tenants to own the lands they worked. The convention raised $500,000 to support the cause, an astonishing sum for 1881 and equivalent to more than $12 million today. At the same time Finerty founded *The Citizen* newspaper in Chicago, a weekly sheet devoted to Ireland, Irishmen, and Ireland's political sufferings. An old colleague on the *Times* once asked Finerty why it was that he so stridently embraced the cause of Irish freedom and so hated the British government. His reply was simple: "If your father had been thrown into prison because he had nailed up a window of his newspaper office, to escape British taxation, you would be a rebel." That perhaps, plus careful mentoring by Irish radicals, helps tell a more complete story.[27]

Finerty's time in the nation's capital as a *Times* correspondent may have sparked another opportunity. In 1882 he ran for Congress as an Independent representing the Second Illinois Congressional District (mostly Chicago) and was elected that fall. He quickly immersed himself in the business of the chamber, delivering effective speeches and committee work in advocacy of such issues as the new navy and coastal fortification. Finerty ran for reelection two years later but was defeated. His Republican leanings and his support for the Republican presidential candidate, James Blaine, who in his own campaign inadvertently alienated Catholic voters, proved insurmountable obstacles for Finerty, whose district was mostly Democratic, mostly Irish-American, and mostly Catholic.[28]

In the years to come, Finerty remained fully occupied. He had his weekly paper, and he had a second wife, Sadie Hennessey, and children. He also attended the affairs of the Chicago Press Club and various Irish-American societies in Chicago, and busied himself with book writing and lecturing. Friends remembered him as a popular lecturer on Irish, cosmopolitan, and historical subjects. They said he never used notes or manuscripts but relied upon his memory for words fitting the subject. One speaking opportunity in 1905 took him to Helena, Montana, for the dedication on the state capitol grounds of a heroic-size statue of Thomas Francis Meagher, Irish-American patriot (whom Finerty knew well) and erstwhile Montana pioneer. Finerty's hour-long address, well received, was a full discourse on Irish history.[29]

Finerty published three books in his lifetime and bequeathed to his heirs one other book manuscript that was published decades after his passing. Of his published works, *War-Path and Bivouac, Or, The Conquest of the Sioux* was unquestionably his standout. He drew its story from his many essays appearing summer-long 1876 in the *Chicago Times*. He had a phrase in those stories, repeated often, referring to the "thread of his narrative," meaning simply his diary-like day-to-day journal. It was that chronological thread that formed the basis of the book. In his newspaper accounts Finerty often obligingly digressed from his day-to-day thread, particularly after combat and when Crook's campaign stalemated on Goose Creek in July. While still providing his editor with news copy from the front, on those palpably slower occasions he featured campaign anecdotes, assessments, and asides that did not always fit his running narrative. Many of those digressions are not in the book, and that they are published here allows Finerty to serve history once again, this time more fully.[30]

In studying Finerty's life, one obviously confronts and accepts his unbridled Irish patriotism. But what pervaded his life and legacy all the more, and what proves to be his lasting contribution, are his ties to the Great Sioux War. Beyond the confines of Chicago, even he must have recognized this fact. Crook's aide, John Bourke, celebrated the point repeatedly in his diaries, remembering his frequent encounters and spirited conversations with a friend who so greatly distinguished himself with such cool courage on the campaign.[31] When Finerty encountered Carr in Arizona the exacted memories were of Slim Buttes and Whitewood Creek in the Black Hills.[32] Veteran cavalryman and literary titan Charles King mentioned Finerty often in his writings. In a series of articles penned in 1889 for his hometown newspaper, the *Milwaukee Sentinel*, for instance, King recalled "that prince of good fellows and journalist, Finerty, of the Chicago *Times*," who at Slim Buttes "dropped his pencil for the minute and is blazing away with his rifle."[33] In King's classic memoir of the Fifth Cavalry's service with Crook in the centennial campaign, Finerty is affectionately embraced variously as that "reckless Hibernian," the newsman who flashed "pencil and carbine with equal facility," and "the gem of the lot."[34] Decades later and well after Finerty's passing, then General King still fondly remembered his friend from Chicago, telling an Order of Indian Wars dinner audience in 1921 of that "gallant and gifted Irishman who represented the *Chicago Times* all through that summer's meanderings," and who quipped with a sickly irony in the darkest days of the Starvation March that we'd live, since "we still have our horses!"[35]

In Denver in 1879, when Finerty was returning from his adventure in Mexico, he chanced onto Robert Strahorn of the *Rocky Mountain News*. The two newsmen had ridden together with Crook in 1876. The conversation Finerty recalled had nothing to do with Mexico, but focused instead on memories of Tongue River bluffs, Rosebud Creek, and Slim Buttes. We "knew each other well," Finerty chimed.[36] In Strahorn's own reminiscence written many years later, he too recalled the Chicagoan as a "brilliant newspaper man," who on the direction of his publisher, Wilber Storey, joined Crook's camp and not Custer's. "How narrowly a war correspondent sometimes escapes death," he rightly observed. Strahorn added one other charming detail that speaks volumes about this gem of the lot. Having almost miraculously survived the danger-fraught Sibley scout in early July 1876, Finerty blurted to his friends, "'I lost my saddle and bridle. I lost my pipe and blankets, and I lost my horse.' Then, bursting out with a loud cry, he reached the climax by raising his voice to its utmost pitch with 'But the worst of it all is I LOST MY TOOTHBRUSH!'" Strahorn's wife, Carrie, had her own recollections of her husband's Sioux war days, recording in her reminiscence in

1911 an encounter with Finerty: "There was old Jack Finerty of the Chicago *Times*. I have always had a notion that he stepped out from some place in Lever's novels; he was brave to rashness, and devoted to the interests of his great journal," meaning certainly the *Chicago Times* newspaper. Readers encounter mentions of Charles Lever and his novels repeatedly in Finerty's Sioux war letters. In the day, Lever was a version of Tom Clancy of another era.[37]

And what of Finerty's Sioux war stories appearing in the *Times*? They are of two types. Storey had instructed Finerty to use the telegraph wires as often as practicable, and that occurred . . . when practicable. Sometimes doing so was almost effortless. When the newsman passed Omaha and Cheyenne, he had immediate access to public wires. When at Fort Laramie and Fort Fetterman, he again had access to the wire, although now civilian traffic ran secondarily to government traffic. When in the field in the days before and after the Battle of the Rosebud, Finerty again had access to the telegraph but was first dependent upon couriers, and then priority military use of the line. His points of contact changed along the way. Instead of a routing by way of Fort Fetterman and Cheyenne, as was the case in Wyoming, messages from the trail in Montana and Dakota in August and September were still dependent upon couriers, but now routed to Fort Abraham Lincoln on the Missouri River, and after the Slim Buttes battle by way of Deadwood and Custer City to Fort Laramie. One determines in these essays that the communication occurred via telegraph when, second to the story's headline, one reads obviously "*Special Telegram*." This is an inconsistency, however. Telegrams were shorter and the words precise since each was costly.

One distinguishes Finerty's letters more easily. Invariably they were introduced with the line "*From Our Own Reporter*" second to the story's headline, and they were considerably longer. These were Finerty's running narratives, begun one day and perhaps continued the next and the next. Place and date lines are consistently present in Finerty's telegrams and letters and serve to document pauses on the trail or moments around an evening campfire when the scribe dutifully put pencil to paper and recorded the day. Letters required delivery by courier to the nearest mail service, whether post offices at Fort Fetterman, Bozeman (in the instance of one of Finerty's fellow newsmen and perhaps he also), Fort Abraham Lincoln, or Fort Laramie. (As yet, no Black Hills mail service existed, and in 1876 almost all written communications with the outside world relied upon independent express couriers and package services carrying mail to post offices at Fort Laramie, Wyoming; Camp Robinson, Nebraska; and Sidney, Nebraska.)

When one studies Finerty's Sioux war communications, several distinct matters bear consideration. For one, readers encounter disturbing words about Indians both in his news copy and his 1890 reminiscence. In Finerty's June 20 letter from the Goose Creek camp, written in the quiet lee of the Big Horn Mountains juxtaposed against a presumptive lingering adrenaline rush from the Rosebud battle, he digressed from his day-to-day narrative and wrote jarringly, seemingly thoughtlessly, about the Sioux—the enemy on this campaign—and about Indians generally. Finerty saw little virtue in this enemy. They were a "mysterious, untamable, barbaric, unreasonable, childish, superstitious, treacherous, thievish, [and] murderous" lot. Warriors were "fat, tall, and good looking, except in a few cases," while the squaws were "squatty, yellow, ugly, and filthy looking." The men were "lazy brutes," and the women "used as so many pack mules." Were such words not jarring enough, Finerty continued, branding the Sioux "veritable children of the devil," and all of them "lousy, greasy, gassy, lazy, and knavian." Extermination, he allowed, was an acceptable outcome on the Plains.[38]

Finerty's words are upsetting, and that they were penned in the immediate wake of a day-long battle where the outcome was so plainly disputed seems incredible. This is the first language of the sort known in Finerty's writings. One might remember that on the 1876 campaign he first encountered Indians of any sort just two days ahead of the Rosebud battle, when Crow and Shoshone auxiliaries joined Crook's column as scouts. Nowhere in Finerty's known history had he had such intimate contact with Indians before, let alone the people of the Plains and particularly the Sioux. That he could write so recklessly, even callously, is hard to fathom.

Such rhetoric beckons a simple question: Why? It seems way too simple to allow merely that Finerty was a nineteenth-century urban intellectual and a product and reflection of his day, an excuse offered by others in his case and commonly in such instances. But one wonders whether Finerty's character and outlook can be so easily distilled. Ironically, his employer, Wilbur Storey, had quite the opposite take, consistently embracing a moderate Indian viewpoint aimed at citizenship, agricultural providence, and individual land ownership, much in line with President Grant's Peace Policy. Storey saw the humanity in Indian people. Finerty's venom appeared to moderate slightly later that summer, particularly when reporting from the Slim Buttes battlefield in September. There he had his own unsettling brush with humanity after encountering for the first time on the campaign both living and dead Sioux women and children, the inevitable consequences of combat in a season when the morally charged strategy of total war played out on the Plains.[39]

Despite other contact with Western tribesmen in the coming years, Finerty's bleak outlook proved rather consistent. In rapid succession he returned to the West after the Sioux war to join other military campaigns, against Sitting Bull in 1879, the Utes that same year, and the Apaches in 1881. Also in 1881 he had close contact with Indians in Canada, intimate enough to discern and appreciate musical similarities between the Ojibwas in the north and the Plains tribes. And yet through it all, his condescending characterizations of the continent's natives barely changed. When exploring Sitting Bull's camp on Mushroom Creek in the Wood Mountain in 1879, while allowing that some of those Sioux had been cheated, cajoled, and robbed by their American interlopers, his balance played straight to an innate prejudice. He stood in the midst, he wrote, of "some of the greatest cut-throats on the plains, demons whose names are written in the shame and blood of the helpless and innocent, and who deserved to die a thousand deaths for their nameless crimes against decency and humanity." Each of these monologues, from 1876 and 1879, made their way virtually unaltered into his book *War-Path and Bivouac* in 1890. The passage of years had not softened his view.[40]

The passage of decades, not mere years, also invites a fresh look at John Finerty in the realm of battlefield journalism. By the time of the Great Sioux War, the role of war correspondent had come into its own, partly evolving worldwide out of journalistic exploits during the Crimean War in the mid-1850s, and in America gaining full flower during the Civil War. Great newspapers spurred the movement, driven by a thirst for dramatic, saleable news, and abetted by technological advances like the telegraph and undersea cables that enabled the timely dispatch of news from war front to office and continent to continent. Two distinct practices had emerged, one focused on the overall scene of the battlefield, a telling of how battles were won and lost, and the other much more intimately focused on the individuals involved. In one of Finerty's letters from the Sioux war, he invokes the name of William Howard Russell of *The Times* of London. Russell, a stocky Irishman with a flair for battlefield reporting, was his newspaper's "special correspondent" in the Crimea. Before Russell's emergence, wartime newspaper coverage commonly relied on shared news, or letters from junior officers, sources that were neither timely nor principled in the hallmarks of journalism and what constituted genuine news. With a mixture of cunning, persistence, and solid effort, Russell wrote frankly from the Crimea, providing stories often at odds with the British army's own accounting of affairs. In so doing he established himself as an exemplary war reporter, the first of his sort, while certainly enhancing his newspaper's prestige.[41]

The Times of London sent Russell to America at the onset of the Civil War, and early on he cut a highly visible path, with an introduction to Lincoln, a tour of the South (where he reported his own revulsion at the institution of slavery), and a full and frank report of Bull Run, which, as he saw it, amounted to a resounding Union rout and defeat. He earned the derisive and unshakable nickname "Bull Run Russell" for the effort. But Russell was hardly alone. Drawn by a tremendous demand for news coupled with ever-growing newspaper circulations in America, publishers flooded the conflict with correspondents. By one tally as many as 500 reporters covered the war for the North alone. The *New York Herald* fielded sixty-three men. The *New York Times* and *New York Tribune* each had at least twenty correspondents providing coverage, and smaller papers in cities like Cincinnati and Boston each had their own men at the front. After Wilbur Storey acquired the *Chicago Times* in 1861, he had no less than three reporters covering the war full-time, mostly focusing their attention on the Western Theatre, where a preponderance of Illinoisans served.[42]

The war coverage provided by this burgeoning Bohemian Brigade, the tongue-in-cheek name this crowd bestowed on itself, had its rough edges. The journalistic standards of objectivity and the core reporting of who-what-when-where-why were rarely adhered to. Reports from the field were often more imaginative than real, and speckled, as one critic put it, with "sensationalism and exaggeration, outright lies, puffery, slander, faked eye-witness accounts, and conjectures." Many senior officers on both sides distrusted the newsmen in their camps, fearing especially the betrayal of campaign intelligence. Correspondents were reviled if they somehow encouraged defeatism or took unpatriotic swipes at their respective governments. Some reporters savaged officers. Sherman and Grant each had rough goes with newsmen and Sherman despised them, vilifying the whole lot as "buzzards." Other officers learned that courting their trailing correspondents often benefited careers. The reputation of the youthful and flamboyant George Armstrong Custer as the "very epitome of a cavalryman," for example, was earned on the battlefield but made by the press.[43]

Despite such tribulations, Civil War newspaper coverage was devoured word for word and passed from hand to hand, the greater the detail the better. A large New York City newspaper could sell five times its normal daily circulation when it ran details of a great battle. The *Philadelphia Inquirer*, nearer the front, often sold 25,000 copies of a single issue to troops alone. Despite the Bohemian Brigade's scalawags, many correspondents measured up, providing solid coverage of battles won and lost, facts as they saw them, and poignant vignettes from the camps and battlefield.[44]

One gains the sense in reading Finerty's writings that he and fellow journalists were swashbuckling poet-warriors, proverbial "knights of the quill." Finerty particularly loved the thrill of riding at the head of the column, whether on the day-to-day trail, with Mills charging in the Gap at Rosebud, or prowling the Slim Buttes when shots still stirred the air. A fellow reporter on Crook's Rosebud campaign, Reuben Davenport of the *New York Herald*, wielded a weapon too, though out of sheer self-defense during Royall's panicked fight on Kollmar Creek. But such derring-do was not particularly common during the Civil War or on the western frontier. While neither the Union nor the Confederacy recognized correspondents as noncombatants, frontline battlefield exploits were the exception, and invariably remembered. At Bull Run, a *New York World* reporter picked up the fallen colors of the Fifth Massachusetts and attempted to rally the troops. During the Wilderness campaign, in an emboldened moment Henry Wing of the *New York Tribune* donned a Rebel butternut uniform to infiltrate Confederate lines and carry his report of a battle going poorly for the Union to the nearest telegraph station. Grandest of all was Junius Henri Browne of the *New York Tribune*. Browne took potshots at Rebel artillerymen at Fort Donelson, and at Vicksburg, when attempting to sneak past Confederate cannon aboard a Union barge. He was nearly killed when the boat was fired upon and destroyed. The correspondent was fished from the Mississippi and taken prisoner. Remarkably, after twenty months of incarceration in seven different Confederate prisons, Browne and fellow journalist Albert Deane Richardson escaped their confinement and made their way more than 300 miles through the Deep South before reaching Union lines near Knoxville in January 1865. Browne promptly wrote up his adventure in a sensational and enormously successful book, *Four Years in Secessia*, published in Chicago in 1865. It made him famous. Did bookworm Finerty read Browne's tome? It is hard to imagine not.[45]

There is no evidence that Finerty reported the Civil War, although his association with the *Chicago Republican* dates to the conflict's closing hours. That he was drawn to journalism in America in the first place may simply derive from a good education and the seemingly ever-present shadow of his father's own work in newspapers. That Storey sent Finerty to the Sioux war in 1876 seems to have occurred entirely by chance. Already by then, however, a new Bohemian Brigade of Indian war correspondents was making its own mark in the West. As with the Civil War, American newspapers devoured the great Indian battles, campaigns, and treaty events scoring the Trans-Mississippi in the postwar years, invariably relying on a mixed bag of coverage scooped from individuals on the scene or gained secondhand.

The intermittent and broadly scattered nature of western Indian intercourse and warfare presented unique reporting challenges, and yet despite all, a remarkable lot of newsmen met the test. Ridgeway Glover, writing for the *Philadelphia Photographer*, a monthly publication devoted to the photographic arts, went west in 1866, chiefly to photograph distinguished chiefs and Indian life. He reached Fort Phil Kearny, Wyoming, but was killed by Indians quickly thereafter. Glover penned three published letters, but none of his photographs from the Bozeman Trail are known to survive. Joe Wasson of the Silver City *Owyhee Avalanche* accompanied Crook to the field in Idaho in 1867, and joined him again in 1876. Henry Morton Stanley of the Saint Louis *Missouri Democrat* trailed across Kansas with Winfield Hancock in 1867. Debenneville R. Keim of the *New York Herald* accompanied Sheridan and Custer in Kansas in 1868, and although he was not with Custer at the Washita he reported the action fully. H. Wallace Atwell of the *Sacramento Record*, Edward Fox of the *New York Herald*, and several others reported the Modoc War of 1873. Atwell and Fox did not witness the murders of Brigadier General Edward R. S. Canby and other peace commissioners but were on the scene minutes later and broke the gruesome news. No less than five full- and part-time correspondents accompanied Custer to the Black Hills in 1874, including Nathan H. Knappen of the *Bismarck Tribune*, Aris B. Donaldson corresponding for the *Saint Paul Daily Pioneer*, James B. Power writing for the *Saint Paul Daily Press*, William E. Curtis representing both the *Chicago*

Inter-Ocean and *New York World*, and Samuel J. Burrowes reporting for the *New York Tribune*. A year later Thomas C. MacMillan of the *Chicago Inter-Ocean* and Reuben Davenport of the *New York Herald* accompanied Richard Dodge's expedition to the Black Hills to survey its mineral worth as a prelude to a government attempt at purchasing those rights from the Sioux. Keen with writing instruments alone, none of these individuals flashed "pencil *and* carbine with equal facility," as Charles King remembered Finerty doing so uniquely, a quality that seems to have been Finerty's alone. Soon enough, of course, Finerty would encounter Wasson, MacMillan, Davenport, and other newspapermen on the Sioux war trail.[46]

Veteran newsman John Frederick Finerty died at his home in Chicago on June 10, 1908, following a long bout with cancer. He was sixty-two years old. His passing was reported in newspapers nationwide, where he was invariably recalled as an adventuresome newspaper correspondent during the Indian wars, a popular lecturer and writer, a radical advocate for Irish independence, and a devoted American. On the day of his funeral a mile-long procession escorted his coffin to Holy Angels Church in the heart of Chicago's South Side. The local G.A.R. and Irish organizations took prominent roles in the day's proceedings. Honorary pallbearers included Chicago's mayor, six judges, leading Democratic politicians, and well-known ministers of many faiths. He was survived by his wife, Sadie (1861–1933), son John F. Jr. (1885–1967), and daughter Vera (b. 1886). One who knew him well summarized a life well lived: "No one could be intimately acquainted with Colonel Finerty [he was a colonel in the Fenian Brotherhood] without becoming fondly attached to him for his many noble qualities of head and heart. He was a fascinating conversationalist, a brilliant writer and a truly eloquent orator. The great storehouse of his mind unfolded itself in private conversation with the freshness of the running brook, in his writings with the diction and elegance of the classics, and in his oratory like a mountain torrent."[47]

Those fine words were offered by Patrick T. Barry, a fellow Chicago newsman and Irish activist, and were doubtless an apt reflection of an extraordinary individual as Chicagoans tended to remember him. But perspectives sometimes sharpen over time. For all of Finerty's lifelong exuberance for all things Irish, his gifts as a journalist, and a charming personality, modern-day western historians are driven to question his plain and consistent racially charged views of American Indians, which seem so inconsistent with the views of enlightened Americans even then, not the least his foremost patron, Wilbur Storey, as well as so many of the army officers he rode with. Such compromising, undistinguished rhetoric was probably of little or no consequence to contemporary Chicagoans or even many contemporary westerners, who might only have added a resounding "You bet!" But the incongruity prompts pause today, especially when driven to exalt the legacy of this "gem of the lot."

CHAPTER 2

Preparing for War

WITH APLOMB, John Frederick Finerty went to war. An all-out confrontation with the Sioux beckoned on the northern plains. A beat reporter before this for the *Chicago Times*, but summoned now by his editor, Wilbur Storey, to cover the war, the twenty-nine-year-old Irish-American headed west. His opening telegrams and letters to his newspaper reported straightforwardly his railway journey from Chicago to Omaha, and on to Cheyenne, and his transfer there to the dusty trails into the Sioux Country. Along the way, Finerty regaled readers with his meeting with Brigadier General George Crook in Omaha. He found the general an amiable man, but jovial only to a point. The two accepted each other without question or hesitation, and in the days and weeks to come Finerty had open access to this renowned if stoic Indian fighter and his inner circle.

Physically, Finerty was a striking man. In later years friends and associates remembered a stocky gentleman, and that is how he is seen in many period photographs. But in 1876 Finerty, not yet thirty, was in his prime, standing six foot, two, of slender build, with a rosy complexion, brown eyes, curly auburn hair, and a slightly receding hairline. His most distinguishing feature was a full moustache and chin puff. He was rarely apart from his pipe and enjoyed a toddy when offered one by messmates, which seems to have occurred often. It was said, with perhaps only a bit of hyperbole, that Finerty was always thirsty—for liquids and news, and that he could hold any quantity of either.[1]

Finerty was much taken by Cheyenne, a boisterous, rough-and-tumble gold rush town where, as he noted, the smell of gunpowder was in the air. Since the time of Custer's exploration of the Black Hills in the summer of 1874, reports of gold and this beckoning Eldorado held full sway in the nation's newspapers. There were many avenues leading to that luring countryside, but none more lustrous than that starting in Cheyenne, a community of some 3,250 on the Union Pacific Railway, with Fort D. A. Russell nearby, and a veritable expressway leading north.

From Cheyenne, the heralded Black Hills Road, a wide and deeply rutted scar across the landscape, had many localized names: Fort Laramie Road, Red Cloud Agency Road, Custer City Road, each reflecting one's destination. Sequences of ranches and landmarks along the way marked the journey like mile markers. At the Hunton Ranch on Chugwater Creek, some sixty-seven miles from Cheyenne, the road forked. A cutoff branch or left fork led in a northwesterly direction to Fort Fetterman, eighty-four miles beyond. The more heavily traveled right fork continued another twenty-seven miles to Fort Laramie at the confluence of the Laramie and North Platte Rivers. A telegraph line paralleling the road from Cheyenne to Fort Laramie connected the post to the nation's wires.[2]

Finerty found little to love at Fort Laramie, a venerable old post established by the army in 1849 during the heady days of the overland migrations. While the bustle and sprawl of the place was impressive in those days of the gold rush and Indian campaigns, one gruff sergeant in Lieutenant Colonel William Royall's command, with whom Finerty rode, thought the neighborhood looked bleak, the soil mostly gravel, and growing only prickly pears, rattlesnakes, and prairie dogs.[3] A new three-span iron bridge across the North Platte River helped renew Fort Laramie's vitality and on its account alone Finerty's route to the Sioux war came this way, expressly to avoid crossing a high-flowing springtime river at Fort Fetterman. On the far bank of the new bridge, the road split in three directions. Finerty's column followed one of the old overland roads to Fort Fetterman. A lesser fork led northeasterly to Camp Robinson and the Red Cloud and Spotted Tail Sioux Agencies in Nebraska's Pine Ridge country. The more heavily traveled route continued nearly straight north to the Hat Creek Breaks, Red Cañon, Custer City,

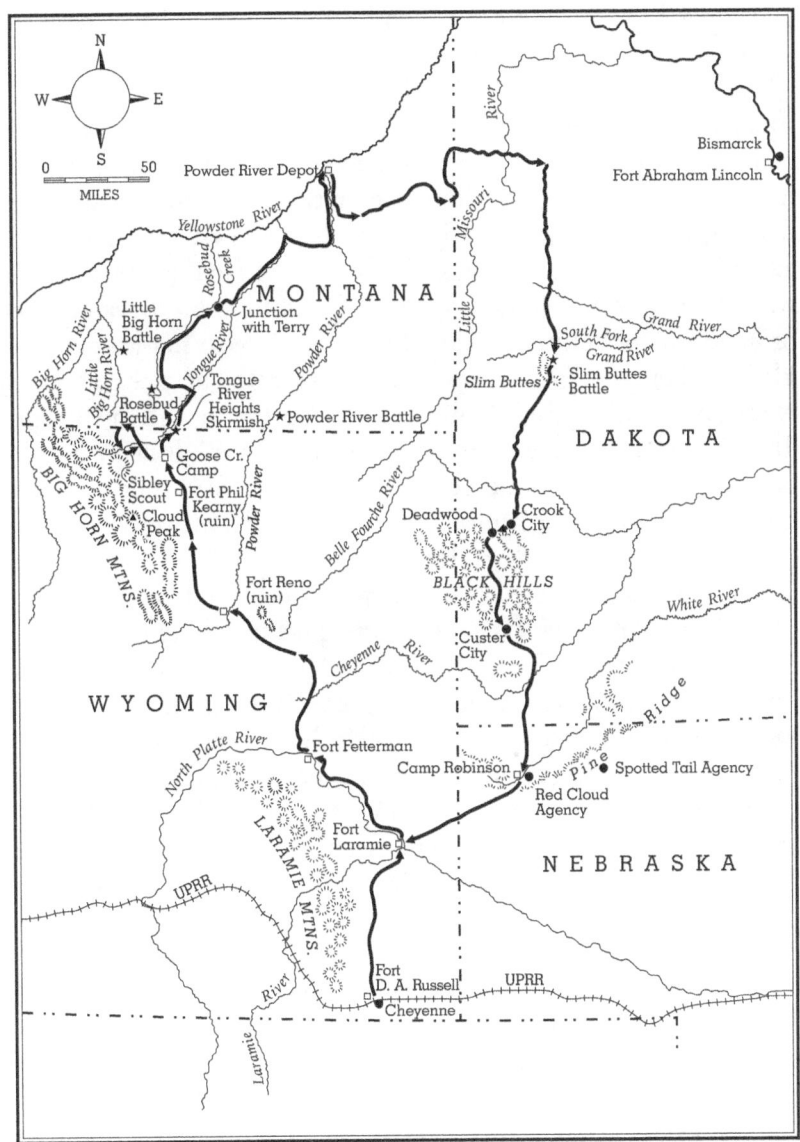

John Finerty's Great Sioux War. Map by Robert Pilk.

and the gold rush diggings beyond. Finerty would have more to say about each of these roads in his coming letters.

The matter of gold in the Black Hills captivated the nation, and Finerty had much to say about it in his letters. Initially he reflected a reporter's skepticism. In Cheyenne and on the road to Fort Laramie he mostly encountered disillusioned citizens returning from the diggings. The rush was slowly maturing. The easy placer ground along French, Spring, Rapid, and Castle Creeks in the central Hills was either claimed, worked-out, or suffered for want of water. The prospects along Whitewood and Deadwood Creeks in the northern Hills beckoned mightily now, but even then the best claims were taken and the days of mechanical mining still loomed in the future. This was a disconsolate-seeming crowd on the trail, Finerty wrote, but this observation came before he explored Deadwood and the northern diggings for himself, an eye-opener that would change his sense of it all rather strikingly.

News of Indian treachery on the roads to the gold country also filled the local newspapers, and Finerty quickly reflected that quandary in his own reporting. Crook's winter campaign had stirred a hornet's nest at the Red Cloud and Spotted Tail Agencies, unleashing a tide of local Indian raiding and killing that threatened commerce, agency management, and even Crook's own ability to recruit desirable Indian allies for the coming campaign. While the killing of young rancher James Hunton by Sioux horse raiders east of the Hunton Ranch was startling in its brashness, occurring as it did so far south of Fort Laramie and so near Cheyenne, the attempted assassination of General Crook on the White River just west of Camp Robinson was of far greater importance. In that instance, Indian traditionalists from the agency caught up in the unrest of the season attempted to waylay Crook soon after his difficult and unsuccessful attempt at enlisting Sioux allies as scouts for the coming campaign. Crook's attempt was a simple reflection of a style of Indian campaigning he had perfected in Arizona, where in large measure his successes were attributable to his employment of friendly Indians joining him to fight kin. That prospect failed him now, and that some of those same Indians then sought to kill

Crook speaks openly to the unpredictability and peril confronting the general, Finerty, and everyone else embarking on this extraordinary Indian war. The point would be brought home soon enough in a demonstration on the Tongue River and in the great battle on Rosebud Creek. For an Irishman from Chicago who had never been on an Indian campaign, Finerty did not yet grasp the enormity of it all, but he was set for the experience of his life.[4]

Chicago Times, May 15, 1876

Frontier Fighters
[*Special Correspondence*]

CHEYENNE, Wyoming, May 10. Public attention here is chiefly directed to the proposed expedition of Gen. Crook against the hostile Indians whose recent atrocious acts have roused more than ordinary indignation. Every day adds yet another crime to the long and bloody record in this territory. The red devils have taken up position in the country surrounding what is known as "the Red canon," a pass lying between Fort Laramie and Custer City, the main route from this point to the mining regions among the Black Hills. So imminent had the peril grown that Crook on last Monday sent forward Capt. [James] Egan,[5] of the 2d cavalry, an officer who showed good grit in the recent winter campaign against Crazy Horse, with three companies of his regiment to scour the country in the direction of the harassed point, and clear the canon for the passage of emigrant trains to and fro. Capt. Egan will hold the position until the main body of Crook's command are ready to move.

Next to "the law's delay," the procrastination attending military expeditions—especially of the character now contemplated—is most annoying. The recent brush with the Sioux, and the disappointment consequent on the failure of the campaign, have made the officers cautious, and the next foray, when it starts, will be of formidable proportions.

Everybody knows that it will be a life-and-death fight for the possession of the Big Horn region, which is said by those who have seen it to surpass anything in the northwest for beauty and fertility. It is the richest hunting-ground in the world, which makes it particularly dear to the red man, who will undoubtedly fight like a very devil to retain it. Our soldiers do not by any means underrate the hostility of the Sioux and will be armed at all points to meet them. Since May 1, a board of army officers have been actively employed in the purchase of horses to mount the cavalry, and they have made good progress. All manner of military supplies are going forward to Fort Fetterman, where the grand muster will be held previous to striking out for the strongholds of Sitting Bull, Crazy Horse, and the other dusky scoundrels who have made Wyoming territory a name of gloom and terror—a veritable "dark and bloody ground"—for so long a period. The smell of gunpowder is in the air, and Cheyenne bristles up accordingly. The town is full of all kinds of adventurers—scouts of mixed origin, ugly looking Mexicans who appear to devote all their hours to loafing, miners pushing toward and coming from the Black Hills, troopers lounging around the streets waiting for the tocsin of war to be sounded, and looking as if they were by no means too eager for the experience of Indian hospitality—in the sense that the burnt child dreads the fire. "Why," said a fine-looking fellow in a cavalry uniform to your correspondent, "these Indian rascals won't stand up and fight as we were used to against the 'rebs' under Phil Sheridan. They sneak and skirmish among the mountains and canons like a pack of assassins, and the soldier is picked off before he has even the pleasure of fighting." This is a style of thing that Caucasians do not relish, and this is what makes the philosophical "regular" much prefer the tedium of barracks life to the doubtful glory of an Indian campaign.

However, there appears to be a general feeling of confidence in Crook, whose undoubted bravery and affable manners have rendered him a great favorite with the people of this section. Although the result of the last effort against the Sioux was rather dispiriting, Crook is accused of blame in the affair—his chief fault having been an overweening reliance on the ardor of his troops as opposed to the peculiar Indian mode of fighting. Added to this, the cold was intense, and the men suffered almost as much as Ney's rear guard retiring from Moscow. Had Crook himself been with Reynolds' troops when they surprised the Sioux village, it is universally conceded that there would have been no retreat until a substantial advantage was gained. As it is, the repulse has stung all concerned into military fury, and when next the boys in blue encounter the red-skins, you may look out for very hard knocks on both sides. The fact is, Gen. Crook knows that he cannot afford to fail in the next campaign. His splendid Arizona record must be maintained at any cost. With a general in this frame of mind, backed by a force large and well provided, the issue of the struggle may be looked forward to with cheerfulness.[6]

Perhaps your readers would like a pen-portrait of the famed Indian fighter as your correspondent saw him at military headquarters in Omaha last Sunday morning. I bore letters of introduction from the lieutenant general, and was at once ushered into the presence of Gen. Crook. He sat at his desk busily employed reading reports of some kind. Pausing for a moment in his employment, he took Sheridan's letter from my hand and read it. While he was so engaged I had time to observe that the general was quite young, certainly not more than 40, with a thick, fair beard, parted in the middle; a large Roman nose of the martial contour; gray, quick glancing eyes; hair the color of his beard, straight and rather close cut, and a firm neck, planted on a pair of broad shoulders. He wore semi-military dress, but nothing to denote his rank.

"Ha! you're from THE CHICAGO TIMES," he said. "Are you accustomed to handle fire-arms?"

"Not much, general," I replied. "I might manage to hit a barn at a couple of hundred yards."

"You need to practice then," said Crook with a smile. "Won't take long to break you in, I guess. Can you ride?"

"Fairly," was my answer.

"That's better," said he. "In going out on this campaign it is best that everybody who goes along should be prepared for emergencies. Are you going back to Chicago?"

"No. I have said good-bye to Chicago until the expedition is through with."

"Very well," said the general. "There will be some delay yet. I am going to visit the Indian agencies to get some warriors to accompany us. After that I'll go to Cheyenne. Await me there. You shall go with me. Let me tell you one thing before you go; don't overweight your horse. Light baggage is an excellent thing on an Indian campaign. *Au revoir.*"

Gen. Crook resumed his reports. Your correspondent resumed his hat, and next morning emigrated to Cheyenne to wait patiently upon providence and Gen. Crook, more especially the latter.

Reports from the Black Hills are very conflicting. The miners from the east, as a rule, became disheartened during the bad weather, but the Montana men, great numbers of whom have flocked to the Hills since last November, are more hopeful. It would, of course, be presumptuous in me to offer an opinion on the matter until I have had an opportunity of judging in person. Enthusiastic store-keepers here show gold specimens which, they say, are from the Hills. Perhaps they are, but my short residence here has convinced me of this much: it is rank treason in Cheyenne to say aught against the Black Hills country. Every citizen of this place feels in duty-bound to puff the concern, which is small blame to them, seeing that emigration to that region carries grist to the Cheyenne mill. Wagon trains, large and small, chiefly the latter, keep passing every day. Reports of the slaying of men and the raping of women by the flying parties of the bloody Sioux, appear to have no effect upon the adventurers, who are mostly German or Irish. They go stolidly along, and within a few days will come news of yet other murders and ravishments. The cowardly Indians avoid the strong caravans, but swoop down on detached wagons and enact the most sickening tragedies. It is remarked as singular that the savages have not scalped such whites as they have slain this year up to the present time. Scalping is a polite attention that Fenimore Cooper's friends rarely omit when opportunity offers.

A more God-forsaken country than eastern Wyoming along the track of the Union Pacific road from Julesburg to Cheyenne, the eye of man has seldom passed upon. Your correspondent saw nothing worthy of note except rocks, low sandhills, straggling antelope, and prairie dogs. The only redeeming feature is the majestic view of "the snowy range" and Long's peak of the Rocky mountains, as the train approaches Cheyenne. Our Chicago moralists would be shocked out of their appetites if they saw bunko, faro, keno, and the rest of it, openly practiced here day and night. The infatuated miners furnish the chief good of the gambling harpies. They stake all their gold dust, lose it, of course, and then go back to dig for more. But Cheyenne, it must be acknowledged, is a quiet kind of hell. Half a dozen peelers suffice to keep people's throats from being cut. Yet the saloons never close, that I have seen, and the devil in the shape of harlotry makes "The Varieties Theatres" places of moral pestilence. Their closing hour is 8 o'clock in the morning; and, on Sunday nights, being closed during church hours, their curtains roll up, and their overture makes discord at midnight. Long John ought to come out here and run for mayor. Perhaps he could do for Cheyenne what he once did for "the sands."7

Crook is expected here to-day or to-morrow, and when he arrives the chances are that he will not long delay his forward movement to Fort Fetterman.

J. F. F.

Chicago Times, May 18, 1876

GOLD AND GORE
[*Special Telegram*]

CHEYENNE, May 17. Everything in the way of military is moving out of here for the front. The pack-train starts at daylight. A farewell ball is being given at Fort Russell by the officers of the 2d and 3d cavalry. Col. [William B.] Royall commands the column going from here, consisting of seven companies of horse. Col. [Andrew W.] Evans commands the column which will move on Friday from Medicine Bow. All are to rendezvous at Fort Fetterman. With Col. Royall's column are the special correspondents of THE TIMES and *The Philadelphia Press*. Very few of the soldiers are around town, nearly all being engaged in packing for the march at dawn. Crook has returned from Red Cloud agency and is at Fort Laramie. He goes thence to Fort Fetterman in the morning. He had a narrow escape from the Sioux. Clark, driver of the stage coach which left Fort Laramie for Red Cloud agency on Monday morning, was killed by the Indians last night, within two miles of the latter point.[8] There were no passengers. The devils were evidently after Crook and his aide, Lieut. [John G.] Bourke, who, fortunately, were a couple of hours faster than the stage. Shaw, a well-known young man about town, was killed near Sand creek on Saturday. Mr. Sanders, one of the oldest settlers of Cheyenne, left here with a train for Custer City 12 days ago, and was butchered by the Sioux on Sunday night.[9] Incessant fighting is reported from the mining regions. Men whose names will never be known have been picked off by the dozen. Such a hornet's nest was never stirred up in this region before. The Indians are also raising hell in Nebraska about 60 miles south of the North Platte. Horses and horned cattle are being run off in droves and there is general consternation. "Let us have volunteers," is the universal watchword in this locality. Unfortunately, reports of desertion from the regular army come in daily. The wind sown by the excursion against Crazy Horse last winter is now being reaped in the shape of a whirlwind of murder. Gen. Crook has his hands full. So far as indicated, the programme is as follows: Terry moves on the Sioux from Montana, Custer from Dakota, and Crook from here. The columns will move cautiously until they form a junction, when they will drive, if they can, the hostile Sioux to the Missouri river. The Indians are, however, well prepared, and may have some objection to being so driven. A long and arduous campaign is before the troops. The Indians, after killing the driver of the stage, stole the six horses, but did not disturb the mails.

Chicago Times, May 20, 1876

Facing the Foe
The Crook Campaign
[Special Telegram]

Cheyenne, Wyoming, May 19. The campaign of Gen. Crook has opened inauspiciously. Without firing a shot his command has already lost 65 men. That number deserted from Lodgepole creek, their first halting place, last night, taking with them their horses, equipments, and arms. They were from the different companies of the 2d and 3d cavalry that left Cheyenne (Fort Russell) on yesterday morning. Some of the lieutenants are in town hunting the rascals up. Col. Royall says he will shoot such as are caught for deserting almost in the face of the enemy. Undeniably, the regulars, especially the recruits, have a very wholesome terror of the Sioux. The desertion of last night has a very demoralizing effect upon the column. If the men begin to run away a couple of hundred miles from danger what will they do when they meet the Indians? This is the general question.

Reports have arrived confirming the news that the Indians of the Red Cloud and Spotted Tail agencies to the number of 100 lodges are on the war path and have broken away from their more pacifically inclined chiefs. Such a hornet's-nest was never stirred up on the frontier. You may confidently look for hot work before this campaign is over.

A deserter just captured says that the men left their colors because it is reported among them that in the event of a battle and defeat the wounded are to be left in the hands of the Indians. Such an order was attributed to Gen. [Joseph J.] Reynolds during the Crazy Horse campaign, but nobody credits the story.[10] Gen. Crook is too brave and too good an officer to tolerate anything so barbarous. If the soldiers will stick by him the general will stick by them, and the whole command will either conquer or fall together.

People at the east may look upon Indian fighting with a somewhat supercilious eye, but that plenty of men are afraid to face the music let the event of last night bear witness. In truth, nobody has much reliance on the regulars, especially the new recruits picked up in the eastern cities. The officers are generally brave and efficient, and some of the men are excellent, but the scalawags and dastards are numerous enough to destroy confidence and make things easy for a stampede. If Crook catches the runaways he will make mincemeat of them. The whole of Royall's column is now on the march to Fetterman.

Chicago Times, May 22, 1876

CROOK ON THE WAR-PATH
[*Special Telegram*]

CHUG WATER, Wyoming, May 21. Col. Royall's column of the Crook Expedition is moving by forced marches on Fort Fetterman. The rear passed this point at 10 o'clock this morning. The campaign will open immediately. Our troops are in excellent spirits, and there have been no recent desertions.

LATER—The citizens at this point have telegraphed for arms to Cheyenne. They anticipate a raid on the unprotected settlements after all the troops have passed into the hostile country. The Indians are cunning, and may play the game of Scipio.[11] In fact, everybody expects a raid in this section.

Chicago Times, May 31, 1876

BOUND FOR BLOOD
THE CROOK CAMPAIGN
[*Special Correspondence*]

IN CAMP ON THE CHUGWATER, NEAR HUNTON'S RANCH, Wyoming, May 22. After a weary wait of 10 days at Cheyenne, the order for the Sidney and Fort Russell contingents of the Crook expedition to march on Fetterman was received with some degree of satisfaction. Col. W. B. Royall, of the 3d cavalry, second in command, a soldier who distinguished himself in the Arizona campaign, arrived from the east on Wednesday, May 17, and next morning the advance guard of his column was en route for the point of rendezvous, 170 miles distant. On Friday morning Col. Royall himself, escorted by company E of the 2d cavalry, and company E of the 3d, left Russell and marched to Pole creek, where they halted for the night, having accomplished 18 miles. At dawn on the succeeding day the march was resumed, and the command,

Preparing for War 37

about noon, halted at Bear springs, 21 miles further north, to allow the wagon train to come up. We were one day's march behind the main body, and Col. Royall determined to keep on until a junction could be formed. Therefore, with daylight on Sunday all were in the saddle, and we made a quick march to Hunton's ranch, nearly 30 miles more upon our route, where we found the five companies that had preceded us encamped.

Upon reaching Chugwater at 10 o'clock Tuesday morning, a courier from the general arrived, changing our line of march from "the cut-off" to Fort Laramie, so that we might escape the delay of crossing the North Platte on the ferry at Fort Fetterman, as there are bridges over both the Platte and Laramie rivers at the fort of the latter name. Orders were issued for an early resumption of the journey to-day, but at nightfall on Tuesday a thunderstorm broke upon the camp. The rain fell in overwhelming torrents, the wind blew a hurricane, and now, as I write, the elemental war continues with unabated fury, making the roads utterly impassable, chilling the poor cavalry horses and mules, and rendering camp existence the very acme of human uncomfortableness. Col. Royall, considering the wear and tear of his horseflesh over bad roads, concluded to remain here until morning, hoping for more favorable weather. Tomorrow, if it were to rain pitchforks, we have got to proceed, as Crook is impatiently awaiting us at Fetterman.

Maj. Evans' column from Medicine Bow must have commenced its movement to-day, so that we shall reach the rendezvous simultaneously. On the first day's march there were some desertions from the command, but the runaways were chiefly recruits. Not a man has left his company since Saturday morning.

This section of country through which we have passed thus far has been described more or less by everybody who had taken any interest in the Black Hills speculation. The most enthusiastic citizens of Wyoming could hardly have the brass to call this region an approach to paradise. This Chug valley is, perhaps, the best strip of land between Cheyenne and Fetterman, and the stream which waters it is so diminutive that a search-warrant can hardly find it. Nevertheless it has a great many branches upon its banks, and along its borders ranges of scrub timber, the only things resembling trees that your correspondent has seen in the territory. Water is scarce, and the absence of forests gives the country a dry and dismal look. It is good pasture land for antelope and such wild game, but a man must be badly off for land who risks his scalp to settle here, unless the Chugwater valley, and a few other fairly watered strips be made an exception.

At this time, the denizens of this locality and the people scattered along this unprotected frontier feel that their lives and property, such as the latter is, are in jeopardy. The Sioux Indians are a sharp and daring breed. They know all our military movements and watch keenly for every advantage. It is well known among their chiefs that this enterprise has drained the country back of here of soldiers and they have nothing to encounter but ranchmen isolated for the most part and not over well armed. If the Sioux do not take advantage [of] our departure to raid the valley, everybody will be most disagreeably disappointed. The settlers already talk of sending their women and children to Cheyenne and other points of the railroad line, while remaining themselves to defend their herds and small farms. Their position is, from any standpoint, undesirable. If the Indians come, they are sure to be burned out, robbed, and butchered. If the savages remain away, the unfortunate people will always keep expecting their arrival until this experiment of fighting George Crook is through with. At this very point, on May 2, Young Hunton, brother of the ranchman, was murdered by the foraging party of red-skins who made things very hot around here for several days.[12]

On our way hither we encountered several disconsolate-looking adventurers returning from the Black Hills. Col. Royall interviewed one party Sunday morning, near Bear Springs, with the following result:

"Hallo, boys, are you going home from the mines?"

"No, sir," one replied, "we never got there."

"How's that? Didn't you start for there?" asked Royall.

"We did pull out for there," the man answered, "but to tell the truth, the Indians met us on the road between Fort Laramie and

Custer and gave us such a hell of a licking we couldn't go ahead, although we had more than 40 men in our train. We did all we could to get through, but we couldn't pass."

"Did you lose any of your party?"

"Yes, sir," said the man. "One man was killed on the skirmish line and two or three were badly wounded. I got this scratch myself."

He exhibited a very well defined bullet scar on his forearm.

"Did you kill any of the Indians?" the colonel further inquired.

"Yes, sir; we shot two or three. One of the bloody thieves rode a white horse. He appeared to be tied to his saddle, but we saw him drop his gun and fall forward on the peak. He never stirred, but the horse carried him off with the rest. Some of our boys say he was Big Little Man. He kept dogging us all the way. At least he exposed himself and we peppered him Oh, he was a—of a——!?"

Col. Royall laughed and, followed by the staff, and correspondents, rode on to overtake the head of the column.

We met about 50 other returning Black Hillers, all of whom wore a most defective expression of countenance. They had all the appearance of a routed army, and were filled with terror of the red skins. Also they spoke most unfavorably of the place called Custer City, and thought that in two or three months not a house would remain there. One very broken-down looking man said, in reply to a question,

"I have lived at Custer for some months and knocked around the mines a good deal. I saw very little gold, and whatever there was to get wasn't worth the trouble. I guess there's some gold around the part of the mountains where the Indians are thickest, but hills are always green far away. When I left Custer, several people that had bought lots there were 'pulling out' intending to return to the states. I want no more of it myself."

We did not meet a solitary person who gave an encouraging account of the Black Hills from any standpoint. Some of them still hanker after the color of the apocryphal gold supply, but all of them feel like giving a wide berth to the Sioux. If any Chicago man thinks more of a little gold dust than of his health and hair, let him try the Black Hills just now.

This enforced halt has had the good effect of giving our riders a chance to heal up, so that it is not an unmitigated evil. After a fellow who has not been on horseback for several years has ridden 70 miles in heat and dust, he feels like taking the world easy; not in sitting position, however. By the time this command reached "the seat of war" their own seats will be more peaceful, even though their hearts be more martial. A military camp on a rainy day would take all the enthusiasm out of a Charles Lever or a Mayne Reid.[13] And yet, it has its redeeming features. Military reserve unbends itself. The laughter of the soldiers is heard from the tents. The officers exchange visits and share cigars and "toddies" with soldier-like hospitality, while the shivering correspondents damn the weather, the mud, and themselves, and begin to look upon "glory" with jaundiced eyes. We have a few young officers in the command who find their first martial experience the very reverse of exhilarating. But this, the veterans assure them consolingly, is heaven itself compared with what they will have to endure on the Big Horn, where it rains nearly half the summer, and burns like a furnace the other half.

Our colonel is a fine-looking old soldier, who has grown gray in the service, and who still rides like a young hussar. The command looks very serviceable, both men and horses. The latter have been selected with great care, but very few of them will be good for anything after they return from this trip. Grain will be almost beyond our reach after we move from Fetterman, and grass is poor feed for what western men call "American horses." Bronchoes (ponies) are much more enduring, but they have to be broken in every morning. They are simply virile mules, and life is too short to undertake their education.

Fort Laramie, Wyoming, May 23. We resumed the march at 7 o'clock a.m. The route was over execrable roads, but we arrived here at 10 o'clock, and went into camp on the north side of the Laramie river, between that stream and the North Platte, which is the boundary of the so-called Indian country.[14] This portion of the country presents the characteristics already described, and there is nothing of note to comment upon. It is, generally speaking, a dry, hilly, sandy, sterile country, having here and there an oasis in which a strong-minded adventurer might hope, after years of toil, to accumulate some wealth. Most people here speak of the Black Hills with doubt, and regard emigrants going in that direction as predestined victims of Indian fury or Caucasian rapacity.

This section of country between here and Fetterman is not very well known, and in a succeeding letter I shall endeavor to describe it.

J. F. F.

Chicago Times, May 24, 1876

Fighting Folks
Movements of Royall's Column
[Special Telegram]

Fort Laramie, Wyoming, May 23. Owing to the tremendous rainfall on Sunday night and all through Monday, Col. Royall's column was delayed in Chug valley, Hunton's ranch, until this morning, as it was impossible to move the wagon train. We reached this point after a march of 30 miles, at 1 o'clock this afternoon. Our cavalry are in splendid condition and Gen. Crook can congratulate himself on commanding the best equipped expedition that ever left this region to fight the Indians. Following is the organization of the entire force:[15] Brig. General George Crook, chief in command; general staff, Capt. A. H. Nickerson, 23d infantry, A.D.C,; Lieut. J.G. Bourke, 3d cavalry, A.D.C.; Capt. Randall, 23d infantry, chief of scouts; Capt. Stanton, engineer corps, chief engineer; Maj. John V. Furey, expedition quartermaster; surgeon, Albert Hartsuff; doctors, Stephens and Pease; chief packer, Mr. Moore; quartermaster's agent, Charles Russell.

Royall's Column—Lt. Col. W. B. Royall, 3d cavalry, second in command; company E, 2d cavalry, Maj. Wells, captain commanding; Lt. Sibley, company B, same regiment; Capt. Rowelle, company A, 3d cavalry; Lieut. Lawson, company D, same regiment; Capt. Henry, company E, same; Capt. Alexander Sutorsus, company F, same; L. F. Reynolds, company M, same; Col. Mills, captain commanding, Lieuts. Paul and Schwatka; adjutant, Lieut. H. R. Lemdi, 3d cavalry; quartermaster, Lieut. George A. Drew, 3d cavalry.

Evans' Column—Maj. E. A. Evans, 3d cavalry, commanding; 3d cavalry company B, Capt. Meinhold and Lieut. Simpson; company C, Capt. Van Vliet and Lieut. Von Ludweitz; company G, Lieut. Crawford; company I, Capt. Andrews and Lieut. Foster; company L, Lieuts. Vroom and Chase; company D, 2d cavalry, Lieuts. Sweigert and Huntington.

At Fort Fetterman are the following: Company A, 2d cavalry, Capt. Dewees and Lieuts. O'Brien and Pearson; company I, same regiment, Capt. Noyes and Lieut. Kingsbury; infantry, company G, 9th regiment, Capt. Burrows and Lieut. Carpenter; company H, same regiment, Capt. Burt and Lieut. Robertson; company C, same, Captain Munson and Lieuts. Copron and Delaney.

The cavalry companies average 55 men and horses each, and the infantry companies average 50 men each. Some more of the latter may be ordered to join. The pack train consists of 320 pack mules, each carrying 200 pounds, and 106 mule-team wagons each carrying 3,500 pounds. There are five assistant pack-masters and 75 packers; 100 teamsters and ten wagon-masters. The cavalry horses may be averaged at 60 to each company, as there are many extra horses. This would give 900 in all. Of men, there are 825 mounted, 150 foot, and 200 packers, teamsters, etc., all armed, making, including officers, an effective force of 1,200. This organization will not be altered, unless by splitting the command for separate raids after we reach Fort Fetterman. The Indians, it is reported, are crossing the Laramie and Platte rivers, so as to attack our ranchmen in the rear. The boys have now received United States rifles and will be well prepared to receive the red ruffians. The women and children are being removed to places of safety. We will reach Fort Fetterman on Saturday.

Half-breed Lewis,[16] a well-known Indian scout, has just arrived from Red Cloud agency with the following official intelligence. Of the 70 lodges of the agency reported as having deserted to the hostile tribes, 17 have been brought back to their lodges. In all there are of Cheyennes, Sioux, and others, some 3,000 ready to fight out this campaign against Gen. Crook. They have numerous allies, and people well informed place the actual hostile Indian camp at from 7,000 to 8,000 first-class fighting men armed with the choicest rifles, and plentifully supplied with ammunition furnished by post-traders and speculators, who grow rich on helping to shed the blood of the regular army. The Indian rendezvous is at a place called Blue Stone, a stream which empties into the Yellowstone in the Montana country. They are commanded by Sitting Bull and Crazy Horse, both chiefs under 40, and eager to signalize themselves by slaughtering the whites. It is expected that the first serious fight will be at a place called Old Woman's park, between the Blue Stone and the Yellowstone, in view of the Big Horn mountain range.[17] The older Indians of the agencies, Scout Lewis says, discourage the present war, but without effect. Crook has all arranged for a speedy march on the warlike savages, and that of Evans will have to march like lightning. After we move from Fort Fetterman we are cut off from civilization, and judging from present appearances I shall have no little difficulty in informing your readers of the events that may occur.

Chicago Times, May 28, 1876

Crook's Campaigners
[*Special Telegram*]

CROOK'S EXPEDITION, OPPOSITE FORT FETTERMAN, Wyoming, May 27. Col. Royall's command, after a tedious march along the left bank of the North Platte, arrived in camp at noon to-day and formed a junction with Evans' column. The entire force intended for the expedition is now here, having lost only a few horses while en route. No Indians showed themselves on the line of march, which astonished all the officers, as the Sioux fired on the camp on the last trip immediately after crossing the Platte. The red-skins have all withdrawn to the northward on a line with Fort Reno and that section. Gen Crook sent out Sergt. Carr with nine men of the 2d cavalry, under a guide named Grouard, to find the fords in Powder river, but the Indians met them between here and Reno and drove them back. To-day two companies of the 3d cavalry, under Capt. [Frederick] Van Vliet and Lieut. [Emmett] Crawford, were sent forward by Crook to meet the Crow Indian scouts from Montana, who are to assist in the expedition. The main column will move on Monday afternoon. Royall's men made some rapid marching by a circuitous route over a miserable country. With few exceptions the left bank of the North Platte is a desert. Water can be had only by following the river. It is rumored that the peace people at the east are trying to stop the movement, but they are too late.

CHAPTER 3

Life on the Trail

JOHN FINERTY'S LETTERS to the *Chicago Times* in early June brimmed with the excitement, expectation, and reality of the campaign trail. For many individuals in this sizeable martial column of foot and horse, the route north, the old Bozeman Trail, with its many sublime and sometimes harrowing landmarks, were new. Lofty expectations overrode virtually everything at first—the initial dry and woodless camps, the accidental wounding of a cavalryman near the Powder River, the varied curiosity and annoyance of Black Hills miners intruding on the routine, the unbending cold and heat changing day-by-day and invariably tormenting the movement. The failures of Crook's first campaign in March might in part be blamed on the extreme winter weather, added to instances of questionable leadership, particularly on the battlefield, but such matters were irrelevant now. This command was undaunted. It had not yet met its enemy.

Several matters in these early letters stand out. For one, Finerty and many others in the command puzzled over the whereabouts of Crook's Indian auxiliaries. Crook had failed to enlist Oglala and Brulé Sioux allies at Red Cloud Agency in mid-May, almost getting himself killed in the process, but then sought help from the Interior Department, hoping to lure to his command Crow Indians from Montana and Shoshone Indians from Wyoming's Wind River country. Responses from the respective agencies were encouraging, but coordinating those individual movements and then actually welcoming such allies into the expedition's camp tormented Crook almost from the start. Sizeable contingents of Crows and

Shoshones did show at last at Goose Creek on June 14, to Crook's ultimate relief.

Finerty and others puzzled when, north of Fort Phil Kearny, Crook diverted the column from the Bozeman Trail (at that point the leg more commonly referred to as the Fort C. F. Smith Road) onto Prairie Dog Creek. Many in the column had presumed that Goose Creek was that day's destination. Said Finerty in passing on June 6, "We marched on for hours, but no Goose Creek appeared. Crook had evidently changed his mind." Modern-day historians have had a field day with this almost irrelevant point, even asserting that Crook, absent any scouts guiding his command, got himself lost. The ever-stoic Crook apparently told few in the column of his reasoning for this questioned diversion but the matter is really quite clear. At Fort Reno when Crook dispatched his three Plainsmen, Frank Grouard, Louis Richard, and Baptiste Pourier, to the Crow Agency to hurry up or even enlist Indian allies there, they agreed to meet on the Tongue River at the mouth of Prairie Dog Creek. Crook suggested this because he knew the place and so did these three scouts, all having been there on the first campaign in March, and the confluence being a simple and obvious landmark. Notions that Crook had gotten himself lost are plainly wrong. At the same time, shame on Crook for his stoicism.[1]

What is particularly interesting in these pre-Rosebud letters is Finerty's keen eye for detail, here revealing the grist of the trail. Barely into the movement, incongruities like the capacity of dragoons to swear on proper provocation, and the nature of mules, the lot of them obstinate and morose, caught his attention. So did the column's capacity to misread the "signs," meaning signs of Indians. As early as June 1, an officer in the van thought that he had observed a cloud of Indians hovering on the left. The column mustered with "martial ferocity," Finerty exclaimed. But then it was noted that those Indians wore blue uniforms, mere companies returning from a scout. "What a fuss about nothing!" Crook screeched as he collapsed his telescope.[2]

Finerty noted how the mood in the column could be exuberant one day and melancholy the next. His description of the burial of Private Francis Tierney on June 7 was particularly touching. Tierney died of a self-inflicted but accidental gunshot wound in the abdomen and was buried with full military honors on a hill overlooking the confluence of Prairie Dog Creek and the Tongue River. "Three volleys—the soldiers' requiem—pealed above his tomb and there we left him to his enduring sleep. Except a burial far out at sea, the interment of a soldier in the wilderness is the gloomiest of funeral experiences," he penned.[3]

Finerty could turn a phrase well and his letters sparkle with wonderful examples. In his June 4 missive written at the Clear Creek camp he described an instance of soldiers tearing down an Indian scaffold grave for use as firewood, an occurrence repeated commonly on the trail. Two days earlier he had lamented the disheveled look of the soldier cemetery at Fort Reno that he and others attributed to Indian disrespect and vandalism. And yet here was soldier vandalism of a near identical sort. What to make of it, he wondered? Well, "it was all the same to the dead on both sides."[4]

Notions of the fearless, dashing war correspondent had come into their own during the Civil War, and Finerty plainly fit the mold. On June 9 Indian warriors fired into Crook's camp at the mouth of Prairie Dog Creek. The shooting was more an annoyance than harmful, but the episode was audacious no less. Crook detailed Mills's battalion to drive off the attackers, who scampered when the companies—Finerty in their midst—surmounted the bluff and loosed several volleys their way. "To say, the truth, they did not seem very badly scared, although they got out of our way with much celerity when they saw us coming in force." "When they saw *us* coming" places Finerty in the mix, in the best spirit of Junius Henry Browne and the Bohemian Brigade of days gone by. Finerty was in the mix on this campaign again and again.[5]

Chicago Times, July 1, 1876

UNCLE SAM'S CROOK
ON THE MARCH
[*From Our Own Reporter*]

IN CAMP ON CRAZY WOMAN'S CREEK, June 3. My last letter dated Sunday, 28th ult., left us in camp before Fetterman. Gen. Crook hardly gave us time to have our soiled clothes washed, for he marched us northward Monday noon. Capt. Van Vliet and Lieut. Crawford, with their respective commands, had preceded us on the road to Fort Reno, to look out for the expected contingent of Crow Indians from Montana. The remainder, a formidable cavalcade, streamed away from the Platte at a brisk pace and brought up at Sage creek, 18 miles ahead, Monday afternoon. We then considered ourselves fairly on the road for the Indian country proper—the lands secured to them, so far as that intangible thing called a treaty could secure them. The Sioux drove the Crows from the Big Horn region, their legitimate patrimony. The United States undertook to protect the Montana emigrants and build forts along the road from Fort Laramie to C. F. Smith. Then came war, peace, and cession of territory—Uncle Sam, by his peace commissioners, yielding to the Sioux what belonged to the Crows, satisfying neither party, dismantling his strongholds, and rendering periodical military expeditions, at vast expense, necessary to maintain some show of paramount authority. The wily Sioux, the most politic, clannish, and warlike of all the Indian "nations," succeeded ably in palavering "the Yankee commissioners" into this grand and overwhelming muddle.

The number of our commanding officers increased and multiplied as we advanced. First came Crook. Then Col. Royall—a blunt, impetuous, old soldier. Then came Maj. Graves,[6] a melancholy man, who, to all appearances, has registered a vow never to smile—in any sense. Capt. [Henry E.] Noyes was appointed commandant of the 2d cavalry. The 3d was divided into 10 battalions, as it had forty companies in the field.[7] The 1st battalion was commanded by Capt. Anson Mills; the 2d by Capt. Guy V. Henry, and the 3d by Capt. Van Vliet. Maj. Chambers commanded the 9th infantry—five companies. Chief Packer Tom Moore looked after the pack-mule outfit, no small job, and Maj. J. V. Furey bossed the wagon train. Nearly all the aforementioned officers had adjutants, all of whom had orderlies, who blew almost without ceasing huge bugles, and rode madly from one end of the column to the other, as if the devil was after them.

It is astonishing how much dragoons can swear on proper provocation. The sentimental fair ones, who so admire our shoulder-strapped and be-frogged army officers in the brilliant ball-room, ought to see and hear them when out campaigning. They are innocent of boiled shirts, their beards become a stubble, and only for the inevitable stripe—the color of Missouri river water—down their pantaloons, they are hardly to be distinguished from the privates of the army. But in contrast with our professional "mule-whackers" the officers are models of urbanity.

We have along a trifle over 1,000 mules, all immensely loaded. They are unamiable and unattractive animals, awkward and discordant, but Crook could never move in this section without them. In manner the mule is obstinate and morose; in habit he is filthy and lacks modesty. Ears polite would be incurably shocked at the appalling sounds that accompany the starting of a pack-train early in the morning. The beasts are "cinched" or girthed so tight that they are almost cut in two. Naturally they do not like to move under such circumstances. They, therefore, stand stock still. This irritates the drivers, who swear at them in an artistic and perfectly inexhaustible manner. They welt the beasts with raw-hides most unmercifully and the beasts reply with their heels, and from the natural batteries in a most effective, if obscene fashion. Simultaneously they dash forward and matters run more tranquilly during the rest of the day. Such is a part of "the romance of war." The mule-drivers have an excellent time of it, and live far better than do the soldiers. The latter are expected to do all the fighting, while the mule-whackers do the best part of the feasting.

In the account given by me of the part of Wyoming through which Col. Royall's command purveyed before reaching Fetterman, I stated that the country in question was a wilderness. The section through which Gen. Crook's brigade had marched from the fort to this point is not bad, but is hardly good enough to counterbalance the *mauvais terres* or "bad lands." The grass ranges along a few small streams are fair and, at this season, the grazing is moderately satisfactory over all this route, known as the Bozeman or old Montana road, but the soil is poor and sandy, having an arid, starved look. The grass is extremely coarse and disfigured in all directions by the interminable sage-brush and villainous cactus. Ranchmen who care little or nothing for the comforts of civilized life could manage to raise large herds of cattle in these parts—if the Sioux were friendly—but for tillage purposes the land is unavailable. We are now about 60 miles from old Fort Kearny, [8] and since we left Fort Russell, some 300 miles south, I have not seen a 20-acre tract that can approach even the medium lands of Illinois or Iowa in productive power. I have not seen a single acre that could compare with the prime farming lands of those states. If there be any wealth in this soil it must be very deep down. It lacks several essentials to make it reasonably inhabitable. First, water; second, timber; third, climate. In rocks, hills, sand, ants, snakes, weeds, and alkali this part of Wyoming is rich indeed. If there is much gold in the Big Horn mountains God must have placed it there to make up for the worthlessness of so large a proportion of the territory. It needs neither a professor nor a philosopher to predict that the range of country I have described never can become a part of that great northwest, which is called the granary of the world. Its highest destiny is to become a mammoth cattle range—if ever there should be a market in northern Wyoming for that kind of produce. Irrigation of the soil is out of the question—the area being too vast and the rivers and rivulets too few. I will now resume the narrative of our march.

Col. Royall used to have us on the road at 5 o'clock every morning, but Gen. Crook, on assuming command, fixed the morning hour at 7:30 o'clock, in order that the horses might have sufficient rest, as he intends to make night marches in pursuit of the first bands after he cuts away from his wagon train. From Salt Creek the companies of Capts. [Charles] Meinhold and [Peter D.] Vroom were detailed to patrol the country to the west and look up Indian trails if any could be found. They took four days' rations and had orders to join us at Fort Reno.

On Monday we rode as far as the South Cheyenne—a mere rivulet bordering with cottonwood trees and tangled brush. The water is very bad and made several men quite sick. It was at this point the Indians shot the leader of the last expedition, and ran off the herd the next day out of Fetterman. We were allowed to sleep in peace.[9]

On Wednesday, May 31, the weather, which had been quite pleasant for several days, suddenly changed. The thermometer fell to zero and the wind rose to a hurricane. The sky was deeply overcast and clouds of dust made every object appear dirty and filthily obscure. Many tents were blown down and the men shivered around their watch-fires as if it were mid-winter. It was a relief to everyone when the order to resume our march came, and we moved on Wind River—a poor apology for a stream—18 miles due north. Our course lay over an undulating plain. About noon the clouds partially lifted, and as we mounted a high swell to the rolling prairie we beheld in our front, some 120 miles to the northwest, the chill, white summit of the Big Horn range. From this same swell we had an exceptionally fine view of Wyoming. Looking backward we could see the faint, blue outline of Laramie peak sinking below the horizon. On our right, nearly due east, the dark groups of the Black Hills was [sic] visible. On our right front, northwest, the Pumpkin buttes, four long, irregular mountain-like formations, several hundred feet high, rose abruptly from the bosom of "the bad lands." They run very nearly north and south, the northernmost being nearly abreast of Fort Reno. But the storm came back upon us with renewed fury and our prospective view was speedily cut off.

Wind river did not belie its name.[10] A more comfortless bivouac never fell to a soldier's lot. Every inch of ground was covered with cactus. The water was execrable—the wood scarce and the weather bitterly cold. By Gen. Crook's order we had left our tent stoves at Fort Fetterman, and as the thermometer continued to fall, we began to think that we must have accidently marched into Alaska. The tornado increased in violence and nearly repeated the shabby trick it played on the English army in the winter of 1854, when all their tents were swept into the Bay of Balaklava.[11]

When the dim morning of Thursday, June 1, broke upon the Wind river, snow was falling as thickly as it does about New Years in Chicago. The shower did not continue very long, and when it ceased we found the temperature much more comfortable. Our route that day was to a point known as "the dry fork of the Powder River," about 20 miles distant. As every officer and soldier wore a service overcoat, the cavalry looked much better, because more uniform, than usual. The first half of our journey lay over a mountainous region, but when we gained the higher ground and Powder River valley lay stretched before us mile upon mile, we concluded that we had at length struck a part of Wyoming which we could praise with a good conscience. Although the soil is marred by the woods and brush which more or less disfigure the entire territory, the valley shows evidences of fertility. It is periodically watered by mountain torrents, following the snow melts and rain-storms. The grass is of comparably good growth, and a thin line of timber follows the whole bed of both the "dry" and "wet" forks of Powder river from its source among the mountains to where it falls into the Yellowstone, near the Sheridan buttes. We found many traces of Indian villages near where we camped, indicating that the valley was much frequented by the savages in times when buffalo roamed in large herds, which they no longer do. Antelope are about the largest game now found in that locality. The red-skins disdain to chase these, so long as plenty of bison remain in the great ranges between the Tongue and Yellowstone rivers.

As we approached the valley, a staff officer thought that he observed a cloud of Indians hovering on our left. The distance was too great to make out the precise character of the object, which appeared to be moving rapidly. Capt. Henry's company was detached to reconnoitre, and set off at a trot across the fields. Our column struggled somewhat, and the adjutant rode along the line shouting "close up, close up," which we did. Judging from the haste, we concluded that Sitting Bull and all his warriors must be at our heels. An Indian fight was expected. Muskets were examined, carbines unslung, saddle girths tightened, and every man assumed a proper look of martial ferocity. Very soon we observed Capt. Henry's command approaching "the enemy." He halted while they continued to advance, growing larger every moment. Through a field glass we could then see that those dreaded "Indians" wore a blue uniform, rode American horses, and had a pack train with them. They were, in fact, Meinhold's and Vroom's soldiers coming in from their scout.

"What a fuss about nothing!" Crook exclaimed as he closed his telescope. We rode immediately into camp on "the dry fork," and there we learned that the scouting party had seen no Indians or traces of them; that they had no water since leaving Sage creek, 60 miles away; that they had shot some deer, and, for lack of water, had emptied their brandy flasks with military dispatch. Also, that Frank Tierney, one of Meinhold's men, had wounded himself mortally by the accidental discharge of his revolver.[12]

The absence of Indians had surprised the men who had been previously over the road. Around the camp-fires that evening officers and men asked "Where are the Sioux?"

This interrogation was addressed by one captain to another at the bivouac fire of the 3d cavalry.

"Don't be alarmed," said the party addressed, a grim looking veteran. "If they want to find us we shall hear from them when we least expect."

"They have neglected us strangely up to now," remarked a lieutenant. "Last time they serenaded us every evening after we crossed the Platte. You have heard, I suppose, the joke on Lieutenant Bourke, of Crook's staff?"

"No; let's hear it," shouted half a dozen future generals.

"Very well. We were encamped at Crazy Woman—a d—n mean place—and no Indians had been disturbing us for a night or two. The thing was growing stale and we were impatient for some kind of excitement, as we were slowly freezing to death. 'Let's go up to Bourke's tent,' some one suggested that night, and there we all went.

The lieutenant was engaged in marking out a map by the light of a candle. 'Hallo Bourke,' said one, 'ain't you afraid the Indians will ventilate your tent if you keep that light burning?'"

"'Oh, no,' Bourke said. 'The Indians that have been firing into us are a small firing party. You may rely upon it we won't hear anything from them this side of Tongue river. I know their habits. The distance is too great and the weather too cold. Mr. Indian don't care about being frozen. Now, I'll show on the map where they are going to at——'Whizz! Pop! Bang! Zipp!' came a volley from the bluffs above our camp. A bullet struck the candle and put it out. Another made a large-sized hole in the map. The group scattered quicker than a line of skirmishers, and Bourke was left alone to meditate on the instability of Indian affairs. He don't like to have that story told on him."[13]

It doesn't take much to make men laugh around a camp-fire, and there was general hilarity at the expense of the genial and gallant staff officer, who is one of the most efficient men connected with the expedition.

"Now, Lieut. Schwatka, tell us about that Pawnee picket you had on Powder river last March," said Capt. Sutorius to a stout young officer.[14]

"You mean about the watch?" Schwatka inquired. "It happened this way: We were ordered to make a detail for picket duty, and as the Pawnees were doing nothing in particular, we thought we'd give them a turn. My sergeant took half a dozen of them with the guard, and, reaching the picket post, explained that they would be two hours on and four off duty. He said to the Pawnee chief: 'Look at this watch. It is now 6 o'clock. When the short hand goes around twice you will call me and be relieved. Do you understand me?'"

"Hey—hey—good!" said the Indian, and stalked away.

The sergeant, who was very tired, went to sleep and was not disturbed until it was almost day.

Then he was aroused by a hand laid upon his shoulder. He opened his eyes and saw the Pawnee standing over him, watch in hand.

"Well, chief, what do you want?" asked the sergeant.

Life on the Trail 55

"Pawnee heap cold, much heap stiff," replied the warrior. "Ugh! That thing (indicating the watch) much lie. Long finger (the minute hand) him all right. Short finger (the hour hand) he heap damn tired!"

"The sergeant laughed, and tried to enlighten the Indian as to his mistake. 'Ugh!' was all the disgusted chief would say, but he would have no more to do with the picket."

Next morning we started for old Fort Reno, only 16 miles, a very short march. This was one of the three forts abandoned by the government, under treaty with the Sioux in 1868. The others were Phil Kearny and C. F. Smith. We approached the ruined fort through "Dry Fork canon," which extended about three-fourths of the way. The bottom land is almost covered with cotton[wood] trees, and shows remains of Indian villages. Emerging from the canon, we came upon a bluff and saw, three miles ahead, a small line of shelter tents. They belonged to Van Vliet and Crawford's companies who marched ahead to meet the Crows. Above their camp, on the other side of Powder river, we observed the ruins of Fort Reno, nothing but bare walls and blackened chimneys. We forded the river, which was at low water, and soon reached the camp-ground. Powder river is narrow but rapid. In the rainy season it rises beyond its natural banks and inundates the country for miles. Then it is difficult and dangerous to attempt crossing. Some of the clay along the banks is about the color of gun powder, from which circumstance, it is said, the name is derived. The water is extremely muddy, and is thoroughly impregnated with alkali, as many soldiers discovered to their sorrow before and after we left the place.

Fort Reno was beautifully situated. It commanded a view of the country far and near, and to surprise it was impossible. The low lands surrounding the site are plentifully wooded, which caused the death of many a brave fellow of the garrison—as the Indians used to cut off the wood parties with great skill in other days. The grazing is [exceptionable]—the best I have seen in the territory up to date. The entire mountain barrier of the Big Horn, softened and beautified by distance, is visible to the westward. Fort Reno was the main bulwark of the old Montana road. Since its abandonment few white people have been venturous enough to travel the route. It had a strong stockade and must have been quite a fortress. Loads of old iron, wheels, stoves, parts of gun carriages, axles, and other debris sufficient to make a Chicago junk-dealer rich are lying there uncared for.

Two hundred yards north of the site is the cemetery where some 35 soldiers and one officer—all victims of the Sioux—are interred. Since the fort was forsaken, the Indians have not respected this "Bivouac of the Dead." A monument of brick and mortar, erected by the departing garrison to the memory of their slain comrades, is defaced and mutilated. The slab on which was distinguishable, "Erected as a memorial of respect to our companions in arms, killed in defense——," is shivered into a hundred fragments. The stones upon the graves are uprooted and many mounds are leveled. All the head-boards are broken, but the names of Privates Murphy, Holt, Slagle, Riley, and Laggin, nearly all of the 18th infantry, killed May 27, 1867, can be distinguished by putting the pieces together. The most stoical of mortals hardly fail to look with some degree of sympathy at the lonely and defiled resting-place of those hapless young men, untimely, and ingloriously butchered. They sleep far away from home and civilization. For them Decoration day never dawns, and neither mother, wife, sister, nor sweetheart can brighten the sod above their bones with tributes of affectionate remembrance. "The Indian knows their place of rest," but follows them with his implacable hate beyond the eternal river. He will not allow repose, even to their poor remains.[15]

En route to Reno we came upon the trail of a party of Montana miners going through from Fort Ellis to the Black Hills. We found several rifle-pits that had been thrown up by them showing that they were old soldiers and up to all species of Indian deviltry. Capt. Van Vliet while in advance picked up the following, written on pieces of board:

> DRY FORK POWDER RIVER, MAY 27, 1876. Capt. St. John's party of Montana miners, 65 strong, leave here this morning for Whitewood, Black Hills. No Indian troubles yet.

Tony Pastor's Opera Troupe of Emigrants, from Montana, on their way east, encamped here last night. Don't know exactly how far it is to water. Filled nose-bags and gum boots and rode off singing "There's room enough in paradise."

These documents were signed by Daniels, Stillman, Clark, Barnett, Morrill, Woods, Merrill, Buchanan, Wyman, Busse, Snyder, Jackson, A. Daley, E. Daley, Konitze, and others.[16]

The captain (Van Vliet) further informed me that he had seen no Indians, hostile or friendly. The Crows had failed to come, which leaves Gen. Crook in a very awkward dilemma. Last night he detailed his three scouts—the only guides we had left—Frank Grouard, Louis Richard, and Baptiste Pourier, to set out for the Crow agency, Montana, about 300 miles away, to bring the Indian allies into camp. The men, each having an extra horse, started cheerfully on their perilous mission. If any men can succeed in an undertaking so arduous, the three already named will accomplish their object. Richard is a half-breed. The others are of French extraction, and all are familiar with the Indian country and its inhabitants.[17] They are expected to meet us on Tongue river about 10 days from now. Should they be cut off, the expedition will be without eyes and must go it blind or return, baffled, whence it came. Could we obtain the 300 Crow Indians promised, their assistance would be invaluable. Without them we cannot hope to find the lodges of the Sioux, who have been their invaders and oppressors, and with whom they have warred for centuries. It is a matter of boast among the Crows that they never killed a white man. They are said to be warlike and reliable, and, if half what is told of them be true, they may be classed as "truly good" Indians—just such fellows as Cooper used to write about.

Than the morning of Saturday, June 3, a lovelier never dawned in any clime. It was 6 o'clock when our entire command—no company detached—struck their tents and saddled up for the road. An hour later we turned our backs on Powder river, the three branches of which Lieut. Schwatka facetiously named "Charcoal," "Spitfire," and "Sulphur" forks. We had to go 27 miles to the point from which

I date this letter, called Crazy Woman's creek, on account of some obscure Indian tradition.[18] There is no water between this stream and the Powder river, yet there is an abundance of good grass, because there is a considerable rainfall in this section, where the vaporish influence of the mountains is felt. We saw many traces of buffalo, but none of the animals showed themselves that day.

Our column, including the infantry, the pack and wagon trains, extended between four and five miles. The foot—or "walk-a-heaps," as the Indians call them—moved two hours in advance with the wagons. The 3d cavalry formed the van of the horse brigade, the 2d forming the rear guard. Crook and his staff were several miles in advance. Col. Royall, one of the fastest marchers in the United States army, regulated the time of the column, and we went like greased lightning. Were I to live to the years of a patriarch, I shall never forget the beauty of that scene. A friend and myself allowed the soldiers to file ahead so that we might have a complete view. The cavalry rode by twos, in the intervals between each of the 15 companies, excepting the extreme rear guard behind the pack mules, being just enough defined to indicate the various commands. The wagons, 120 in all, with their white awnings and massive wheels, covered the rising ground in front of the horsemen, while the dark infantry column was dimly discernable miles in the van. Our route was over a gently swelling, or billowy, plain, destitute of trees, but sufficiently carpeted with young grass to render it fresh and vernally verdant. A white frost of the previous night, just evaporated, laid the dust and appeared to cover the prairie with countless diamonds.

The sun shone with a radiance hardly ever witnessed in the denser atmosphere of the east. Fifty miles to our front—we were marching westward—rose the mighty wall of the Big Horn mountains, Cloud Peak, the loftiest point of the range, seemingly to touch the sapphire canopy of the sky, its white apex standing in broad relief against the firmamental blue. The base of the mountains, timber-covered as we saw on nearer approaches, had that purple beauty of coloring sometimes seen in the master-pieces of the great landscape painters. The snow line, under the influence of the solar rays, gleamed like molten silver, all of which, taken in conjunction with the green fore and dark-middle ground produced an effect of dazzling grandeur. Even the rudest of the soldiery appeared impressed by the spectacle. It was like a glimpse of the promised land. Perhaps never again will the panorama of the Big Horn appear so magnificent to the eyes that gazed upon the fullness of its glory on that brilliant morning in "leafy June."

My vision has since grown accustomed to the scene and a nearer view, for we are now within 20 miles of the base, has dissipated much of the glamour that embellished that first grand vista from the heights above Fort Reno. Our pickets have been doubled since crossing Powder river, but no Indians have molested us. That they have observed our march we are assured by the signal fires which we have noticed burning all yesterday and to-day far toward the east.[19] It is suspected that the main body of the Sioux are in Montana, observing Gibbon's column. The old officers say that when they hear of Crook's rapid advance, they will, most likely, move southward, and, if they intend fighting at all, will make up for their singular neglect by welcoming us with bloody bands, etc., at every opportunity.

This creek is a mountain stream, nearly all snow-water, which renders it intensely cold. Only in that respect is it desirable as a halting place. Where we encamped is entirely encircled by ravine and scrub-wood—both admirable adjuncts for an Indian ambuscade or night attack. The Montana men had been there, for we observed their fortifications. There were two wagon tracks, which showed that in passing the ravines the practical miners had walked between their teams, so as to be prepared for instant defense. Our pickets were posted and despite gory imaginings, we went to sleep as peacefully as if we occupied the best rooms in your palatial hotels. No matter how warm the day may be in this northern latitude, the night is always cool. Mosquitoes are not early in their attacks, and are seldom troublesome except along the margins of the rivers.

J. F. F.

Clear Creek

Crook's Expedition, Camp on Clear Creek, Wyoming, June 4. We arrived here, after a ride of 22 miles, at about 12:30 o'clock. The name of our camping ground is no misnomer. A more translucent stream than that on which our tents are pitched never flowed in any land. The bed is gravel, and every object in the water is plainly discernible, although in many places the stream is quite deep. It abounds in fish, chiefly of "the sucker" species. Clear Water creek is a tributary of the Powder river and flows from the mountains. It gathers up all the little streams that tumble down the ravine in this section, and they are innumerable. This improves the character of the soil, which grows excellent forage. The country is wonderfully verdant at this season, but in the latter part of July the sun will have burnt it yellow. We have begun to strike the game region and have observed many traces of buffalo and the trails of Indian hunting parties only a few weeks old. Such geologists as we have along here say that the soil and the bed of the creek give indications of gold. Two miners from Pennsylvania experimented to-day and found sufficient to indicate that the gold prospect is not of the worst, but people are very skeptical about this gold business just now. It appears strange that the Montana miners did not make some effort to solve this problem. The [illegible] party to explore the mountain range. Crook has come out for fighting purposes only. He'd rather find an Indian village than all the wealth of El Dorado.

Today, for the first time, I saw an Indian "grave." It was situated on a little bluff above the creek. After dismounting, I went up to observe it. The Sioux never put their dead under ground. This "grave" was a buffalo hide, supported by willow slips and leather throngs, strapped upon four cotton wood poles, about six feet high. The corpse had been removed, either by the Indians themselves or by the miners who had passed through a few days before. Around lay two blue blankets, with red trimmings, a piece of a jacket all covered with beads, a moccasin, a fragment of Highland tartan, a brilliant shawl and a quantity of horse-hair. Scarcely had I noted these objects when a squad of young fellows from the 9th infantry walked up the hill after firewood. They, evidently, were lacking in the bump of veneration, as the following remarks will show:

"Hallo, Sam, what in hell is that?"

"That—oh, that is the lay-out of some d—d dead Indian. Let's pull it down. Here, boys, each of you grab a pole and we'll tear it up by the roots."

They did tear it up by the roots and within ten minutes the Indian tomb was helping to boil the dinners of the 9th infantry.

Thus the relationship of all men to each other in point of savagery was established. The Sioux defaced the white graves at Reno. The whites converted the Sioux funeral pedestal into kindling-wood. It was all the same to the dead on both sides.

In the evening two rough-looking fellows came into camp and reported that they belonged to a party which was coming from the Black Hills to the Big Horn. The main body, they said, was a day's march behind us. It was their fires we saw the day previous. The men went away like Arabs, and only when they had gone did it strike our officers that they were "squaw men" from the Sioux camp, who visited us in the capacity of spies on behalf of their Indian people-in-law. It was stupid not to have detained the rascals as prisoners.

J. F. F.

At Old Fort Kearny

IN CAMP AT OLD FORT PHIL KEARNY, June 5. To-day was one of our shortest marches—only 16 miles. We got into camp about noon, and are located in a most delightful valley, at the foot hills of the Big Horn mountains. This is a celebrated spot. Here it was that Col. [Henry B.] Carrington founded the fort made bloodily famous by the slaughter of Fetterman, Brown, Grummond,[20] and 83 soldiers on Dec. 22 [*sic* 21], 1866. The world has heard the story how the wood party was attacked down Piney creek, half a mile from the post. How Fetterman and the rest, being signaled, went to their relief.

How a party of Indians decoyed them beyond the bluffs and then fell upon them like an avalanche, killing every man, and mutilating everybody except that of Metzger, a bugler who fought with such desperate valor that the Indians covered the remains with a buffalo-robe as a token of their savage respect.[21] They attempted to take this brave bugler alive, but he killed so many of the warriors that he had to be finished. This much Red Cloud's people subsequently told our soldiers. From our camp we can plainly see the fatal ravine on the old Fort Smith road, where those brave but hapless soldiers fell. They call the place surrounding it "Massacre Hill." We march over that road, en route for Goose creek, in the morning. Alas, for glory! I visited the cemetery near the site of the fort this afternoon. The humble railing around it was torn down by the Sioux. The brick monument above the bodies of the officers was half demolished, and a long low mound upon which the grass grew dark, rank, and dismal indicated the last resting place of the unfortunate men who met their dreadful fate at the hands of the very Indians who are now being fed on government rations at the Red Cloud agency. Red Cloud, now old and half paralytic, was a prime mover in that butchery. The event closed Col. Carrington's fame forever, although the court of inquiry acquitted him, chiefly on the ground that he positively ordered Maj. Fetterman not to pursue the Indians beyond the bluffs.

We passed Lake De Smet, called after the famed Jesuit, on our road hither. It is six miles behind us—a sheet of salt water, without visible outlet, about 2½ miles long by about half a mile average width.

Somebody came into camp this afternoon and told Gen. Crook that there were buffalo grazing beyond "Massacre hill." Acting on the information, he, with Capt. [Azor H.] Nickerson, of his staff, and Maj. [Alexander] Chambers, of the infantry, mounted their horses and rode out in pursuit. They went far beyond our lines, saw a dozen deer, one grizzly bear, but no buffalo. Crook, however, shot a cow elk. The general is a very brave man—a little too brave for the position which he occupies. He ought to bear in mind the rude philosophy of the pitcher going so often to the well and getting broken at last. Some fine morning we may wake up and find no Crook. His passion for hunting may leave his scalp hanging in some Indian lodge for squaws to stare at.

Fort Phil Kearny was situated in a most exposed and defenseless place, commanded by bluffs on every side. Indians could come within a couple of hundred yards of the stockade without being observed. A dozen better sites could have been selected in the immediate neighborhood. The officers of the expedition explain the matter this way:

Col. Carrington commanded the 18th infantry. When he was sent out by the government to "prospect for a site," his wife, a lady of some will, accompanied him. From old Fort Caspar, at Platte bridge, they wandered on and on, northward, until they reached this point on the old Montana road. Carrington always carried a bugle, as he loved to sound the calls himself. One morning he arose from the bivouac, as usual, and was going out of the tent, bugle in hand, when Mrs. Carrington said:

"Henry, Henry, where *are* you going with that bugle?"

"Why, Margaret, my dear," he replied, "I am going to sound the call so that our march may be resumed."

"You may march all you please," said she, "but not one foot further in this direction am I going. This is as good a place for your fort as you can find."

"Henry" laid down the bugle. The march was not resumed. "Margaret" had her way, and so Fort Phil Kearny, of gory memory, came to be built.

When Capt. Grummond, of the dragoons, went to the rescue of Fetterman and got killed for his pains, Mrs. Grummond gave Carrington a terrible tongue-thrashing, called him a poltroon and many other names. The colonel had her, Mrs. Carrington, Mrs. Orton, and two other ladies—all that were in the fort—placed in the magazine, laid the train, and was ready to blow them and the whole concern up in case the Indians forced the stockade, which they were quite capable of doing had they attempted the feat. It was a miracle that they did not, as Carrington had less than 90 men left. The colonel is now on the retired list. His wife,

Margaret, died a few years ago, and, strange to relate, the second Mrs. Carrington is no other than Mrs. Grummond, widow of the dragoon officer, on whose account she insulted her present husband so grossly.

Thus, you see, military heroes, the chivalry of the land, as it were, can gossip about as much as the members of a Massachusetts sewing-circle.

J. F. F.

Beaver Creek

Beaver Creek, Wyoming, June 6. Crook wants to establish his permanent camp at a place called Goose Creek, reported to be only eight miles from Phil Kearny. The whole command—wagons and all—started out to find it early this morning. We crossed the "Great Piney," a rapid mountain torrent, and marched through the fatal ravine in which Fetterman's column got cut to pieces. So perfect a trap was never seen. There was no way out of it. A small party had no more chance of escaping those 1,500 Sioux, in such a position, than an exhausted fly has to break away from the strong spider who has her fast in his web. Fetterman, it is said, was in bad humor with his commanding officer when he left the fort, and hence his rashness and the tragic result thereof. "Not unavenged he died," however, for 180 Indians, by their own acknowledgement, were killed or wounded. Every man of the expedition looked with interest at a spot scarcely second to Fort William Henry as a gloomy memory of Indian warfare.[22]

Our road lay through one of the richest grass ranges that I have ever seen. It is capable of high cultivation. The air is laden with perfume, the ravines being filled with wild flowers of many species. We marched on for hours, but no Goose creek appeared. Crook had evidently changed his mind for we diverted to the northeast somewhat abruptly, following the course of a stream called Beaver creek. It ran at the base of a range of red hills, scraggy and wild, and we were not long in leaving the beauteous scenery of the morning far behind us. We found out that we were on the old Bridger trail, and marched five and twenty miles before halting at this point. En route we struck a buffalo herd and our men killed six of the animals—all in prime condition. We saw a number of deer, and wild fowl spring up at almost every step. The plain was indented with buffalo tracks, showing that we had struck a belt of the hunting grounds. The veterans say that where you find the buffalo there you find the Indians too. But we saw no red-hides that day. A heavy thunderstorm, accompanied by fierce rain, made our camp rather dreary. At the camp-fires an adjutant told us that Crook was marching on Tongue river.

The continuous marching over rough roads had told severely on our stock. Many of the pack mules are half flayed alive, their loads having galled them dreadfully. Several cavalry horses look worn out, and not a few of the men are suffering from inflammatory rheumatism—a disease quite prevalent in Wyoming. We have only one cavalry and four infantry ambulances, and three doctors to look after the whole command. "Put the sick in the wagons," is now the order, the ambulances being full. A sick man might as well be stretched upon the rack as in an army wagon. But a man has no business to be wounded or taken ill while engaged in this kind of enterprise. In the words of Marshal Massena, before Torres Vedros, the soldier on an Indian campaign must have "the heart of a lion and the stomach of a mouse."[23]

J. F. F.

The Junction

CAMP, JUNCTION OF TONGUE RIVER AND PRAIRIE DOG CREEK, June 7. We came upon Prairie Dog branch of Beaver creek early this morning, and followed it over hills and rocks for about 18 miles. It was an execrable road, the creek being very winding, which necessitated the crossing of it at numerous points. Added to this the trail was over a hilly country, and the wagons had a hard time getting in. What brought Crook up here nobody knows.

Perhaps he is "prospecting." We are within three or four miles of the Montana line, and no white people ever camped in this spot before. It is an out-of-the-way place.

Tongue river winds around us like a horse-shoe, north and east. The creek bounds us on the south. A ridge rises toward the west. The low land by the river is fairly wooded with the eternal cotton-tree. Above us on the north rises a bold, steep bluff, overlooking camp and river. Grazing is not over-luxuriant. Such is our present location. What we are here for no one has, as yet, been able to find out. The Crow Indians have not been heard from. Without them we are next door to helpless. The Sioux will never let us find them—unless they want to be found.

No miners have, so far, attempted to explore the Big Horn range. Even the heartiest appear afraid to approach those mysterious mountains. A small party would have a poor show among them, for the Sioux would soon discover their weakness and massacre the whole outfit. People who pretend to be familiar with the region say that gold exists there in abundance. I have met no one who is able to prove the assertion. As for Gen. Crook, he'll never go up there without orders, and he has none to that effect. He is out to hunt the Sioux, not to dig for treasure. Which will prove the more profitable is a matter for the future to determine. Our commander appears to be, physically, a man of iron. He endures heat or cold, riding or walking, with Indian stolidity. If he feels discomfort he never expresses the feeling. While apparently frank with all who approach him, he is never communicative, except occasionally to his aides. To all others he is a sphinx. The general is a born Nimrod, and always rides miles ahead of us, attended only by a few officers, chasing such game as may turn up along the road. The Sioux have missed several opportunities of capturing this "Gray Fox," as they call him.

Private Francis Tierney, alias Doyle, of Albany, N.Y., a recruit belonging to "B" company (Meinhold's) 3d cavalry, died from the effects of a gun-shot wound accidently inflicted by himself at the dry-branch of the South Cheyenne river, on the evening of May 30. He was buried this afternoon with full military honors. Every officer and soldier not on duty attended the funeral. His grave was dug in a lonely spot among the low hills that surround this place. Capt. Meinhold shoveled the first clay upon his body. They wrapped him in his overcoat and blanket, for "no useless coffin enclosed his breast."[24] A rough granite slab shut him out forever from the living world. Three volleys—the soldiers' requiem—pealed above his tomb and there we left him to his enduring sleep.

Except a burial far out at sea, the interment of a soldier in the wilderness is the gloomiest of funeral experiences. It was a sad destiny that led this young man, first of all this command, to lay his bones in the *terra incognita* of Wyoming.

J. F. F.

Lo's First Appearance

Tongue River Camp, June 8. Some Indians appear to have found us at last. At about 11 o'clock last night the howling of a pack of "coyotes"—animals the Indians often imitate when approaching a camp—was distinctly heard. Soon afterward, some of the wagoners down by the river were shouted to in an Indian dialect from the bluff. Arnold, a half-breed,[25] went down to the bank and attempted an interview. He recognized the Crow idiom, but thought it rather imperfect. The savages were invisible, being concealed among the cliffs and brush on the other side.

"Any half-breeds there—any Crows?" asked the Indian spokesman.

Arnold gave an indefinite reply.

"Have the Crows come yet?" the Indian asked louder than before. Arnold did not immediately reply, but, when he did, spoke in Sioux, whereupon the redskins suddenly ceased talking, and no more was heard from them. They left as mysteriously as they came. Why, if they were hostile, they did not fire is very strange. Why, if they were friendly, they did not try to get into camp is equally inexplicable. If they were bona fide Sioux the chances of hearing from them again are very promising.

We have not half a dozen "prospecting miners" in our camp, as follows: William Wyant, Charles Calderbaugh, Frederick Smith, and H. C. Meyers, from McKeesport, near Pittsburgh, Pa.; Ernest Hornberger, from Pittsburgh, and John Rees,[26] from Georgetown, Col. Interviewed most of them to-day, and all are confident that there is gold in the Big Horn region, and most of the streams flowing from the mountains. They have discovered traces of gold in many of the rivulets already. Wyant told me that the two miners suspected of being "squaw men," who followed us to Clear creek, said to him that they were from Montana, and four of them had left there for the Black Hills early in the spring. Being a small party, they were afraid to keep the lower road, and, therefore, footed it through the mountains, living on game. When they reached "Crazy Woman's fork," they saw a bar in the middle of the river and determined to prospect it. Having no pan, they extemporized one out of a blanket and a willow hoop. In two days, they told Wyant, $70 in gold was "panned out." Then they left for the Black Hills, where one of the party died. Matters not being prosperous there, they organized a party of 60 men and started for "Crazy Woman," which they reached one day after we left. They had followed Crook's command to buy sugar and coffee, of which they obtained a small quantity. They did not show Wyant any gold specimens. It was their intention, they said, to keep track of this expedition and to let Gen. Crook know what success they might meet with. Wyant gave their story for what it was worth, but was not prepared to vouch for the truth of all they said.[27]

Some soldiers have come in and report that they found a fresh Indian trail on our side of the river, a mile below the camp. A party of cavalrymen, out hunting buffalo, found a sore-back pony, which the redskins—a small body—had abandoned in their retreat.

Capt. [Thomas B.] DeWees, with his company of 2d cavalry, has gone into camp on the other side of Tongue river to look after any straggling Sioux that may be prowling around. The camp was disturbed about 10 o'clock by firing on the part of his pickets. It subsequently turned out that the warrior in question, against orders, fired at a clump of sage brush, supposing they were going to be eaten up by Indians.

Life on the Trail

JUNE 9. Two couriers with dispatches to the general have arrived from Fetterman. One telegram from Sheridan states that 120 Snake Indians have left Sweetwater valley to act as our scouts and guides. They are commanded by two white men and are at Fort Phil Kearny by this time. Another dispatch conveys the information that 3,000 Sioux warriors have left the lower agencies (Red Cloud and Spotted Tail) to go into the country of Crazy Horse, and, in conjunction with the wild bands, give battle to Gen. Crook. This would make a very strong opposing force. The same couriers inform us that eight companies of the 5th cavalry, from Kansas, have occupied the agencies; and that the Sioux have made a dash on Sweetwater valley and killed several of the inhabitants, also running off their herd. No news from the Crow Indians. The couriers think that Grouard and his party, who left for Crow village from Fort Reno, will be unable to cross the Big Horn river which is much swollen by melting snow. In fact it is not improbable that the scouts may have fallen into the hands of Sitting Bull's people, in which case their scalps are drying in some Indian hovel by this time. But they are old hands on the frontier and can save their bacon if any men can.

Camp rumors are now the order of the day. That Indian business the other night has swelled into gigantic proportions. Belief is gaining ground that the Sioux have spies among our packers, many of whom are half-breeds, and that they got all the information they wanted relative to the strength of this command. Neither Crook nor Royall take any stock in these rumors. It is feared that the Indians will lay for our wagon train on its return to Fetterman. Should they succeed in "jumping" it, either going or coming back, our situation will be anything but agreeable.

JUNE 10. At about 6:30 o'clock last evening, "stable call" having just been sounded, our attention was attracted by firing on the right, facing the northern bluffs above Tongue river. It came up all of a sudden—first a single shot from an infantry picket and then a succession of volleys, with the peculiar whistle and scream of bullets around our ears in the different company tents. A band of Indians were attacking the camp. It is useless to deny that we were taken by surprise, and, for a few moments, everything was confusion.

The cavalrymen were grooming their horses "on the line," having brought them in from grazing a few minutes before.

Hell appeared to have broken loose in the bluffs and all around the north side of the camp. On our extreme left, the pickets of the 2d cavalry kept up an incessant fire which was very spiritedly responded to by the Sioux. The higher bluff, which commanded the entire camp, situated almost directly north, seemed alive with redskins, judging by the number of shots, although only two Indians, mounted on fleet ponies, were visible on the crest. They rode up and down in front of us repeatedly, and appeared to act in the double capacity of chiefs and look-outs. Although a great number of soldiers fired upon them, they appeared to bear charmed lives. But the savages were rapidly getting the range of our camp, and making things uncomfortably warm. Crook's headquarters and the infantry lines were immediately below them, while our tents, on the northern slope, offered a very attractive target. Their guns carried admirably and made loungers, who thought themselves comparatively safe, hop around in a very lively, if not over-graceful, manner. The firing had lasted 10 minutes when a brilliant flash of inspiration came upon some officer in command. Of course it took some time to come, but it was good that it did come sometime. The men had instinctively fallen in line—the worst thing they could have done under the circumstance. All at once a young staff-officer, excited and breathless, rode into the camp of the first battalion of the 3d cavalry.

"Col. Mills! Col. Mills!" he shouted.

"Here, sir," replied the commander of the battalion.

"Gen. Crook desires that you mount your men instantly, colonel, cross the river and clear those bluffs of the Indians."

"All right, sir," said Mills, and he gave the order.

All at once the four companies of our battalion—"A," Lieut. [Joseph] Lawson; "E," Capt. Sutorius; "I," Capt. [William H.] Andrews and Lieut. [James E. H.] Foster, and "M," Lieuts. [Augustus C.] Paul and Schwatka, were in the saddle. "Forward," shouted the colonel, and forward we went.

A company of the 2d cavalry was extended among the timber on the left to cover the attack upon the bluffs. In a minute our charging companies were half wading, half swimming through Tongue river, which is swift and broad at that point. The musketry continued to rattle and the balls to whiz as we crossed. Partially screened by cottonwood-trees in the bottom-land we escaped unhurt. In another minute we had gained the base of the bluffs, when we were ordered to halt and dismount, every eighth man holding the horses of the rest. Then we commenced to clinch the rocks under a scattering fire from our friends—the Sioux. The bluffs were steep and slippery, and took quite a time to surmount. Company A took the extreme right; M the right centre; G the left centre, and I the extreme left. We reached the plateau almost simultaneously. The plain extended about 1,000 yards north and east, at which distance there arose a ridge and behind that, at, perhaps, the same distance, another ridge. We could see our late assailants scampering like deer, their fleet ponies carrying them as fast as the wind up the first ascent, where they turned and fired. Our whole line replied, and the boys rushed forward with a yell. The Sioux gave us another salute, the balls going about 100 feet above our heads, and skedaddled to the bluff further back. There, nothing less than a long-range cannon could reach them, and we could pursue them no further, as the place was all rocks and ravines in which the advantage lay with the red warriors. The latter showed themselves at that safe distance, on the east of the ridge, and appeared to take delight in displaying their equestrian accomplishments. I borrowed a field glass and had a look at them. Not more than a dozen were in view, although at least 50 must have fired upon us in the first place. Those that I saw were dressed in a variety of costumes. One fellow wore what seemed to be a tin helmet, with a horse-hair plume. Another chap wore a "war bonnet," but most of them had the usual eagle feathers. To say the truth, they did not seem very badly scared, although they got out of the way with much celerity when they saw us coming in force. Our firing having completely ceased, we could hear other firing on the south side of the river, far to the left, where the 2d cavalry had their pickets. This, we subsequently learned, was caused by a daring attempt made by the Indians to cross a ford at that point and take the camp in [the] rear, with the object of driving off the herd. They failed signally and lost one man killed and some wounded. Whether our party killed any of the Sioux I don't know. They did their best, which is all that could be asked of them. One thing is certain—the redskins killed none of us, but they slightly wounded Private [John E.] Collins, I company, 2d cavalry, and Sergt. [John C. A.] Warfield of F company, 3d cavalry. Likewise they killed a valuable horse belonging to Capt. [Andrew S.] Burt of the 9th infantry, disabled some others, and perforated the bowels of a pack-mule.

This is a full, true, and particular account of "the battle" (such as it was) of Tongue River Bluffs.

What a pity that so much wind and valor should have been so uselessly expended!

In justice to the officers and soldiers employed in the affair, I think it necessary to remark that if the Indians had remained within rifle-range they would have shot them with right good will. After "the battle" our battalion was withdrawn to camp, and Capt. [William C.] Rawolle's company of the 2d was detailed to garrison the bluff—a very unpleasant duty, as it rained all night. It is wonderful how many precautions military men take after all trouble is over. A picket stationed on the bluffs from the first would have prevented surprise. As it was, had the Indians waited until dark, hell would have been to pay. Our herd would, most likely, have been stampeded and, by this time, we should be in full retreat on foot—"walking a heap" back to Cheyenne.

J. F. F.

Change of Base

Goose Creek, W.T., June 11. Convinced that Tongue river is an unhealthy place for a permanent camp, Gen. Crook last night ordered a change of base to this point, 14 miles from our last bivouac. The change is for the better in every way. The creek which bears so undignified a name is really a fine, clear mountain torrent, two branches of which flow around our position. Goose creek is hardly inferior to Tongue river in depth, although not quite so wide. We have abundance of wood and a superfluity of forage. The country around is absolutely delightful—about such a country as you meet with on the finest sections of the Hudson river. This fertility is due to the plentiful rainfall—we are almost directly under the Big Horn range, within a few miles of the Fort Hills. Our camp presents quite a cheerful appearance, but the best kind of a bivouac becomes monotonous when there is nothing to do and not much prospect of doing anything. If the Indian scouts would only come we could see our way. As it is everyone, from the general to the private, appears dissatisfied. Crook is confident that Grouard and the Crows will appear in due time.

J. F. F.

The Crows

Goose Creek Camp, June 15. Just as we began to give up all hope of ever again seeing our scouts or hearing from our Indian allies, Frank Grouard and Louis Richard, accompanied by a gigantic Crow chief, rode into camp at noon yesterday, and, amid the cheers of the soldiers, rode direct to the general's headquarters. I proceeded there at once and had an interview with the celebrated scout, Grouard, who is half a Frenchman and half a Sandwich Islander. He was brought to this country from Honolulu when a mere boy; ran the mail for the government on the Pacific coast for some years, and, when only 19 years, was captured by Crazy Horse's band of Sioux. The chief spared the young man's life, and he lived in the Indian village, having espoused a handsome squaw for some years. A misunderstanding with his wife's relatives made the village too hot for him, and, being allowed comparative liberty, he took the very earliest opportunity of taking "French leave." He is now about 28 years of age; is familiar with every inch of this country, can speak nearly every Indian dialect, and is invaluable to Gen. Crook, who would rather lose a third of his command, it is said, than be deprived of Frank Grouard. The scout told your correspondent that he and his companions had had a hard time of it since they left Fort Reno to search for the Crows. A band of Sioux got sight of them the second day out, and chased them into the mountains. They eluded their pursuers, and after four days' hard riding, reached the Big Horn river, which they had to swim with their horses. A few miles from that stream they saw an Indian village, full of women and warriors. The latter, to the number of about 300, charged down upon them, mounted on ponies. The scouts had a river between them and the Indians—a small river, but sufficient to insure their safe retreat. The red men fired upon them without effect, and then Grouard, by their large, bushy heads, entirely different from the handsome Sioux, recognized the Crows. He immediately shouted to them in their own language, and very soon the three scouts were in their midst, saluted by a storm of "Hows?" Then they learned that five Crow scouts had started to find our camp. It was this party that attempted to speak to us from Tongue river bluffs Wednesday night [last] week, but when Arnold spoke Sioux they became alarmed, suspecting a trap, and retreated. They would have come in only that Grouard told them we were going to camp on Goose Creek. They saw us leave Fort Kearny, but when we took the Tongue river road they concluded we were not the party they were looking for, and turned back. Grouard soon set matters right, and before many hours had nearly 200 warriors ready for the road.

They were, he said, within 10 miles of our camp, but, with the Indian caution, declined to come in until perfectly assured that it would be a safe proceeding. Baptiste Pourier had remained behind with the Indians to give them confidence. Five Snake, or Sho-sho-ne, scouts sent from their tribe at Sweetwater valley to notify the Crows that they were coming to help us, and should be treated as friends, were with the party. Louis Richard, the Indian scout, and Maj. Burt went back for the Crows. We waited impatiently for their arrival. At 6 o'clock a picket galloped into camp to notify Crook that his allies were in sight.

Then we saw a grove of spears and a crowd of ponies on the northern heights, and there broke upon the air a fierce, savage whoop. The Crows had come in sight of our camp, and this was their mode of announcing their satisfaction. We went down to the creek to meet them, and a picturesque tribe they were. Their horses—nearly every man had an extra pony—were little beauties, and neighed shrilly at their American brethren, who, unused to Indians, kicked, plunged, and reared in a manner that threatened a general stampede. "How? How?" the Crows shouted to us one by one as they filed past. When near enough, they extended their hands and gave ours a hearty shaking. Most of them were young men, some of whom were handsomer than some white people I have met. Three squaws were there on horseback—wives of the chiefs. The head sachems were "Old Crow," "Medicine Crow," "Feather Head," and "Good Heart," all deadly enemies of the Sioux. Each man wore a gay, colored mantle, handsome leggings, eagle feathers, and elaborately worked moccasins. In addition to their carbines and spears, they carried the primeval bow and arrow. Their hair was long, but generally tied up and gorgeously plumed. Their features, as a rule, are aquiline, and the Crows have the least prominent cheek bones of any Indians I have encountered. The squaws wore a half-petticoat and parted their hair in the middle, the only means of guessing at their sex. Quick as lightening they gained the centre of our camp, dismounted, entered, and lariated their ponies, constructed their "tepies," or "lodges," and like magic, the Indian village arose in our midst. Fires were lighted without delay, and the Crows were soon devouring their evening meal of dried bear's meat and black-tailed deer.

In the middle of this repast, we saw several warriors raise their heads and say "Ugh! Ugh! Sho-sho-ne." They pointed southward, and, coming down the bluffs in that direction, we saw a line of horsemen, brilliantly attired, riding at whirlwind speed. Crook sent a scout to meet them. Hardly had he time to start forward when the new-comers crossed the creek, and, in column of twos, like a company of regular cavalry, rode in among us. They carried two beautiful American flags, and each warrior bore a pennon. They looked like Cossacks of the Don, but were splendidly armed with government rifles and revolvers. Nearly all wore magnificent war bonnets and scarlet mantillas. They are not as large as the Crow Indians, nor as good looking, but they appear to be hardy and resolute. The meeting between them and the Crows was boisterous and exciting. Demoniacal yells rang through the camp, and this wild cavalry galloped down to headquarters, rode around Crook and his staff, saluted, and, following the example of the Crows, were soon bivouacked and deep in their rough-and-ready suppers. Tom Cosgrove, chief of scouts in the Wind River valley, accompanied them. His lieutenant is Nelson Yarnell and the interpreter is a young half-breed, called Utah Clair.[28] The Indian chiefs of the Snakes present are Wesha and Nawkee, with the two sons of old Washakie.

Last night an immense fire was kindled near Crook's tents, and there all the chiefs of both tribes, together with our commanding officers, held "a big talk." Louis Richard acted as interpreter, and had a hard time of it, having to translate in three or four languages. A quarter of an hour intervened between each sentence. The chiefs squatted on their heels, according to their ancient custom, and passed the long pipe from man to man. Crook stood in the circle, with his hands in his pockets, looking half bored, half happy. Maj. [George M.] Randall, chief of scouts, and other members of the staff were with him. The Indians were quite jolly, and laughed heartily whenever the interpreter made any kind of blunder. The Snakes retired from the council first. They said very little. "Old Crow," the greatest chief of the Crow nation, made the only consecutive speech of the night, and it was a short one. Translated, it was as follows: "The great white chief will hear his Indian brother. These are our lands by inheritance. The Great Spirit gave them to our fathers, but the Sioux stole them from us. They hunt upon our mountains. They fish in our streams. They have stolen our horses. They have murdered our squaws—our children. What white man has done these things to us? The face of the Sioux is red, but his heart is black. But the heart of the pale face has ever been red to the Crow. ('Ugh!' 'Ugh!' 'Hey!') The scalp of no white man hangs in our lodges. They are thick as grass in the wigwams of the Sioux. ('Ugh!') The great white chief will lead us against no other tribe of red men. Our war is with the Sioux and only them. We want back our lands. We want their women for our slaves—to work for us as our women have had to work for them. We want their horses for our young men, and their mules for our squaws. The Sioux have trampled upon our hearts—we shall spit upon their scalps. ('Ugh!' 'Hey!' and terrific yelling.) The great white chief sees that my young men have come to fight. No Sioux shall see their backs. Where the white warrior goes there shall we be also. It is good. Is my brother content?"

The chief and Crook shook hands amid a storm of "Ughs" and yells. All the red men then left the council fire and went to their villages, where they put on their war-paint and made night hideous with a war-dance and barbarous music. They imitated in succession every beast and bird of the North American forests. Now they roared like a bison bull. Then they mimicked a wildcat. All at once they broke out with the near, fierce howling of a pack of wolves; gradually the sound would die away until you would imagine that the animals were miles off, when, of a sudden, the howling would rise within a few yards, and in the darkness you would try to discern the foul "coyotes"—next to the Indians the terror of the plains. All night long, despite the incredible fatigue they must have endured coming to join us, the savages continued their infernal orgies. Their music is fitter for hell than for earth. And yet these are not the worst red men existing. These are "the truly good" Indians. Our young soldiers appeared to relish the yelling business immensely, and made abortive attempts to imitate the Indians, greatly to the amusement of those grotesque savages. I fell asleep dreaming of "roystering devils"[29] and lakes of brimstone.

Crook is bristling for a fight. The Sioux are encamped at Rose Bud, on the Yellowstone river, holding Gibbon at bay. "They are numerous as grass" is the definite Crow manner of stating the strength of the enemy. We march to-night to attack them. Each man carries four days' rations. For the rest we want we must trust to luck. The infantry are to be mounted on pack mules, and 100 men, commanded by Maj. Furey, are to remain behind and guard what we leave at this place. Stirring times and some vacancies in the army list are, doubtless, ahead. If the Sioux mean fight we shall have "a day worth a warrior's telling." Whoever loses, the motto will be *vae victis*.[30]

J. F. F.

Chicago Times, June 21, 1876

OLD CROW
CROOK AND THE CROWS
[*Special Telegram*]

CROOK'S EXPEDITION, GOOSE CREEK CAMP, W.T., June 15, via FORT FETTERMAN, June 20. At last after dreary days of waiting for his appearance Grouard, the scout, has arrived in camp, and with him 180 Crow Indians from Montana. They arrived late on yesterday afternoon. Among the notable Crows who put in an appearance at that time are the famous chieftains, Old Crow, Medicine Crow, Feather Head, and Good Heart. Scarcely had the excitement that the arrival of this band of warriors created in camp, quieted down, when it was announced that another body of Indians were approaching, and a few moments later, in dashed 86 more of the Crow [*sic* Shoshone] tribe, headed by Tom Cosgrove, the chief of the scouts in the Wind river valley. It is reported that 50 more of the same tribe turned back when they had arrived at Crazy Woman's creek, on being informed that we were beyond Fort [C. F.] Smith. From the moment of the arrival of these allies the camp assumed a different appearance; and it was evident to the dullest intellect that action would take the place of the present inertia. No sooner had the band arrived, than there was a hurried consultation between Gen. Crook and the scouts and chieftains, which lasted nearly an hour. That same night there was a grand council of war held at Crook's headquarters, which was participated in by the officers of the army and the chiefs of the Crows. At this council every plan for the coming campaign against the hostile and powerful Sioux was agreed upon. The Crows are eager for the fight with their old enemies, the Sioux, for they see hope of revenging themselves by the aid of their white allies, and in wiping out in the blood of their foes all the wrongs and indignities that have been heaped upon them for so many years past. The very mention of the hated name of Sioux roused them to uncontrollable rage, and the thought that they might soon be able to be tearing at his scalp-lock or driving a deadly knife into his heart kindled within their hearts a feeling of fiendish delight that found expression in fierce and savage shouts, of still more savage gutturals, that only could find a comparison in the growls of tigers whose jaws reeked with the warm blood of dying victims. The stoicism of the grave warrior was not proof against the terrible and overmastering passion of revenge.

The conference between the officers and warriors was maintained by the aid of interpreters, and as usual on such occasions speeches were made by both officers and chieftains. The most notable speech of the evening was made by the veteran warrior Old Crow, who spoke substantially as follows:

> These are our lands by inheritance. The Great Spirit gave them to our fathers, but the Sioux stole them from us. They hunt upon our mountains; they fish in our streams; they have stolen our horses, they have murdered our squaws and our children. What white man has done these things to us? The face of the Sioux is red, but his heart is black, but the heart of the pale face has ever been red to the Crow. (Ugh, and cries of "Good.") The scalp of no white man hangs in our lodges; they are thick as grass in the wigwams of the Sioux. (Ugh.) The great white chief, Crook, will lead us against no other tribe of red men. Our war is with the Sioux, and only them. We want back our lands, we want their women for our slaves to work for us as our women have had to work for them. We want their horses for our young men, and their mules for our squaws. The Sioux have tramped upon our hearts, and we shall spit upon their scalps. (Terrific yelling.) The great white chief sees that my young men have come to fight. No Sioux shall see their backs. Where the white warrior goes there shall we be also. It is good. Is my brother content?

As the old chieftain finished his harangue, the fierceness of which no type can describe, Gen. Crook arose from his seat, and advancing to where he stood, shook hands with the battle-scarred warrior.

At this juncture the yelling became fiercely frantic, and it was not such shouts as one hears issuing from the lips of civilized men, but it was wild and demoniacal in its fierceness, full of suggestive horrors. Simultaneously with this the warriors rose to their feet, and began a war dance, which they kept up with uncoated zeal until the gray dawn of morning put an end to their wild orgie. During their dance they gave vent to the most unearthly shouts and whoops, which nearly stampeded the horses belonging to the army, and did effectually put to flight all of the cattle, who stuck up their tails, and incontinently fled from sounds so unearthly and savage.

There ensued the usual wild race over hills and mountains, and after much hard work, and any amount of still harsher cussing at the cause of the stampede, the cattle were recovered. As was predicted, there will be an immediate move of the command. The order has been issued to prepare to march for the Sioux camp at the Yellowstone, between Rosebud and Tongue rivers, to-night, and now the camp is rapidly breaking up, and preparing for a march. The united Indian bands will be under command of Maj. Randall, while Weesha and Waukee, the Snake chieftains, will act as aids [sic] to him

The Crows say that the Sioux are encamped in strong numbers, and are fully prepared for a desperate resistance. Of this fact there can be no doubt for they have completely held Gibbon's column at bay, and it might be said that they have completely checked the advance. Terry is reported to be on the south side of the Yellowstone, trying to join Gibbon, but he is harassed on every side by the Sioux. He has a steamer with him. Rations have been issued for four days and it is evident that the march will be a fatiguing and a forced one, as only blankets are given to the men, while 100 rounds of ammunition are furnished each soldier. Crook will endeavor to form a junction with Gibbon and Terry. This is absolutely necessary in our case as we are nearly out of meat, and should the Sioux interfere with this plan we shall be compelled to eat our horses, which is not a very alluring prospect. The 9th infantry, five companies of which will be mounted on mules, will go with us. The wagon train will remain here until we return, under command of Maj. Furey, who, with 100 men will garrison this place. The march will be a severe one as it is over a rough and rugged country, and one that will be beset at every turn by lurking foes. Should the Sioux continue to maintain their present position we shall have a battle with them before a week is gone by.

Gen. Sheridan arrived from Fort Laramie and left for the east to-day.

The 5th cavalry, now at Fort Laramie, are ordered to move northward along the Powder river trail and cooperate with Gen. Crook, more particularly in intercepting the Indians coming southward. Col. Stanton joins this command.[31]

CHAPTER 4

The Rosebud Battle

TWO DETAILS ARE WORTH remembering when reading or utilizing the numerous Rosebud battle accounts penned not just by the five dedicated newsmen accompanying George Crook that day, but by every other diarist and recorder documenting the action, whether in letter, diary, report, or reminiscence. The first is simply the need to carefully position each of these individuals on the field during the battle so as to understand what they observed firsthand. Rosebud was an enormous fight sprawling an equally enormous landscape, by one estimate spanning some fourteen square miles of battlefield. At times on June 17 three distinct fights were underway simultaneously, even while lesser actions played out on three other segments of the field. No one individual, not even General Crook himself when situated on the hilltop now bearing his name, could see it all.

The simple notion of not seeing it all folds into the second observation critical to comprehending the work of Rosebud's journalists and documentarians. What each individual witnessed firsthand and what they learned about secondhand requires careful acknowledgment. Fortunately, the five dedicated newsmen were spread widely that day and accordingly provided their readers with compelling narratives of the battle action playing across their respective fronts. As the fighting ensued, Finerty and one other reporter rode with Captain Anson Mills. Reuben Davenport, writing for the *New York Herald*, accompanied Lieutenant Colonel William Royall. Two others rode with Crook. Finerty and Davenport seemed driven to be in the midst of the action. Finerty expressed the matter understandably in the second of his Rosebud battle reports, reminding his readers that "the position of a newspaper correspondent in an Indian expedition forces him to go in with the rest. There is virtually no such thing as rear."[1] These modern-day cautions are simple enough—a need to recognize where individuals were on the field, and a concern, foremost, with what individuals witnessed firsthand and not what they learned by hearsay, suggesting, of course, that secondhand information is sometimes suspect. And yet despite these simple cautions, the fact remains that personal observation and hearsay comingled in the day's news reports, even in Finerty's accounts.

John Finerty saw plenty on June 17. Barely had the battle opened when Crook ordered Captain Anson Mills and the First Battalion of the Third Cavalry to attack Sitting Bull's warriors in the Gap, that distinctive landform on the eastern perimeter of the field. Finerty carefully reported Mills's two successful charges in the Gap along with instances of close combat and heroics deep in that sector. He chronicled, as well, Mills's and Captain Henry Noyes's foray into the Rosebud Narrows later in the battle. Finerty accompanied both of these actions, invariably riding at the front. He added other details to his cumulative battle narrative in subsequent reports written from Crook's Goose Creek camp, particularly then focusing on individual valor and tribulation. Meanwhile, two other acclaimed journalists, Davenport and Robert Strahorn, the latter writing for the *Rocky Mountain News*, rode with Royall and Crook, respectively, and chronicled the action occurring along Kollmar Creek and on Crook's Hill, in the western and central portions of the battlefield. Both brought to their narratives the same vibrancy that Finerty delivered in his accounts, reporting what they experienced personally, in addition, of course, to what they also learned of later.[2]

Ever mindful of the admonition from *Chicago Times* owner and senior editor Wilbur Storey to utilize the telegraph freely, Finerty's first communication reporting the Rosebud fight captured its essences, sometimes with cryptic brevity. One pictures Finerty feverishly scribbling in his notebook as Crook quickly established camp on the battlefield that afternoon, intent on having his dispatch to the *Times* in the hands of the courier leaving for Fort Fetterman that evening. Finerty's initial telegraphic report concluded with a listing of the day's killed and wounded. History, of course, tells us that this lone courier, apparently Louis Richard, did not ride far that evening before encountering Indians and returning to camp, delaying by many days the dissemination of this and other initial filings.[3]

Finerty communicated by telegraph again after Crook's command reached Goose Creek on its return from the battlefield, briefly adding several critical details, not the least that Crook's Indian auxiliaries were abandoning him and that he had called for reinforcements and mountain cannon, the latter a reference to small, light-weight mountain howitzers. Crook, in fact, never called for such ordnance and no artillery of any sort was received in his camp.

Finerty's second report on the Rosebud Battle and the third covering the movement was a running narrative in typical form, penned on the banks of Goose Creek. In it, he adds diary-like observations on the movements of June 16 and 18, and characteristic digressions and prosaic references. He meant his telegram and this letter to be read in relative unison, the pair comprising his report from the field of the Rosebud battle. One might note, as well, that these jottings were entirely rewritten when Finerty prepared his book, *War-Path and Bivouac*, and that tome, too, must be added to the mix to appreciate Finerty and the Rosebud fight as he knew it in their entirety.

Chicago Times, June 24, 1876

A Bull Fight
The Battle
[*From Our Own Reporter*]

Crook's Expedition, Rosebud Creek Camp, Montana, June 17, via Fort Fetterman, Wyoming, June 23. Pursuant to order, this entire command, excepting 100 men, left with Maj. Furey to defend our wagon train, broke camp on Goose creek, Wyoming, at dawn on June 16, and accompanied by the Snake and Crow Indians, marched over 40 miles that day, and halted for the night in Montana territory. Our objective, so far as we can learn from headquarters, was a strong Indian village situated in a deep canyon, through which Rosebud creek runs due north. We hoped to take the Sioux by surprise, but the Crow Indians were inaccurate as to distance, which left Gen. Crook in ignorance as to the exact location of the hostile camp. The Indian scouts failed to reconnoiter according to orders on the night of June 16, and could only be induced to go forward next morning, losing much time in exercising their war ponies. Finally, Grouard, our ablest guide, got them beyond the bluffs in our front, and we followed them for more than four miles further on, halting on Rosebud creek, in a valley commanded on every side by high, steep bluffs, covered with large boulders. Each man had a single blanket, 100 rounds of ammunition, and four days' rations. Everything superfluous was left behind so as to lighten the horses.

Two companies of the 9th infantry, mounted on mules, accompanied the cavalry.[4] Our whole force, including the Indians, was in the neighborhood of 1,200 men. We had been halted about one hour, our horses unsaddled and grazing, when at 8:30 this morning the report of firearms was distinctly heard from behind the northern bluffs in the direction of the canyon. Soon afterward the Snake and Crow scouts came running over the hill to inform Crook that Sitting Bull, with his whole available force of Sioux, was advancing in quick time to attack us right in camp. Two companies of the 2d cavalry and the same number of infantry were ordered to deploy as skirmishers and support the Indian pickets. Hardly had they reached the crest when volley after volley from the Sioux announced that the fight had commenced in earnest. From our camp we could see the enemy swarming in crowds upon the higher range of bluffs in every direction on a line of at least two miles. They were all mounted and fired with wonderful rapidity. Maj. Randall, our chief of scouts, aided by Lieut. Bourke, rallied our friendly Indians and led them to attack the centre of the Sioux. The latter received them with successive volleys, and after a gallant fight Randall's redskins were compelled to keep within shelter of the lower range of hills, the number of Sioux opposed to them being overwhelming.

Observing this state of affairs, Col. Royall ordered the first battalion of the 3d cavalry, consisting of A, E, I and M companies, under Col. Mills, to advance, mounted, and charge the central bluffs, so as to drive back the enemy in that direction. This order was executed with a brilliancy and celerity seldom equaled, under a sweeping hostile fire, which made a volcano of the plateau between the lower bluffs above our camp and the higher ones occupied by Sitting Bull. The battalion charged at full gallop with fierce ringing cheers, halted for a moment to pour in a withering volley, and then galloped up the ascent to the crest of the ridge. Despite their great numbers and splendid position, the Sioux centre broke and ran like a pack of wolves, taking shelter on other bluffs, 1,200 yards behind, for this battle-ground is a succession of ridges for miles on miles. The battalion then dismounted and deployed as skirmishers along the position they had carried.

While this was being done on the centre and right, the second battalion of the 3d cavalry, consisting of companies B, D, F, and L, under Col. Henry, was ordered to attack Sitting Bull's right, which they did, driving it back even with the Sioux centre and left. The third battalion of the same regiment, companies C and M, under Col. Van Vliet, was ordered to occupy the northern [*sic*, southern] bluffs in our rear, so as to checkmate any attack from that point. The fight now became general, and continued until past noon almost without interruption, the Sioux proving themselves the best fighting Indians that ever fired a shot. Beaten on one ridge they retired behind another, so that we were compelled to keep following them up, exposing our line all the time. Firing from their ponies, their shots were generally a little too high until late in the action—a fortunate thing for us.

At a quarter past 12 o'clock Mills' battalion, excepting I company, detached after the first charge to support the left, was ordered to vacate its position on the right centre, and make eastward first and then north, down Rosebud creek, through the canyon, at the end of which four miles distant, was situated the Sioux village. To enter the canyon the left of the hostile line had to be forced and Mills ordered company E of the 3d, under Capt. Alex Sutorius, to charge up the bluff and carry the position, which was speedily accomplished.

The Rosebud Battle

The Indians, however excellent as skirmishers, have not yet learned the art of standing a cavalry charge. Mills then moved down the canyon rapidly toward the village, according to orders. His place on the bluffs above the camp was supplied with only a few infantry, as the 2d cavalry were detained to sustain his movement.

Crook now determined to charge along this whole line, and for that purpose ordered Henry's battalion to fall back and get their horses, left some distance in the rear. Fortunately, Sitting Bull mistook this preparatory movement for a retreat. Henry retired across an exposed hollow, and the Sioux fought desperately right into his command. L company, of the 3d, Captain Vroom, was rear guard, and some men did not hear the order. They were immediately surrounded, and almost in a second 15 of our bravest fellows lay dead and wounded on the bluff. F, I, B, and D companies of the 3d instantly countercharged, and the wounded, except one man, were rescued by Capt. Andrews and Lieut. Reynolds' command. At that moment the brave Henry, a most accomplished officer, who was an acting brigadier during the civil war, was shot in the face, the ball entering above the right cheekbone and coming out at the left. He was mounted, as nearly all officers were, and was a prominent mark. His wound is dangerous, if not fatal.

Sitting Bull now discovered the advance of Mills and Noyes on the village. At least 50 warriors and 100 of their ponies lay dead along the ridges. The number of wounded embarrassed the Indian chief. He had most of the killed and all of the injured strapped to horses and carried off. The Sioux then broke and ran in a northwesterly direction, but despite all their efforts the Snakes and Crows took 13 scalps. Information reached Crook that the Indian village was deserted, and he immediately sent Capt. Nickerson, of the staff, to countermarch. This was done very reluctantly. The command faced southward once more. Sitting Bull fought to cover the retreat of his women and children, which was rapidly accomplished. He also hoped to beat Crook in open flight, but the command slept on the field of battle.

Our ammunition was failing, our rations nearly out. The Indians could not then be surprised, so it was decided to rely on our base of supplies and recuperate. Gen. Crook is now satisfied that the Sioux can and will fight. They are better armed than his own soldiers. Of the latter it must be said that braver men never faced an enemy. They would charge the Sioux to the gates of hell had they been allowed. The action occupied five hours.

Following is a list of our killed and wounded:

> D company—Sergt. O'Donnell, severely wounded. I company—Sergt. Meagher, seriously injured; one private, severely wounded.
>
> Third Cavalry, First Battalion, E Company—Private Henry Harold, dangerously wounded. I company—Killed, privates Wm. Allen and Eugene Flynn; wounded, Sergt. Grosch, severely; Corporal Cardy, severely; privates Smith, Linskoski, O'Brien, Stewart, and Reilly, severely. M company—Wounded, Bugler Snow, dangerously.
>
> Second Battalion—Wounded, Col. Guy V. Henry, commanding battalion, and captain of D company, dangerously. B company—Wounded Private Jacob Stiener, severely. L company—Killed, Sergt. Nankerchen; Privates Mitchell, Conner, Mannett, and Potts; wounded, Sergt. Cook, severely; Private Krazmer, severely; Private Edwards, seriously. F company—Killed, Sergt. Marshall, Private Gilbert Roe; wounded, Private Town, severely; Private Fischer, severely; Private Rutlen, slightly. Fourth Infantry—D company, Private James A. Devine, Private John H. Terry, Private Richard Flynn, all severely wounded.[5]
>
> Shoshone Snake Indians—Killed, one warrior; wounded, four warriors, severely.
>
> Crow Indians—Wounded, three warriors, one mortally.
>
> Total, including Indians, 10 killed and 30 wounded. Several of the slightly wounded are not mentioned.

We also lost 19 horses killed, and the same number more or less injured. Between 15,000 and 20,000 rounds of ammunition were fired by this command. The Sioux have expended twice that amount—one cause, doubtless, of their retreat. Thus we celebrated [the anniversary of] Bunker Hill.

[From Our Own Reporter]

Goose Creek Camp, W.T., June 23. We left Rosebud yesterday morning and arrived here at 3 o'clock this afternoon, carrying our wounded on traverses [*sic*, travois], an Indian contrivance.

The Sioux have not molested us since Saturday night's fight although they watched our retrograde movement from the hills. We camped last night at Beaver creek. The Crow Indians deserted. They fear the Sioux have reached their village, as some of their ponies were found with the enemy. The Snakes will also go home. This compels Crook to wait here. He will send for five companies of mounted infantry and some mountain cannon. Our wagon train leaves for Fort Fetterman to-morrow, and we remain till it returns, when the campaign will be renewed. This business begins to string out.

Chicago Times, July 5, 1876

Braving the Braves
[*From Our Own Reporter*]

CROOK'S EXPEDITION, GOOSE CREEK CAMP, BASE OF BIG HORN MOUNTAINS, WYOMING, June 20. Our column, as stated in my last letter, left this creek some eight miles further east on the morning of June 16, and marched 45 miles that day, halting in Montana on Rose Bud Creek, at a point situated about 20 miles north and 25 miles east of fort C. F. Smith. We moved at first five or six miles through a strip of Wyoming bad lands, all red clay and sand; but, passing beyond that sand belt, we reached one of the finest countries for pasture and water that could be seen in either hemisphere. We soon entered magnificent Montana, a land that would maintain millions of people in living if there were enough emigrants to settle it and if the whole tribe of Indians, friends and otherwise, were exterminated. I have seen the rolling prairies of Iowa and the rich farming lands of Ohio and Illinois, but the portion of Montana territory through which we marched compared to richness with the best soil of the states indicated. We moved over an undulating surface—a rich carpet—[of] buffalo grass beneath the horses' feet for many miles. There were very few trees, except where springs bubbled up or rivulets ran, and these were sufficiently numerous for all purposes of agriculture.

Immense herds of buffalo covered the slope and crowned the crests of the hills. No wonder that the Sioux hold dear such a patrimony and risk their lives to maintain it. We had just begun to enter the great northern hunting-grounds, which extend all the way northward from this creek and Tongue river to the Yellowstone and beyond it. Our march was enlivened by the Snake and Crow hunting parties, which chased the bison all along the road, producing considerable excitement among the soldiery, who were restrained by discipline from breaking ranks and following that superb game. The bison, for an awkward, hump-backed, short-headed animal, can run amazingly well, and needs a horse of long wind and fleet limbs to outrun him. Nearly every one of our Indians has two equines—one a pony for pack work, the other a horse for war and the chase. The latter can go like a meteor and has wonderful endurance. Mounted upon him, the Indian warriors could secure a retreat from the *Chausseurs de Afrique* of MacMahon, with all their Arab horses.[6]

The Indian war-horse is not as beautiful a beast as the Arabian, but he has more toughness than an ordinary mule. These combined qualities of strength, speed, and "hold out" make him the main stay of the red men of the plains, whether he be Sioux, Cheyenne, or Snake. Where the breed came from, or of what blood compounded, nobody seems to know. It is not a mustang, neither is it an Arabian—perhaps a combination of both. It may be for aught we know, indigenous to this region—a theory sustained in the fact that the Indian can get more work out of such a horse than any other race of men, white, black, or yellow.

In the buffalo hunt, the Crows took the west side of our road and the Snakes the east. Both had plenty of work on hand, and they all wasted ammunition—only 100 rounds per man—with true Indian improvidence. Sometimes they would chase a single bison for an hour, firing 20 or 30 shots each at him, and even then he would escape. These were the younger warriors. The old "bucks" act more coolly, shoot less, and kill more game. That night when we went into camp buffalo steak was plentiful, for our Indian allies are by no means greedy. They kill their beast, cut out his tongue, liver, and heart, and, unless very hungry, leave the carcass to rot upon the prairie. They don't want to load their horses much unless near their villages, where the squaws can dry the meat, for the average Indian is still unchanged—still the same mysterious, untamable, barbaric, unreasonable, childish, superstitious, treacherous, thievish, murderous devil that he has been since first Columbus set eyes upon him at San Salvador. Whether friendly or hostile, the Indian is a plunderer. He will first steal from his enemy. If he cannot get enough that way, he steals from his friends. While the warriors are fat, tall, and good-looking, except in a few cases, the squaws are squatty, yellow, ugly, and filthy looking. Hard work disfigures them, for their lazy brutes of sons, husbands, and brothers will do no work, and the unfortunate women are used as so many pack mules. Treated with common fairness, the squaws might grow tolerably comely, figures being generally worse than their faces. It is acknowledged by all that the Sioux women are better treated and handsomer than those of all other tribes. Also they are more virtuous, as the gayest army officers confess that the girls of that race seldom yield to the seducer.

The Sioux abhor harlots, even treat them in a most inhuman manner—even as they treat white captive women—when they are discovered. If they do not kill them outright they injure them for life and then drive them from the tribe. Among the married, such as their marriage is—for polygamy is a recognized institution in the tribe—adultery generally means death to the female concerned if she is discovered, when among the interested "braves" it begets a feud that only blood can extinguish. The Sioux hold it a sin against nature—according to their ideas of sin and nature—for a woman to remain unmarried, and they sometimes punish her, if she continues obstinate, in a very cruel and indelicate fashion. Fortunately for the Sioux women, they, for the most part, believe in matrimony and are spared all trouble on the score of their prolonged virginity.

Imagine all the old maids in New England being punished because the men of their generation did not have the good taste to woo and marry them. The Sioux will not have any old maids hanging around their wigwams. This is a truly patriarchal way of providing husbands for the fair sex. Massachusetts ought to send her stale virgins to Sitting Bull.

The other Indian tribes are more lax in their ideas of female propriety, and care much less whether a woman is married or the reverse. Taken all in all, the Sioux must be descendants of Cain, and are veritable children of the devil. The rest are a very little behind them, except in point of personal appearance and daring, in which the Sioux excel all other Indians. All of them are lousy, greasy, gassy, lazy, and knavian. That they have strong family and tribal-affection, I have seen proven on this trip, but every Indian looks upon the white man with a jealous, distrustful eye.

Crook tried to keep his wild allies under discipline, without avail. We were ordered to make no fires so as to avoid alarming the Sioux village, which we hoped to surprise next day or evening, but our Indians took no notice of the order and lit all the fires they listed. Then they attacked their buffalo meal like a flock of vultures and gorged themselves to an extent that rendered them utterly useless as scouts for the time being. Crook could not afford to fall out with them—he had enough of Indians to fight. He begged them to go forward that night and post him on the exact location of Sitting Bull's camp, which we came to find. The savages refused, and, instead, chanted some of their infernal war songs—"melodies" that combine the braying of a mule, the neighing of a horse, and the roaring of a bull—to the annoyance of the whole camp, for our men were tired after their long march and wanted to sleep. But nobody could stop their mouths, and we were forced to submit.

In that northern clime, the summer nights are very nearly as cold as those of Illinois in late October, when the leaves have fallen. But the days are as warm as those of Georgia or the Carolinas. Each man of the expedition had a single thin army blanket to protect him from "the midnight dews and damps." As we had heavy frosts every night of our Montana "scout" we "slept cool" and awoke not only unrefreshed, but feeling worse than when we lay down. In this way we prepared for what was coming.

I sent you by telegraph, per Gen. Crook's courier, via Fort Fetterman, a full account, some 1,800 words, of the engagement of

The Rosebud Battle

June 17. If it has miscarried, so has the official report of the fight sent by Crook to Sheridan. It is not my intention to go into details here, as the news will be stale, doubtless, before this better letter can reach you. In order to preserve the thread of my narrative, that is, if all the couriers got safely in, and if all were honest, which is a matter of some doubt, I will briefly state the facts in the case, as your lawyers would say.

Let me say, by way of preface, that the position of a newspaper correspondent in an Indian expedition, forces him to go in with the rest. There is virtually no such thing as "rear," unless with the reserve, which is generally called into action before the fight is over. Besides, if the journalist does not share the toil and the danger, his mouth is shut, for if he presumed to criticize any movement, some officer would say to him, "what the devil have you to say about it? You were skulking in the rear, and got everything by hearsay. We don't care what you think." Let no easy-going journalist suppose that this Indian campaign is a picnic. If he comes out on such business, he must come prepared to ride his 40 or 50 miles a day, go sometimes on half rations, sleep on the ground with small covering, roast, sweat, freeze, and make the acquaintance of such vermin or reptiles as may flourish in the vicinity of his couch, and finally, be ready to fight Sitting Bull or Satan when the trouble begins, for God and the United States hate noncombatants. Thus was I, who am peaceably disposed, placed in the position of an eye-witness, my "mess" being with the 3d cavalry, which had all the hard knocks last Saturday. The four regiments were just as brave men, but, for some reason, were not extensively used, although as things turned out there was no lack of employment.

"Reveille at 3 o'clock. We march at 4:30 in the morning," was gallant old Royall's order on the night of the 16th. Precisely at the appointed time the trumpet aroused us from bivouac. We were allowed some coffee boiled in tin cups and then waited for orders to saddle up and go. As usual, the Indians were hard to get forward, but our brave guides, Frank Grouard and Tom Cosgrove, persuaded a few to precede us on the march. The sun rose red, heralding an unusually warm day, rich in dust. We were not disappointed. The brigade marched four miles further to the north on Rose Bud creek and halted, in order that the horses, which were half starved, might have a chance to graze, before making a final march on Sitting Bull's village. We were halted a little over an hour in that deep valley, commanded by mountain bluffs on every side, and all within easy range. Our Indians were running mad races with their war ponies, which amused us very much, when, without warning, a rattle of musketry was heard beyond the northern-slope. Another and another followed in quick succession, "They are firing at buffalos," said the recruits. In a minute or two the singing of bullets around our heads convinced us that those buffalo hunters could fire with uncommon accuracy. Wild yells came to our ears on the morning breeze, and simultaneously, the Snake and Crow scouts came flying over the bridge shouting, "Heap Sioux—heap Sioux!" and indicating with their hands the position of the advancing enemy. The other friendly Indians rushed to assist their pickets, and the firing became almost deafening.

The war whoops of the opposing redskins could be distinctly heard above the roar of the conflict. But the Sioux soon obtained the mastery and beat back the Crows and Snakes in great confusion. Then, Crook ordered two companies of the 2d cavalry and Cain's company of the 4th infantry to deploy as skirmishers on the left.[7] They were half-way up the hill when we, having bridled up and saddled, awaiting orders, from the centre of the camp saw the whole range of bluffs from east to west, over two miles, covered with hostile Indians, while a perfect blaze of musketry made the hills seem on fire. Our skirmishers took possession of the lower range of bluffs and considerably annoyed the enemy, who, however, continued to advance with fury. Then an aide-de-camp came riding madly from headquarters to Maj. Evans,[8] commanding, under Royall, the 3d cavalry, the last-named officer commanding, under Crook, both regiments. The order, in effect was, "Maj. Evans, the general commanding orders that the First battalion mount at once and charge the heights in the centre of the Indians so as to clear them. When that is done, let the Second battalion support the skirmishers on the left, and, let the Third battalion cross Rose

Bud creek and occupy the heights in the left rear, so as to prevent us being surrounded."

Those orders were instantly obeyed. Mills headed the First battalion up the heights and charged the enemy at full gallop, driving him from the centre ridge to another crest 1,200 yards in rear—the country being a succession of ridges far as the eye can reach. Henry,[9] with the Second battalion, advanced and drove Sitting Bull's right back to the centre. Both commands were then ordered to dismount, and having placed their horses under shelter were advanced again and deployed as skirmishers. Maj. Randall, chief of scouts, and Lieut. Bourke, of Crook's staff, rallied the Shoshones and Crows and led them up against the new line formed by the Sioux. They maintained a very spirited fight for some time, but gradually retired before outnumbering foes, to the main line. The plateau between our ridge and that of Sitting Bull was much exposed and only a general charge could drive the enemy. Officers and men chafed at the delay, for the white soldier detests, as a rule, the slow work of skirmishing—a military art of which the Indians are thorough masters. For several hours, up to noon, the battle ranged along the whole line, the Sioux's fire far exceeding ours in volume, for they blazed away without ceasing. A chief, with a mirror in his hand, directed their movements by signal. He was well obeyed, for the Indians showed admirable pluck in every instance, except when we charged them right home. That their bravest could not or would not stand. Fresh swarms of Indians appeared every moment. Some attempted to cross the creek in our rear, but our Third battalion, under Col. Van Vliet, kept them in check.

At about 10 minutes past noon, Mills' battalion except one company ("I") detached, was ordered to vacate the position it occupied, mount and move down Rose Bud creek, through Dead canon, one of the most dangerous and difficult of passes for a military column, being about 14 miles long, and having on each side steep hills, covered with pine trees and huge rocks. It looked a regular death valley.

Half-way down its course, the Indian camp, or village, was reported to be situated. Capt. Sutorius with "E" company of the 3d cavalry, led the van. He was ordered to make a charge at full gallop up the hill commanding the canon on the right of the line and occupied by a strong body of Indians. The charge was perfectly successful and the First battalion moved down the Dead canon, followed by the entire 2d cavalry, five companies under Maj. Noyes. Grouard acted as guide. When within two miles of the village, Capt. Nickerson of Crook's staff, overtook Col. Mills with an order to return and fall on the Indian rear, which was exposed by our movement. He also learned that the Indians had abandoned their camp. Mills was reluctant to return, but obeyed, and we crossed over the western side of the canon, though a ravine, to attack Sitting Bull's unprotected point.

That astute Indian, however, was not going to be trapped in such a manner. He was aided in escaping by an awkward movement of Henry's battery under orders from headquarters. Crook wished to charge the enemy all along the line, and commanded Henry's men to fall back and get their horses, which necessarily had been left some distance behind. The Sioux, seeing the retrograde movement, thought our men were retreating, and took heart to charge them. Henry retired over a hollow, very much exposed. A portion of company "L," commanded by Lieut. Vroom, either did not hear or did not understand what was going on. They were late in getting out of the way, and a swarm of Sioux instantly surrounded and cut nearly the whole of them to pieces. Companies "I" and "F" countercharged and recovered the dead and wounded, killing many Indians at the same time. Col. Henry, a very brave officer, received an ugly and dangerous wound in the face. The general charge was about to be made when all at once the Sioux quitted the field, having suffered very severely. Dead ponies strewed the ground on every side. Thirteen dead bodies of the enemy remained on the field, and through the field glasses we could see their wounded and such dead as they had picked up strapped to their horses and borne away. They retreated in a northwesterly direction.

Clots of blood all along their trail showed the extent of their loss. They had fought, in the first place, to cover their village while it was moving out of the canon. In the second, they hoped to surprise us right in camp, stampede our horses, and sweep us all away by their overmastering numbers. They gained their first point; the second they utterly failed in. We occupied the field of battle, and slept that night in the camp of the morning. Our horses were too exhausted to pursue the Indians far. From where the battle began we drove their right and centre three and their left five miles, when they retreated. It is supposed that some of their high chiefs must have fallen. Had they not been severely handled, we would have been again attacked that night, but we were not molested in the least.

I have sent you by telegraph the names of our killed and wounded, so I will only recapitulate here, as follows:

Second Cavalry—Two sergeants and one private wounded.
Third Cavalry—Two sergeants and seven privates killed. One captain, two sergeants, one corporal, two trumpeters, and eight privates wounded.
Fourth Infantry—Three privates wounded.
Snake Indians—One warrior killed and three wounded.
Crow Indians—Five warriors wounded.

Of the horses, 19 were killed and as many more or less injured. Nearly 20,000 rounds of cartridges were expended. The dead we buried in camp, taking precautions to prevent their being dug up by the Sioux. The latter could have no less than 50 warriors killed, 150 wounded, and 100 horses left dead or dying on the ridges.

Our rations being nearly exhausted—we carried food for four days only—we were obliged to come back to our permanent base and retire from Rose Bud on Sunday morning, June 18. Some of the Sioux appeared upon the hills around, but did not venture to attack us again. The Crow and Snake Indians kept up a perpetual howling over their dead and wounded. They did well enough in the fight with the Sioux. We halted in the afternoon on an obscure creek, about 25 miles from here, where the Crows winged their flight back to the agency. The Snakes came with us this far, because it's on their way home to the Wind river valley. They go with the wagon train, which leaves here for Fort Fetterman in the morning. Maj. Furey, Capt. Nickerson, and Maj. Chambers, one company of the 4th and two companies of the 9th infantry will accompany.[10]

Five additional companies of infantry, one of cavalry, and some mountain howitzers are ordered for the next campaign, which will begin when the wagon train returns, which will be in about twenty days. The pack train remains here with us. Our camp is within a few miles of the Big Horn range, and, doubtless, some attempt at exploration will be made while we are idle. We have no geologist, except Lieut. Bourke, and the miners all turned homeward when fighting was talked of. Thus our chances of doing anything satisfactory are very slim, but I will do all I can to explore this much-talked-of gold region. Crook could serve the country to more advantage searching for gold mines than fighting the Indians, who, as we have seen, are brave enough to anticipate our attacks and warm our hides into the bargain.

I cannot help admiring the pluck of the red devils, although I detest the race. "Sitting Bull" ought to change his name to "Charging Bull." He fully answers the wish of the poet (Russia had not sold us that heap of ice called Alaska when the lines were written):

> Oh for a steed—a rushing steed,
> And a rifle that never failed,
> And a tribe of terrible prairie men,
> With desperate valor mailed—
> Till "stripes and stars"
> And Russian czars
> Before the Red Indian quailed.[11]

With soldiers less brave, Crook, on Saturday, June 17, would have been whipped so badly that a cloud would rest forever on the anniversary of Bunker Hill. No one doubts the general's valor, but he has underrated his enemy—a very grave fault. The Sioux have fine arms, and know how to use them.

Our stubborn leader will, no doubt, fight it out on this line *a la* Grant, all summer. Well, let him go ahead. He is a brigadier general, and his scalp ought to be proportionately precious, according to military ideas. If he is willing to risk his hair and bushwhack around this region, and further on, for several months to come, the rest of us can make no objection. I am going to see the thing through, for two reasons: First, I have received no orders from THE TIMES, as no mail has reached us since May 30; second, if I receive orders to return after the train leaves, I cannot get back at all. Added to this I hope to get into the mountains with some hunting parties, if nothing more, and find out whether there is any precious metal among them. If Crook moves out again, I hope he will go to the Yellowstone. It is a pity to have this country unoccupied save by wild bears and savages. We expect, in any case, to get back to Fort Russell by the middle of August or beginning of September. Carriers are very unreliable and are the chief annoyance of correspondence. Therefore, if any of my communications got lost or delayed you must attribute it to accident or neglect. It is 200 miles from here to Fetterman. The country is full of prowling Indians, and a man going alone, or even with a small party, takes a risk.

In connection with Saturday's fight, it would be unfair to omit the names of Adjs. Lemly, Chase, and Morton, who carried orders all though the action to the most exposed places. Being detached from their companies to serve with Col. Royall and Maj. Evans, they were mounted targets all through the engagement. So were the various gentlemen composing Crook's staff. Mr. Lemly's horse was killed under him.[12]

Whatever else may be said of our fight with Sitting Bull, no officer or man engaged can be charged with cowardice. Some mistakes, perhaps, were committed, but in a fight which was next door to a surprise these were inevitable. We are all wondering what has become of Gibbon and Terry. When last heard of, both were stuck in the mud somewhere on the Yellowstone.

J. F. F.

CHAPTER 5

Loafing Hangs Heavily upon Us

FINERTY'S CONCERN WITH LOAFING weighing heavily on Crook's Big Horn and Yellowstone Expedition in midsummer 1876 hit the mark soundly. With no news from the outside world to excite the command aside from occasional official dispatches delivered by harried couriers, the men of the expedition knew only the monotony of camp life, hunting and fishing forays on Goose Creek and into the Big Horn mountainside, and days hauntingly overshadowed by the news of Custer's death. Each of the remaining newsmen commented upon this intolerable malaise, as did most of the expedition's diarists and occasional correspondents. Finerty's summer letters are heavy with laze.

One topic remained fixating. As the days turned to weeks, the men in the Goose Creek camp sparred over notions of victory or defeat at the Rosebud. Most agreed that Sitting Bull's warriors had stymied Crook in that calamitous fight. Finerty straddled the middle. In his view Crook undeniably held the field that day and inflicted many casualties, while incurring plenty of his own. That alone smacked of victory. But Finerty coyly remembered, too, that Crook's primary objective when launching the Rosebud movement was striking a crippling blow on Sitting Bull's village. Doing so was a classic tenet in Plains Indian warfare. That ambition had been wholly thwarted. Unable to close on the village on the morning of June 17 as Crook had so plainly imagined, or to follow up later that afternoon when his scouts refused to lead him down the Rosebud Narrows, the general returned the next day to his base camp, soon dubbed Camp Cloud Peak, where he ordered forth reinforcements and resupply and then idled away the summer.

Victory at Rosebud had truly been in Crook's grasp, but he frittered away the opportunity. By Crook's own inaction subsequently the glimmer of victory at Rosebud turned to defeat and a cloud that henceforth shadowed the general for the rest of his days.

In Finerty's summer letters he returned again to his rather caustic view of Sitting Bull's Indians, a matter he discussed in a Rosebud context. "Let no man accuse me of Indian worship," he plainly confessed. Unworthy as Indians may have been as a people and an enemy, Finerty saw the enormity of the task at hand, and questioned Sheridan's and the army's mettle when squaring against opponents powerful enough to stop Crook and crush Custer. Why not instead kill off the Indians' meat supply, he pondered. "Exterminate the buffalo," he charged, as while the buffalo last, Sitting Bull will last. Finerty hammered this theme in one of his letters. He may simply have been echoing common camp chatter but already the extermination of buffalo was well underway elsewhere on the Great Plains. Buffalo still roamed plentifully in the north, but not much longer, and the consequences of the slaughter there and in the south were not just pivotal but indeed wholly devastating to Indians across America's heartland.[1]

Finerty made two forays during the summer lull, one a crossing of the Big Horns that was purely idyllic, and another with Frederick Sibley and Frank Grouard that was little short of harrowing and nearly fatal. The Sibley episode is remembered primarily as a scout, a reconnaissance of sorts orchestrated by Crook aimed at locating Sitting Bull's village. While the thirty men of that adventuresome crew saw no tipis, they stumbled onto hundreds of Sioux and Northern Cheyenne warriors in the headlands of the Little Big Horn River. Those warriors unhorsed the soldiers and pushed them high into the Big Horn Mountains. In the midst of this breathtaking escape Bat Pourier, another of Crook's Plainsmen with Sibley, jokingly chided Finerty that now, at last, he would have something newsworthy to send to his paper.[2]

Finerty was the only newsman accompanying the Sibley foray, and his several accounts prepared for the *Times*, and his later reflection in *War-Path and Bivouac*, are centerpiece contributions for reconstructing that narrative, itself another signature episode in Crook's second campaign against the Sioux. Almost immediately a good deal of credit accrued to Sibley for extricating his men from sure death, unharmed aside from utter exhaustion and the loss of their horses and all equipment except for weapons. Finerty's accounts added greatly to the luster. But Finerty also warmly praised Frank Grouard, the Plainsman who shepherded the young Second Cavalry officer and for the most part led the retreat. Finerty's praise of Grouard was unique and amply justified.

While Finerty's narrative of the Sibley scout may have been the most gripping episode in his midsummer letters, his description of the army's carbine cartridge extraction problem may be his most charged. By later-day reckoning, Finerty seems to have wholly misunderstood the issue, and yet his first-hand description of desperate soldiers at the Rosebud prying spent cartridge cases from their carbines while under hot fire from the Sioux is gripping and adds measurably to a debate that rages to this day. In his newspaper account he leveled a charge at the army's single-shot .45–55 Springfield breech-loading cavalry carbine, a simple, dependable, short-barreled weapon capable of great destruction. He focused his vent on the weapon's asserted failure in battle, when spent cartridges would stick in breeches, necessitating frantic prying with knifes or other implements. The infantry carried similar but heftier single-shot .45–70 Springfield breech-loading rifles, capable of even greater destruction because of their longer range. The rifle also featured a cleaning rod, a slimmed-down version of the ramrod of old. Finerty labeled them iron wands, and a great tool for extricating jammed cases. Whether carbine or rifle, each weapon featured a spring-loaded extractor hinged in the breech. Finerty faulted these alleged wimpy extractors, when in truth dirty breeches and soft copper cartridges were central to the problem, not spring-loaded (and actually rather stout) extractors. These points were recognized then but often ignored. And yet even while misunderstanding the fundamental details of the matter, Finerty's colorful firsthand description of frantic troopers manhandling weapons that "failed to throw out the shell of the exploded cartridge," making them "virtually disarmed," adds measurably to a controversy of continuing interest and importance.³

Chicago Times, July 12, 1876

SOUND ON THE GOOSE
WITH CROOK
[From Our Own Reporter]

CROOK EXPEDITION, CAMP CLOUD PEAK, Wyoming. June 28. Following our recent exciting scout into Montana has come a period of enforced apathy which is physically and mentally nauseating. We are counting on our fingers the weary days that must still elapse before that wagon train, with its snail pace, can return. Until then we must solace ourselves with such fishing and hunting as can be found here—neither very abundant at this season. As regards location we have nothing particular to growl at. Our tents are pitched on both sides of a deep ravine, 27 miles distant from the Big Horn range, through which a brilliant mountain torrent rushes with savage vigor. Our horses have plenty of forage and we ought to be comparatively happy, but we are not. A duller camp never made war boresome. Except for the bugle calls, a cemetery could hardly be more desolate of life and sound. The days run into one another unmarked, except for their length. In your civilized world Sunday chapters off the time—gives you a weekly beginning and end—freshens you up, as it were, every seventh day; but here that day is like every other—sullen, lazy, lonely, and cheerless. No "Charley O'Malley" or other "Irish dragoon" could ever flourish in an atmosphere so irksome.⁴ Indian solemnity appears to oppress everybody, and the fierce, furrow-browed old hills appear to drown reproach on all that is light, or gay, or happy.

Sad, desolate old hills that have no history. Old as the pillars of Hercules, massive as the Apennines, snow-robed like the Alps, and yet without a memory save that of the nomadic Indian, with his hideous painted visage, his wolfish howl, and his vermin-garrisoned wigwam. Around their gigantic figures are no gleams of the heroic past; no Hannibal with his mighty oath and mightier achievement; no Scipio with his Roman genius and terrible revenge; no Caesar with his devouring ambition and swarming legions; nor Horace, nor Virgil, nor Tasso, nor Dante, with their deathless symphonies and souls of poetic fire; nor Rienzi with his eloquence; nor Angelo with his creative glory; nor Bonaparte with his eagle pinions, catching on their golden plumage the famous of the ancient world. These mountains that we look upon to-day are mere heaps of rock, sand, and clay, destitute of all that can appeal to the imagination from the magic lights and shades of antique story. But despite this historic barrenness, our mountains are not without their natural attractions, pine-tree forests, foaming cataracts, gloomy canons, and towering pinnacles, showing almost at every step

> A red deer's wild and rocky road;
> An eagle's kingly flight.[5]

Besides they have that mysterious gold-concealing reputation which charms the adventurers, and which has led many a would-be Monte Christo to "jail 'neath alien skies and tread the desert path" in pursuit of the world's *ignis fatuus*,[6] only to find a tomb in the bowels of the wolf and the raven, or leave his miserable bones, those ghastly land-marks of mortality to grin solemn warning at those who may follow his fatal "trail." But thousands will follow that "trail," even though they tread on skeletons at every step. The love of gold is stronger in men than the fear of death.

Yesterday we received the first mail that has reached us since May 29. It was rather weak—no newspapers whatever having come, except a few for headquarters, and even those were old. Dearth of reading matter is the greatest deprivation we endure. Nobody expected that Crook was going to make an all-summer affair of this campaign, but it looks very like it now. Our wagons are to bring supplies for four months, which looks somewhat tedious. Meanwhile a kind of informal "post" will be established here, or in this vicinity, under the name of "Camp Cloud Peak" (Goose creek is not sufficiently heroic it would appear) so that our scouting parties can draw for supplies whenever they get run ashore, which will be pretty often. Everybody sighs for a renewal of active work, as the time then will not appear so long. Loafing hangs heavily upon us, for, unlike nearly all other campaigners, we are utterly cut off from the feminine world, which means civilization, and will be until we return to Fort Fetterman. Mars, when coming on this campaign, left Venus at home to look after the house.

Lieut. [Walter S.] Schuyler, of the 5th cavalry, recently appointed on Gen. Crook's staff, joined us on the 23d, and brought some news relative to army movements. Gen. Sheridan has been at Red Cloud agency and must have missed Crook's dispatch. Gen. Carr, with eight companies of the 5th cavalry, is on the Little Powder river, hunting up Indians. I have no doubt he will find them, if he only goes far enough. If he does, he'll wish he hadn't, for if Crook with 1,200 men found enough to do in repulsing Sitting Bull, what chance can Carr have with only 400? By the way, a rumor from Indian sources states that some big Sioux chief, either Sitting Bull or Gray Eagle, was killed in the fight of the 17th. This was why, they say, the Indians retreated so suddenly and simultaneously, after holding their own for so many hours. Arnold, the mail carrier, states that Sheridan has returned to Chicago.

Terry, we are told, had a fight also, and the Sioux at the agencies say it was a drawn battle, with many killed on both sides. Sitting Bull had 1,800 lodges, about 5,500 warriors, on Rosebud creek, and doubtless, most of those gentlemen joined in giving us that warm reception last Saturday week. We intend to trespass on their good nature once more when the wagon train comes in, unless the peace commissioners, appointed, as we understood, by congress, spoil the game.[7] I think Crook fears this, because he is reported to be rather dissatisfied with the defeat of the recent scouts. To surprise the Indians is now admitted to be impossible. We must fight them openly if they choose to allow us, because they are masters of the situation and will follow whatever policy best suits their interest. Looked at from an impartial stand-point, the Sioux are on the defensive. They stand for their hunting grounds—for their subsistence. They refuse to go to the agencies, where they are systematically starved and cheated, except in a few cases. Apart from their cruelty, common to all Indians, the Sioux are to be admired for the bold stand they have made. They have not skulked. They have not run away disgracefully or avoided the long-promised fight. On the contrary, they have been the attacking party when their territory—theirs either by privilege, or conquest, or treaty—was invaded. Sitting Bull, through the agencies, sent word to Crook to come on if he wanted a fight. He would wait for him. The Indian was as good as his word. Crook came and they fought. We gained a barren victory, leaving the campaign as undecided as if no shot had been fired.

True, the Indians suffered severely. Otherwise they would have followed up our retrograde movement to the bitter end, but they still hold their position between us and the Yellowstone river, and, after re-entering Montana, we will have to fight our way mile by mile to the banks of that powerful stream. Of course the Sioux will have to succumb finally—they are the last of the Indians, that is in the sense of serious resistance to the national authority and the unending incursions of the whites. They despise the "friendly," or degenerate tribes, and they make no secret of their undying hostility to the pale-faces. But they have a barbaric virtue which must command the admiration of their bitterest foes—fidelity to each other. When Crook, at the beginning of this expedition, went to Red Cloud after warriors to serve against the Montana Sioux, the agency Indians laughed at him. Did he think they were going to fight their own kith and kin—their brothers and cousins—for the pale-face? Not they. He might get the facile Pawnee, or the small Shoshone, or the gasconading Crow, but Sioux against Sioux—never.

And so the proud savages battled the white chief, and, no doubt, agency warriors and agency ammunition figured in the affair of the 17th on Rose Bud. It is certain that all the "young men" left Red Cloud to join Sitting Bull. The old men, squaws, and papooses remain. Why does not the government transport the latter to the Missouri river, if it means business? How strange that our civilized administration should permit its post traders and agents to arm the Indians, provide them with ammunition, feed their women and children, place them, in a word, on a war footing, and then enlist unsuspecting white men in the regular army, arm them, train them, feed and clothe them for the purpose of shooting down the very warriors whom the government itself has rendered formidable. Thus we have the interior and war departments fighting each other in the field. The men killed on both sides fall by government bullets.

The chief "Spotted Tail" is the most sagacious, friendly, and honorable of the Sioux leaders. He has firmly maintained the treaty of 1868 and is content to live in peace with the whites, because he sees, and knows, the absolute uselessness of resistance. Neither he nor his have had anything, so far as is known, to do with the present troubles, which, indeed, as is generally acknowledged, were stirred up by Gen. Crook himself, when he attacked Crazy Horse's band last March. Then was sown the wind—now we are reaping the whirlwind.

The pretext of this war is to drive the Indians to the reservations on the Missouri river and make them come into the agencies. The Sioux object to this for several reasons, chief of which are, first, the hunting-grounds on the Missouri are inferior to those on the Tongue and the Yellowstone; second, at the agencies they are treated as beggars and are cheated and half-starved; third, they hate being cooped up in reservations, where they die of inaction and bad food; fourth, they think the country belongs to them and not to the whites; fifth, they love their wild freedom and abhor the paleface's civilization; sixth, they look upon work as a cardinal vice fit only for squaws; seventh, they like hunting and bloodshed. Under these circumstances, it would appear sensible for the government to adopt one of two courses. Either withdraw all troops from the disputed lands and leave the hunting grounds, from Powder river to the Yellowstone, to the Sioux, or move in a sufficient army—say 10,000 men—to sweep them root and branch from the face of the earth. With our present force, the war may drag its weary length along for years. Better to make one grand swoop and be done with the wretched business than be going to the expense and annoyance of annual expeditions, such as those now on foot—none of them so organized as to accomplish anything decisive. The days are gone when one white soldier could whip 10 Indians. The latter are now better weaponed than our own army, and a smart savage, with a first-class rifle, a keen eye, plenty of powder and lead, and courage sufficient for all military purposes, is quite enough for one good "regular" to look after. If any fireside hero thinks that he can come out to the region and get away with a score of Sioux, Crook will give him plenty of chances before the summer is over. A regiment of such "invincibles" would be a god-send just now.

"Buffalo Bill" is with Carr's cavalry. He says: "Th . . . [illegible] . . . Indian war," from which it is to be presumed that "Bill" is going to devour the Sioux nation body and breeches.

As we are growing tired of inaction, a party is being organized to go into the mountains and hunt for gold. The general himself is going along. Should the yellow tempter be discovered in any reasonable quantity, the influx of miners to this section would be tremendous. There is ample room here for a fine settlement, and an army of miners, rooted to the soil as it were, would be more effective in settling this Indian question than an army of soldiers, tired of the campaign and counting the hours until they can return to "the railroad" and go upon an unmitigated military spree.

We have no whisky in camp, and are, therefore, going to have a dry Fourth of July. But the rainy season has commenced, making all things look dreary, encouraging rheumatism and giving men's thoughts a suicidal tendency. To banish dull care we are advised to go fishing. Oh, Isaac Walton—gentle, complacent old fraud!—even your patience would become exhausted sitting on the pebbly banks of Goose creek, rain dripping from your garments, your teeth chattering, "waiting for a bite." Even Nimrod's pastime grows monotonous in this vastness of mammoth desolation and preternatural silence. So oppressive, when away from camp, is the latter sensation, that I fancy a shot fired by the man in the moon would be heard among these mountains. We virtually pine for something to read and would not cast away even a dime novel, a "poem" by Walt Whitman, a lecture by Deacon Bross, or a tract by Brother Moody.[8] Rather than this should last, welcome anything—tornado, earthquake, flood, or storm.

To a man used to the bustle of a great city, camp-life, inactive, is the most damnable of bores.

I have been astonished at the few amusement resources displayed by the officers of this outfit. Only for the occasional "rubbing up" given them by "commanding officers," subalterns would sink into a Van Winklish lethargy, and be eternally lost to "glory" and the "service." Nowhere does "the little brief authority" of man display itself in such "capers before high heaven" as in the regular army of this republic. In sooth, a man to be either an officer or private in Uncle Sam's legions must say: "Be calm—be calm, indignant heart" almost every day of his life; must muzzle his tongue, quell his spirit, and hug to his breast that granite idol, "discipline." In military parlance, the corporal "sits down" upon the private; the sergeant upon the corporal; the lieutenant upon the sergeant; the captain upon the lieutenant; the major upon the captain; the lieutenant colonel upon the major; the colonel upon the lieutenant colonel; and the general upon the whole pile. Thus, the nethermost man gets pretty well flattened out, if the others are in bad humor, and at no time are "commanding officers" so "cross and contrary" as when lying around camp, tormented by "blue devils," and nothing to do.

A more unromantic looking set of military heroes, the eye never rested upon than ours. Dust, rain, sun, and sweat have made havoc of the never very graceful uniforms. The rear portions of the men's pantaloons are, for the most part, worn out. The boots are coffee-colored. Such a thing as a regulation cap is not seen in the whole camp—everybody, from the general down, wearing some kind of a *sombrero*, picturesque enough, but rather unmilitary. Every face is parched—nearly every beard unshorn, and the eye is wearied by the unending display of light-blue pants and dark blue shirts, all in a more or less dilapidated condition. Our hours are regulated by the bugle, our only means of ascertaining the time. The mornings are chilly, the days hot and the nights wondrously cool for the latter part of June. But we generally have a lovely mountain breeze, highly invigorating, and vastly agreeable, except when it grows unruly and blows down our tents. I wish some enterprising company would lift those superb mountains en masse, move them to Chicago, and plant them for all time on the northwestern prairie, say five miles from Bridgeport.[9] How grand it would be to have the Big Horn giant scanning his tremendous countenance in the resplendent mirror of Lake Michigan!

A party of miners have been prospecting some of the creeks flowing from the hills around here, but have found no striking indications of gold. Some are going with Gen. Crook into the middle of the range in a few days. If nothing golden is discovered by them, the Big Horn region will cease to interest the fortune-hunting public for many a year.

J. F. F.

Chicago Times, July 26, 1876

In a Horn
In Lonely Lands
[*From Our Own Reporter*]

Crook's Expedition, Camp Cloud Peak, Wyoming, July 11. My desire to penetrate the Big Horn mountains has, at length, been gratified. On Saturday morning, July 1, Gen. Crook, with Col. Mills, Maj. Burt, Lieuts. Bourke, Schuyler, Carpenter, Lemly, half a dozen packers, and some newspaper correspondents, left this camp on a hunting and exploring expedition into the mountain ranges. The entire party were mounted on mules and went provisioned for four days. The weather was very fine and we were not annoyed by the heavy rain-storms which prevail here at this season. Two hours' ride brought us to the plateau of the eastern slope and we found a rich table land carpeted thick with grass, begemmed with countless flowers and watered by innumerable ice-cold streams. Thick pine forests covered most of the ground, but there were numerous natural parks, laid out by the hand of nature with a grace and beauty seldom seen in the artificial works of landscape gardeners.

From the plateau we could see three or four snowy ranges, the breezes from which rendered the July atmosphere cool and bracing as the early May zephyrs in less elevated latitudes. Not a man of the party had ever been two miles in the mountains previously, and we followed the trail left by the Snake Indians after they left us for Wind River valley on June 19. This led us into the very roughest parts of the Big Horn range, for the Snakes took the most inaccessible route in order to avoid the hunting parties of the Siouxs [*sic*] who periodically go into the mountains to cut lodge poles and kill game. Our mules, nevertheless, were equal to all emergencies, and by 3 o'clock in the afternoon of our first day out, we reached a lovely dell on the main branch of Goose creek where we went into camp until the dawn of Sunday. Starting forward again, we reached the beginning of the snowy range about 10 o'clock and were considerably impeded in our course by the melting snows, which converted the mountain valleys into so many quagmires in which our animals floundered at about every step. As we ascended higher we noticed several immense layers of quartz, some of which gave indications of gold, but not sufficient to gratify a rush of people in this direction with the expectation of growing rich in a day or a week. In fact the gold indications were no greater than those to be observed in almost every great chain of mountains on the continent.

A gentleman of this party, who had traveled much in Europe, particularly in Switzerland, said that the pass through which we moved reminded him in almost every feature of the St. Gotthard pass. Below us were the dark, green woods and golden streams, above us and around us were the eternal snows and the tremendous rocks, from which, and through which burst and thundered a thousand cascades, forming the head-waters of the splendid rivers that fertilize the slopes of this mountain region through-out its entire extent. Picturesque lakes, none of them completely frozen over and all of immense depth, so far as we could judge, met the eye at almost every half mile, so that there was no difficulty to recognizing the inexhaustible reservoirs that fed the countless torrents which swelled the volume of the Big Horn and Tongue rivers.

At 3 o'clock in the afternoon we reached the highest pinnacle of the snow range, almost on a level with Cloud Peak, and saw several other immense ranges toward the west and north, which, however, looked more like cloud banks than the mountains of Idaho, Utah, and Montana. Resting on this crest for half an hour, we commenced to descend the western slope and struck into one of the loveliest canons that can be imagined, indented by a glorious stream, and garnished by groves of cedar through all its extent. In the middle of this wild paradise we halted and went into camp. Gen. Crook and Lieut. Schuyler shot a couple of mountain sheep, genuine "big horns," so that our commissariat was well supplied. We had along three or four pack mules, which carried the heavier portion of our bedding and subsistence. The mosquitoes bothered us terribly while the sun continued visible, but at night the intense cold compelled them to cease their labors and allow us repose.

The general felt anxious to get back to camp by the Fourth, so he announced that he would allow us until noon next day to prospect for gold and do such hunting as we felt disposed for, after which our homeward march would begin.

At 5 o'clock on Monday morning Col. Mills, Lieut. Lemly, Messers. Wasson, Davenport,[10] and your correspondent, left the camp and rode down the canon to the west until we reached a point six miles distant from where Crook had established his headquarters. There the party got separated in an unaccountable manner, and Col. Mills and myself found ourselves alone. We supposed that the others had ridden forward to a prominent mountain peak about six miles further on, and we determined to proceed in that direction. As we advanced, the valley progressed in beauty. We passed lake after lake and stream after stream. The trees increased in size and variety, and the vegetation assumed a tropical richness. We saw hundreds of bear, elk, and buffalo tracks, indicating that the country was full of large game, but the beasts kept successfully out of sight.

Dozens of American eagles rose magically from the rocks and soared proudly above us, screaming with all their might, for, doubtless, they had never seen white men before. We kept on until we reached the base of the mountain, which was our objective point, but still we saw nothing of our late companions, which very much surprised us. Having gone so far, we determined to ascend the peak, the lower part of which was covered with large juniper trees—the crest being a bare rock which rose several hundred feet above the forest. We tied our mules in the trees about two-thirds of the way up, and then scaled the remainder of the almost perpendicular ascent. Thoroughly exhausted with the heat and climbing, we finally reached the summit, and each of us uttered an involuntary exclamation of astonishment. We had actually crossed the verge and stood upon the western-most outpost of the Big Horn mountains. Below us to the west lay the tremendous valley of the Wind river and Big Horn, bounded by a wall of mountains half covered with snow, while two other ranges, of similar character, rose beyond it. We observed the great river winding around the northwest, where it meets the Yellowstone, while the Gray Bull and countless other streams running from east and west, were distinctly discernible. Along the Big Horn river, for 15 miles on either side, appeared a strip of rough, sterile lands, similar to what I had already seen in Wyoming, but the western slope of the mountains and the mouths of the canon were natural gardens, studded with evergreen groves and beautiful by-parks in which the grass appeared to be several feet high, looking rich as green velvet. The water courses ran from every rock, and the noise of rushing waters could be heard in the sublime solitude—the only sounds that broke the awful stillness of that beauteous desert.

The lakes studding the valleys, looked like pieces of the blue sky which had fallen from the heavens, as if to contest their ethereal beauty with the lovely earth beneath. My enthusiasm was aroused, and looking down the slope and along the canon, I said to Col. Mills, "Bring along your Italy." The colonel laughed, but acknowledged that even in his extensive experience he had never looked upon anything so picturesque. He pointed out to me several ledges of quartz and remarked that gold almost invariably accompanied that particular geological formation. He also took a sketch of the scene for the benefit of the service. Then we took a last lingering look at the scene and prepared to descend to where the mules were tied to the juniper trees a thousand feet below. Having found the animals, we faced toward the camp, Col. Mills acting as guide. We had not proceeded down the slope very far when, on reaching an opening in the forest, we saw two huge bull buffaloes grazing at some distance, and the killing instinct common to masculine humanity immediately suggested the beasts as victims. The mules were tied up again. We approached the edge of the wood, leveled our rifles, and in a minute both bisons were wounded. Mills killed his at the first shot, but, being a young hunter, it took three cartridges to settle my buffalo. Then we cut out their tongues, as we had no means of carrying any other portion, and proceeded on our journey.

We reached camp in the canon at 3 o'clock and found that Crook had been gone for some hours, but had left one of his scouts behind to show us his trail, as he struck out a new route over the mountains, which we found much more practical than the one we first came over. We overtook the rest of the party at 6 o'clock, and went into camp for the night. Then we learned that Lieut. Lemly and Mr. Davenport had missed us in the woods and turned back, supposing that we had done the same, while Mr. Wasson's[11] mule was so tired that he could urge it no further and was obliged to return. Thus, by accident, Col. Mills and THE TIMES correspondent had the honor of being about the first pale faces that ever crossed the Big Horn range completely from the eastern to the western slope. Had we known that the rest had turned back, to confess the honest truth, we should have done the same.

The gold prospectors examined some of the streams and lakes, but found no great encouragement, although there were plenty of "indications." We saw some Indian trails but none of very recent appearance. Next morning, after experiencing a July snow-storm during the night, we resumed our march, and, without further adventure, reached camp about noon on the centennial Fourth. We had nothing wherewith to drink to the memory of George Washington, but we had a banquet on elk, deer, and mountain sheep, killed by Crook and his officers during the time that Mills and I were wandering through the Cedar canon. Taken altogether the trip was a delightful experience.

Capt. Graves, of Montana,[12] with a company of some 30 miners, followed our trail into the mountains, determined to decide the gold question once and for all. The captain told me that his party had explored every stream on the eastern slope of the range, from Crazy Woman's creek to Tongue river, and had not found a single grain of gold. He thought that if the precious metal existed in this region at all it must be in the Wind River valley, where the streams from both mountain ranges converge. Reports since received from his party state that no gold has been discovered by them find the chances are that they will all turn back and give up their explorations. Nearly every man in camp is satisfied that there are no gold mines in this vicinity. Several men experienced in mining have tried their hands at prospecting, but nothing, except disappointment, has come of it.

Apart, however, from this question of gold, there is no richer tract of country in America, and scarcely any more beautiful than the portion skirting these mountains and contained in their valleys. The summer season is short, it is true; the winters are long and rather cold, but an industrious population would soon conquer the difficulties produced by these circumstances. Hundreds of thousands of cattle could be raised here, grain could be grown in abundance—with powerful streams in such profusion manufactories would soon spring up; but to counterbalance all this there is one real drawback—the Sioux nation. They absolutely hold this country in the teeth of our government up to the present writing. Our campaign against them has been a failure more or less, so far, and no small party of us dare venture five miles from camp without the almost certainty of being cut off. I had some experience in that direction last week, which I will now relate.

The day after Crook's party returned from their hunt, the general, expecting the wagon train every moment, determined to send out a reconnoitering party along the base of the mountain, northwest, to discover where the Indians were and to take a general observation of the country. Lieut. Frederick W. Sibley, of E company, 2d cavalry, with 25 picked men drawn from the regiment, was detailed to accompany the scouts, Frank Grouard and Baptiste Pourier, on the reconnaissance. John Becker, a mule-packer who had some experience as a guide, was also of the party. The scouts had ventured forward some 20 miles two nights before, but saw Indians and returned. An officer came around to my tent on the morning of July 6 and informed me of the plan. He said the party were going in the direction of the Little Big Horn river, northwest, and if no Indians were discovered they would proceed still further.

As I was sent out here to see the country and not to dry-rot around camp, I made up my mind to go with Sibley, who is a fine young officer and a son of the late Col. Sibley, of Chicago.[13] I obtained Crook's permission, which he appeared rather reluctant to give, and was ready to start when the party mustered at noon. Each of us carried 100 rounds of ammunition and enough provender to last a week. The scouts led us to camp on Big Goose creek, but 13 miles from Camp Cloud Peak, where we remained until night. When evening had sufficiently advanced, our little party, 30 men all told, moved forward for the most part on the old Fort C. F. Smith road, Grouard keeping a sharp lookout from every vantage point ahead. The full moon rose upon us by 8 o'clock, and we continued our ride along the foot of the mountains until 2 o'clock that morning. Then we halted at a point seven miles from the Little Big Horn, in Montana, and fully 40 miles from our permanent camp, half-corraled [sic]our horses, and slept until daylight, our pickets keeping watch from the bluffs above our encampment.

At 4:30 o'clock on the morning of Friday, July 7, we were again in the saddle, pressing on toward where the scouts supposed the Indian village to be. Reaching the foot of a rocky mound, Grouard told us to halt while he took observations. By this time we had moved about four miles from our late bivouac. We observed Grouard's movements with some interest, as we knew we were in the enemy's country, and might encounter Indians at any moment. Scarcely had the scout taken a first look from the crest of the ridge, when a peculiar motion of his hand summoned Baptiste to his side. Both left their ponies below the bluff, and observed the country from between the rocks on the summit. A minute afterward they had mounted their horses, and came galloping back to us. "Quick, for your lives," cried Grouard. We mounted immediately and followed him. He led us among hills of red sandstone, the footstool of the mountains, and we were obliged to make our horses leap down on rocky ledges as much as six or seven feet to follow his course. Within 15 minutes we reached a hill sufficiently large to conceal our horses, while those of us who were furnished with glasses, namely Grouard, Pourier, Lieut. Sibley, and myself, went into the rocks, and waited to see what was coming. "What did you see, Frank?" asked Sibley of the scout. "Only Sitting Bull's war party," Frank replied. "Knew they were up here without coming at all." We did not have long to wait for the confirmation of his words. Almost at the same instant groups of mounted savages appeared on every hill north and east of us. Every moment increased the numbers, until they seemed to cover the country far and wide. "They have not seen us yet," said the scout. "Unless some of them hit upon the trail we are comparatively safe."

Gradually the right flank of the Indians approached the ground over which we had come that morning and the previous night. We watched their movements with breathless interest. Suddenly an Indian attired in a red blanket halted, looked for a moment at the earth, and began to ride around in a circle. "Now look out," said Grouard, "that fellow has found our trail and they will be after us in five minutes."

"What are we going to do?" asked the young officer.

"Well, we have but one chance of escape," said Grouard, "let us lead our horses into the mountains and try to cross them. Meanwhile prepare for the worst."

Then we left the rocks and went down among the soldiers. Lieut. Sibley said to them: "Men, the Indians have discovered us. We will have to do some fighting. If we can make an honorable escape, all together, we shall do it. If retreat is impossible, let no man surrender. Die in your tracks for the Indians show no mercy."

"All right, sir," said the men, and the whole party followed the scouts and the officer up the steep mountain side, which at that point was steep to a discouraging extent. The Indians must have seen us, they were scarcely more than a mile distant, for hundreds of them had halted and appeared to be in consultation. We continued our retreat until we struck an old Sioux trail on the first ridge. "This path leads to the snowy ridge," said Grouard. "If we can reach there without being overtaken or cut off, our chances are pretty fair." Most of the road was rather good, and we proceeded in a northwestern direction at a brisk trot. Having gone five miles and seeing no Indians on our track, Grouard concluded that they had abandoned the pursuit or else did not care about attacking us in the hills. The horses were badly used up, and many of the men were suffering from hunger. So we halted to make some coffee and to allow our animals to recuperate. This occupied about an hour, when we again mounted and set forward. We crossed the main branch of Tongue river, flowing through the mountains, and were in full view of the snowy range. The same splendid scenery that I had observed when out with Crook's party was visible on every side. The trail led through natural parks, open spaces bordered by rocks and pine trees on the mountain sides. Here the country was comparatively open. Suddenly John Becker, the packer, and a soldier rode up, exclaiming, "The Indians, the Indians!"

Grouard looked over his shoulder and saw some of the red devils riding on our right flank. We had reached a plain on the mountain range, timber on our left, timber on our front, and rocks and timber on our right, at about 200 yards distant. "Keep to the left along the woods," said the scout. Scarce were the words uttered when from the rocks there came a ringing volley. The Indians had fired upon us, and had stuck my horse and two others. Fortunately the scoundrels fired too low, miscalculating the distance, and not a man was wounded. Our animals, after the manner of American horses, stampeded and nearly dashed out our brains against the trees on our left. The savages gave us three more volleys, wounding more of our horses, before we got the beasts tied to the timber. We gave them a volley back to keep them in check, and then formed a circular skirmish line in the woods. We could see the Indian leader, dressed in what appeared to be white buckskin, directing the movements of his men. Grouard recognized him. He is a Cheyenne, called White Antelope, famed for his enterprise and skill.[14] The Cheyennes and Sioux are firm allies, and always fight together. White Antelope led one charge against us, but our fire sent himself and his warriors back in quick time. Then the Indians laid low in the rocks and kept up an incessant fire on our position, filling the trees around us with lead. Not a man of us ever expected to leave that spot alive. They

Loafing Hangs Heavily upon Us 119

evidently aimed at our horses, thinking that by killing them all means of escape would be cut off from us.

Meanwhile their numbers continued to increase. The open slopes swarmed with Indians, and we could hear their savage, encouraging yells to each other. Cheyennes and Sioux were mixed together and appeared to be in great glee. They had evidently recognized Grouard, who they mortally hate, for they called-out to him in Sioux, "Standing Bear (the name they give him), do you think that there are no men but yours in this country?" We reserved our fire until an Indian showed himself. They were prodigal of their ammunition, and fired wildly. But they were fast surrounding us. We had fought them and kept them at bay for two hours, from half-past 11 until half-past 1 o'clock, but they were 20 to our one, and we knew that unless a special Providence interposed we could never carry our lives away with us. We were looking death full in the face, and so close that we could feel his cold breath upon our foreheads, and his icy grip upon our hearts.

"No surrender" was the word passed from man to man. Each of us would have blown out his own brains rather than fall alive into Indian hands. A disabling wound would have been the same as death. I had often wondered how a man felt when he saw inevitable sudden doom before him. I know it now, for I had no idea of escape, and could not have suffered more if an Indian knife or bullet had pierced my heart. So it was with all of us. It is one thing to face death in the midst of excitement. It is quite another thing to meet him in almost cold blood, with the prospect of your dishonored carcass being first mutilated and then left to feed the fox and vulture. After a man once sees the skull and cross-bones as our party saw it on the afternoon of July 7, no subsequent glimpse of grim mortality can possibly impress him in the same manner. Well, the eternal shadows were fast closing around us; the bullets were hitting nearer every moment, and the Indian yell was growing stronger and fiercer when a hand was laid on my shoulder, and a soldier named Rufus, my neighbor on the skirmish line, said, "The rest are retiring. Lieut. Sibley tells us to do the same."[15] I quietly withdrew from the friendly pine tree which had kept at least a dozen bullets from making havoc of my body. "Go to your saddle-bags and take all your ammunition," said Sibley as I passed him. "We are going to abandon the horses. The Indians are all around us, and we must take to the rocks on foot. It is our only chance."

I did as directed, but felt a pang at leaving my noble beast, which was bleeding from its wound in the side. We dared not shoot our horses, for that would discover our movement to the enemy. Grouard advised this proceeding. With a celerity which was only possible to men struggling for life, and to escape a dreadful fate, our party obeyed their orders, and, in Indian file, retired through the wood and fallen trees in our rear, toward the east, firing a volley and some scattering shots before we moved out, to make the Indians believe we were still in position. Our horses were evidently visible to the savages—a circumstance that facilitated our escape. We ran for a mile through the forest, waded Tongue river (the headwaters) up to our waists, and gained the rocks of the mountain ridge, where no Indian pony could follow us, when we heard five or six scattering volleys in succession. It was the final fire of the Indians before they made their charge at our "late corral" to get our scalps. "We are safe for the present," said Grouard, with a grim smile, "but let us lose no time in putting more rocks between us and the White Antelope." We followed his advice with a feeling of thankfulness which only men in such trials can ever know. How astonished the Indians must have been when they ran in upon the maimed horses and did not get a single scalp.

Even under such circumstances as we were placed in, we had a little laugh at their expense. But we had escaped one danger only to encounter another. Fully 45 miles of mountain, rock, and forest lay between us and Crook's camp. We could not carry a single particle of food, and had to throw away everything superfluous in the way of clothing. With at least 50 Indians behind us and uncounted precipices before us, we found our rifles and 100 rounds of ammunition each a sufficient load to carry. The brave Grouard, the ablest of scouts, conducted our retreat, and we marched, climbed, and tumbled over places that at other times would have been impossible to us, until midnight. Then we halted under an immense pile of rocks on the top of a mountain, and there witnessed one of the most terrible wind-storms that can be imagined.

Long before dawn we were again stumbling through the rocks and forest, and at daylight reached the tremendous canon cut in the mountain by what is called the eastern fork of Tongue river. Most of our men were too exhausted to make the descent of the canon, so Grouard led us through an open valley down by the river, on the left bank, for two miles as hard as we could go, for if discovered there by the savages we could only halt and die together. Fortune favored us, and we made the right bank of the stream unobserved, being then about 25 miles from Crook's headquarters. In our front were the plains of the eastern slope, full of hostile Indians, while our only avenue of escape was to climb over the tremendous precipice which formed the right side of the canon. But the dauntless Grouard was equal to the crisis. He scaled that gigantic wall diagonally, and led us along a mere squirrel path not more than a foot wide, with an abyss 500 feet below, and a sheer wall of rocks 200 feet high above us.

After an hour's herculean toil we gained the crest and saw the point of the mountain, about 20 miles distant, where lay our camp. This, as may be imagined, was a blissful vision, but we were half dead with fatigue, and some of us were almost famine-stricken. Yet the indefatigable Grouard would not stop until we reached the eastern foot-hills, where we made a dive into the valley to obtain water, our only refreshment on that hard rugged road. Scarcely had we slaked our thirst when Grouard led us up the hill again, and we had barely reached the timber when, around the rocks, at the point we had climbed shortly before, appeared another strong party of Sioux. This made us desperate. Every man examined his rifle and looked to his ammunition. We all felt that life would be too dearly purchased by further flight, and following the example of the brave young Sibley and the two gallant scouts, we took up our position among the rocks on the knoll we had reached, determined to sell our lives as dearly a possible. "Finerty," said Sibley to me, "we are in hard luck, but, d—m them, we'll show the red scoundrels how white men can die. Boys (turning to the soldiers), we have a good position; let every shot dispose of an Indian."

At that moment not a man among us felt any inclination to get away. Desperation and revenge had usurped the place of the animal instinct to preserve our lives. In such moments mind is superior to matter, and soul to the nerves.

But we were spared the ordeal. The Sioux failed to observe us, as, very fortunately, they did not advance high enough to find our trail, but kept eastward on the lower branch of Tongue river. Thoroughly worn out, we all fell asleep, excepting the tireless scouts, and awoke at dark somewhat refreshed. Not a man of us, Sioux or no Sioux, could endure the mountain journey longer, so we took our 30 jaded, hunted lives in our hands and struck along the valley, actually wading Big Goose creek up to our arm-pits, at 3 o'clock Sunday morning, the water being cold as the mountain snow could make it. Two men, Sergt. Cornwell and Private Collins,[16] were too exhausted to cross, so they hid in the brush until we sent two companies of cavalry after them, when we reached camp. After crossing Big Goose we were nearly a dozen miles from our camp on Little Goose creek, and, you may judge how badly we were used up, when it took four hours to make six miles. The rocks had skinned our feet and starvation had weakened our frames. Only a few were vigorous enough to push on. At 5 o'clock we saw a few more Indians, but we took no pains to conceal ourselves further. They evidently mistook us for a camp outguard, and being only a handful kept away. At 7 o'clock we met some cavalry out hunting, and we went into camp for horses, as most of the men could walk no further. Capts. DeWees and Rawolle, of the 2nd cavalry, came out to us with led horses, and we reached camp at 10 o'clock Monday morning amid congratulations from every side. The men who remained at Goose creek were brought in some hours later. Thus, after passing through incredible danger and great privation, every man of our thirty, unwounded as by a miracle, found himself safe in Camp Cloud Peak, surrounded by comrades. For conducting this retreat with such consummate success, Frank Grouard deserves the highest place among the scouts of the American continent.

The oldest of our Indian fighters, including Col. Royall, concur in saying that escape from danger so imminent and appalling in a manner so successful is unparalleled in the history of Indian warfare. It was fortunate for the party that an officer possessing the coolness and good sense of Lieut. Sibley commanded it. A rash, confused, bull-headed leader would have disregarded Grouard and brought ruin upon us all.

We found on getting in that Gen. Crook was up in the mountains on another hunting expedition. A messenger was sent for him at once, but did not find him. News reached our camp by the scout, Louis Richard, from Fort Fetterman, on Monday, to the effect that Gen. Custer with five companies of the 7th cavalry had been massacred in an Indian village not far from where Crook encountered the Sioux on June 17. This led Col. Royall, who feared that Crook might be waylaid in the mountains by Indians, to send four companies of cavalry to his rescue. They met the general coming back with some officers, and packers, having killed about 20 elk—a great boon to the camp, as we had been living chiefly on bacon for a month. Crook said very little when he heard of our adventure and Custer's disaster, but he kept up a big thinking.

July 12. Yesterday afternoon, Washkee,[17] the Shoshone Indian chief, with 213 warriors, arrived in our camp as allies. They appear to be in good fighting humor, but complain bitterly that the agencies continue to supply the Sioux with ammunition. While this is permitted the war will go on, for the Sioux will not surrender while they have a shot left. Spotted Tail is the only Sioux chieftain who has kept his entire band from off the war-path. The old man knows that in the long run the game will go against his people, and he has no desire to be at enmity with the whites.

Indians have been firing into our camp every night since our reconnoitering party returned. They are, as usual, after our herd of horses and mules, but we have everything strongly guarded. Our wagon train is expected to-day, and the companies of [Elijah R.] Wells and Rawolle[18] have gone north [*sic*, south] as far as Fort Phil Kearny, some 18 miles from here, to meet it. In addition to this force there are with the train seven companies of infantry, under

Maj. Chambers. By the way, all our so-called companies are short of their legal complement by 25 men on an average. This shows how deceptive a muster-roll can be. When we hear of a regiment we receive hardly a weak battalion. Is this war, or humbug?

Sheridan's dispatch to Crook, after hearing of the Rosebud fight, was: "Hit them again, and hit them harder." Doubtless the fate of the brave and unfortunate Custer will show the lieutenant general [Sheridan] that it takes men as well as valor to fight the combined forces of the Sioux and Cheyennes. This is *the* Indian war, and many a brave man will bite the dust before the matter is decided. "Forty millions" must conquer in the long run.[19]

This morning three scouts from Gen. Terry arrived in camp with full dispatches relative to Custer's catastrophe, and informing Crook of the movements of the army on the Yellowstone. The men belong to Gibbon's regiment and came through in three days from the confluence of the Big Horn and Yellowstone rivers.[20] The whole matter of the Little Big Horn tragedy must have been published by THE TIMES long ago, so there is no need to dwell upon it here. The misfortune has cast a gloom over our whole camp and has had a bad effect on the morale of the men.

Gen. Terry wishes Crook to form a junction with him. He offers to waive all seniority and heartily cooperate for the common cause and against the common enemy. His steamboat has gone for fresh supplies and will be at the rendezvous by the 18th inst. I hope Crook will accept Terry's proposition.

It is now 2 o'clock in the afternoon and our train has not yet arrived. We can see signal fires lit by the Sioux burning along the course of Tongue river and we are expecting to be summoned into action every minute. Within five days we shall know how this campaign is going to turn out. If we form a junction with Terry, I have faith that we shall be finally and speedily victorious. Some Utes and Bannocks are expected with the train. Should they come, our force of Indian allies will be quite respectable.

J. F. Finerty

Chicago Times, July 16, 1876

CROOK SAFE

[*Special Telegram*]

CROOK'S EXPEDITION, CAMP CLOUD PEAK, WYOMING, via FORT FETTERMAN, July 15. On July 1 Gen. Crook, with several officers and all the newspaper correspondents, making up a party of 20 in all, left here and crossed the Big Horn mountains, almost due westward, partly to hunt and partly to explore. They were out four days. Your correspondent, with Col. Mills, crossed three snowy ranges and penetrated to the western slope, whence they had a full view of the Wind river and Big Horn valleys. The gold indications were respectable, but not sufficiently numerous to justify a rush in this direction. The country itself, the slopes and valleys of the mountains, is a second Tyrol.[21]

Lakes, streams, flowers, and grasses of all description abound. The mountains abound with wild sheep and elk, together with buffalo and deer. Along the banks of the Big Horn river there is a strip of rough bad lands, about 20 miles wide, but the rest of the soil is above the average. We were the first white party that ever crossed these mountains. Our means of exploring for gold were necessarily incomplete, but Capt. Graves, with a party of 26 Montana men, is now working the rivulets on our track, so far without success. The mountains are wooded up to the snow level. The party returned safely to camp. They had to use mules and follow old game and Indian trails over passes made as those of St. Gotthard[22] and St. Bernard.

Last Thursday, July 6, Lieut. Sibley of Company E, 2d cavalry, with a detail of 25 picked men, was ordered to escort Frank Grouard and Baptiste Pourier, the scouts, along the base of the mountains, to discover, if possible the camp of Sitting Bull. Desirous of viewing the northern section of the mountain country, your correspondent accompanied the command. We left camp at noon, and marched until 4 o'clock in the afternoon, when we halted until night and pushed on by moonlight. The march was continued for 45 miles, until we reached a point near the Little Big Horn river, when we went into bivouac. At 4 o'clock in the morning we started again, and proceeded about three miles, when Grouard signaled to us from a forward bluff to halt. We did so, and he came riding back to say that a multitude of Indians all on the war-path, were within a mile of us. He led us into the side rocks to see whether we would escape observation. Hardly had we taken position when they came swarming over the hills, and seemed to cover the country. In 20 minutes they struck our trail, and Grouard led us up the mountain side, horses and all. The Indians saw us at once, and a strong party started in pursuit. We crossed the mountains to the northwest, and when about 12 miles from the edge, within a view of the snowy range, we were attacked from all sides but the east. Grouard led us into the timber. We tied our horses and fought the savages for two hours; until they began to close in on us by hundreds from every point. Your correspondent's horse and those of some others were wounded badly by the first volley fired within 200 yards range, but not a man was hurt. Seeing that if we remained longer we must all be butchered, Grouard decided to abandon the horses and retreat on foot. We took all our ammunition and left everything else. The Indians kept firing on our horses, supposing we were there, until we put two miles between us, rocks and trees being our protection. The Indians could not well follow us on horseback.

We had a march on foot of 50 miles over canons and precipices. We were well up in Montana. We marched almost incessantly, without rations, from 2 o'clock on the afternoon of Friday until the same hour on Saturday, when we were again in sight of Indians on this side of the slope. We lay back until dark, marched all night, having to cross several rivers, and reached camp without losing a man, although some were delirious from hunger and fatigue—a most miraculous escape, seeing that an innumerable band of Cheyennes and Sioux, fully armed, were after us. Our escape is due to the skill of Grouard, an unequaled scout, and to the soldierly coolness of Lieut. Sibley, an officer only 23 years old. He is the son of Col. Sibley, who recently died in Chicago. Judging by the number of redskins, we must have seen Sitting Bull's whole force. White Antelope, a Cheyenne chief, was the man who nearly captured us.

This morning three couriers, William [*sic*, James] Bell and two others,[23] from Gen. Terry, now at the confluence of the Big Horn and Yellowstone, arrived with dispatches for Crook. Terry wants the general to co-operate with him, and he will waive all claims of seniority. Full news of the Custer disaster was also sent, but as it has reached you already it can be omitted. Some 200 Snake Indians, under Washakie, their chief, have arrived to aid us. We expect our wagon train and mail to-day, but it has not yet arrived.

The country is full of Indians, and we fear it has been attacked. Two companies of cavalry have gone to Phil Kearny, to meet it. Taken in all, this campaign is growing red hot. Full particulars of everything are forwarded by the courier who brings this dispatch.

LATER—it is feared in camp that Gen. Crook will prefer to act independent of Terry.

Another Account
[To the Western Associated Press]

CHEYENNE, July 15. The following is just received:
CROOK'S CAMP, CLOUD PEAK, July 12. The following is via Fetterman to-night: Three soldiers, couriers from Gen. Terry, at the mouth of the Big Horn, have just arrived. Gen. Terry's dispatch to Crook confirms Custer's fate, and implies very plainly that had Custer waited one day longer Gibbon would have joined him. Terry is anxious for Crook to join forces, make plans, and execute them regardless of rank. The Indians are still hovering about the Little Big Horn, one day's hard march from here. They have fired into camp every night of late, and tried to burn us out by setting the grass on fire all around. On July 6 Lieut. Sibley, Company E, 2d cavalry, with 25 men, and Frank Grouard, and Baptiste Pourier, as scouts, went on a reconnaissance, were discovered and surrounded, and followed into the timber of the Big Horn mountains, where, by hitching the horses to trees and abandoning them, the men were enabled to escape on foot by way of a ravine in the rear. They all got back alive, and probably this diversion saved the camp from a

grand attempt at a stampede or capture. The Snake Indians, 200 strong, joined us here on yesterday, but unless the Utes also come soon no offensive operations will be likely to take place until the arrival of the 5th cavalry from Cheyenne crossing [presumably the Cheyenne River crossing east of Fort Reno]. The wagon train and additional infantry are due from Fetterman to-day. The health of the command is good. Gen. Gibbon's reserve force were met by the victorious Sioux, dressed in Custer's men's clothes and mounted on their horses, firing into the soldiers. The Indian village possessed evidence of white men's presence, kegs of whisky, etc., being found. Signal fires, supposed to be in reference to the incoming wagon train, are visible to the east of Crook's camp on the extreme south waters of Tongue river.

Chicago Times, July 23, 1876

BOOKED FOR BLOOD
IN CROOK'S CAMP
[From Our Own Reporter]

CROOK'S EXPEDITION, CAMP CLOUD PEAK, Wyoming, July 16, via FORT FETTERMAN, July 22. Our wagon-train arrived here all safe on the morning of the 13th, escorted by three of our 9th infantry companies and by the following new companies of the same branch of the service, sent to reinforce us from Salt Lake: Companies B, C, F, and I, 14th, commanded respectively by Capts. Kennington, Burke, Tobey, and Taylor, and company D, of the 4th, commanded by Capt. Powell.[24] All the men are in fine condition.

We expect the 5th cavalry on Bear creek, near the Little Powder river, to join us within a week. It is said to be the finest horse regiment in the service, and is commanded by Col. Wesley Merritt, who commanded a brigade of volunteer cavalry in the Army of the Potomac. The eight companies assigned to us number 400 men all splendidly mounted. Awaiting the 5th delays our northward march. When we start again the numerical strength of our expedition will be as follows: Infantry, 10 companies, 420 men; 2d cavalry, five companies, 270 men; 3d cavalry, 10 companies, 534 men; Snake Indians, 213 warriors; 5th cavalry, 400 men; total, 1,837 men, not including officers, packers, and camp followers. Maj. Noyes still commands the 2d cavalry. The 3d has been reorganized as follows: First battalion, companies A, E, I, and M, Col. Anson Mills; Second battalion, companies C, G, F, and D, Col. Van Vliet; Third battalion, companies B and L, Capt. Meinhold.

We are provisioned until Sept. 15, and the talk now is of having a winter or fall campaign should the next scout fail, and of sending the wagons back for more supplies. Furthermore, it is said that Capt. Nickerson, of Crook's staff, is bringing up a strong force of Ute Indians, but no artillery has been ordered, which most of the officers consider a very unfortunate omission, as after poor Custer's experience the passion for charging into Indian villages has somewhat subsided. A few shells thrown among the rocks or tepees would make the Sioux think the day of doom was at hand.

Gen. Crook officially informed your correspondent to-day that he was going to unite his force and co-operate with Gen. Terry, who is now marching southward from the Yellowstone, to form a junction with this command. Should he, however, fail to arrive on time when our reinforcements come up, Crook will march against Sitting Bull without delay. The chances are, however, that the junction will be speedily effected.

J. F. F.

Chicago Times, July 27, 1876

The Door of Death
[*From Our Own Reporter*]

CROOK'S EXPEDITION, CAMP ON MOUTH TONGUE RIVER, Wyoming, July 23, via FORT FETTERMAN, Wyoming, July 26. We have moved 14 miles north from Camp Cloud Peak since July 16, and are awaiting Gen. Merritt and the 5th cavalry before renewing active operations. That force is now en route here by rapid marches and will arrive within this week. Four Crow scouts arrived from Gen. Terry's command on the 20th inst. with dispatches dated the 16th. All are well, with the general and his party. On that date they were anxiously awaiting dispatches from Gen. Crook. The latter sent a special courier to Terry on the 19th, and if he has had good luck he must have reached the confluence of the Big Horn and Yellowstone rivers by this time. Crook wants Terry to march toward his command at least half way, as the Indians are in this vicinity, mostly up in the mountains, and there the big battles of this war must be fought.

Our Snake allies positively assure us that the Sioux are occupying the mountains above us, just where Sibley's party struck them in full force, and they will compel us to fight them inch by inch. This will be a deadly warfare. They know every foot of those ranges, of which we are decidedly ignorant; can guard every pass and ambuscade us at every step. Having plenty of dried meat, they can, with what game they kill, make a prolonged resistance, and being adepts in all the arts of deviltry, they can burn the forests about our ears while keeping free from the fire themselves. Their hunting parties keep out on the buffalo ranges, adding fresh meat to their stores every day.

Truly this is a nice little war for our newest brigadier general to have on hand. Let us hope for the best. It is the only thing we can do. Meanwhile, the veteran officers here say that it would be wise to accept volunteer regiments if only to relieve the 1st, 4th, 6th, and 8th cavalry, all lying on their oars around the other territories, when they ought to be marched right in here to crush this Sioux devil at one blow. The government ought to finish this campaign with a clap of thunder. We ought to burn Sitting Bull in his mountain fastness, or get chewed up ourselves. A regular tidal wave of troops ought to be on the march now to support our approaching movement. It is to be hoped that our impetuous lieutenant general will avoid the error committed by the government during the first few days of the rebellion—the error of not sending enough men into the field to finish the war thoroughly and at once. In Indian as all other warfares homeopathic treatment is both a blunder and a crime.

Gen. Sherman is right now, just as he was right when he said that 200,000 men would be necessary to keep Kentucky in the union. "I am astounded," says Terry to Crook, "at the numbers and skill of the enemy." May fortune keep us from being more so. The voice of our camp says to Sheridan, "Send out here all your military who are loafing around where there is nothing more formidable than pretty girls to fight." They will cost the government as little here as where they are and will be infinitely more useful. Let this not be construed into a "scary" dispatch. This command will fight to the last man, but the officers and soldiers recognize the formidable character of the task before them and are radically down on all half-way military experiments.

If the lessons of the past month are not thrown away in high places, Custer will not have died in vain. Any one spoiling for a fight had better emigrate to these parts without delay.

J. F. F.

Chicago Times, August 1, 1876

"Lo" Game
in Crook's Camp
[*From Our Own Reporter*]

Crook's Expedition, in Camp, on South Tongue River, Wyoming, July 23. Our thin-ribbed horses and melancholy mules having devoured all the forage around Camp Cloud Peak, we have been making gradual marches to this stream, about 14 miles further north, since Thursday morning, July 16. The heat has been intense and the air and earth are full of enormous grasshoppers, moving down, like a sand cloud, to lay waste Nebraska and Kansas. They have eaten up everything in these endless fields, already burned brown as Moor-land by the July sun, so that the country, or wilderness has changed the verdant hue which greeted our eyes on the march to Rosebud for one closely approaching butternut—a fatal color for "boys in blue."25

Moreover, our ever-attentive friend, Sitting Bull, has been busy burning up the grass for miles north, east, and west of us, for some reason pregnant with Indian deviltry. He may think that he can starve out our horse-flesh—no difficult matter, seeing that our animals, entirely without grain for months, are half-starved already. But his own ponies have stomachs, too, and we can stand the destruction of horse rations about as well as the Sioux leader. Indians never do anything without an object, and, no doubt, before you read this we shall have solved the problem by some disagreeable process. Our Snakes, who scout the country every day, report that the mountains are all on fire down by North Tongue River, and that the Sioux are going to defend themselves in those tremendous ranges, full of canons, boulders, and woods, where an army would be melted away in useless efforts to dislodge them. If it comes down to bushwhacking, I am willing to bet ten to one that the Sioux will give us the best whipping ever a command of this kind got.

If we can get a fair stand-up fight out of them, away from any trees, why then I think we have some show of success, although the Indians must number at least double our present force, and that is a very moderate estimate of their strength. The despised aborigines of three months ago, have suddenly become formidable assassins—foemen more than worthy of our Caucasian steel. To quote the language of an orator, above whom now rolls the turbid tide of the Missouri, when referring to the defense of Algiers—the French Montana—by Ab-del Kaker in 1847—"An outcast tribe has been roused into brilliant heroism and successfully copes with the cross and the sword of the Christian civilizer."[26]

Let no man accuse me of Indian worship. I adore the race so much that I would gladly apply a torch to any mine the springing of which would annihilate them one and all, for they are incarnate devils in mind and act; but "ne'er may valor lose its meed," even though displayed by the most fiendish savages. This particular war has been forced upon the Sioux, and they have responded to the challenge right gallantly, as many a void in the army list and many a ghastly gap in our lately-boastful squadrons can bloodily testify. They have hit our haughty "regulars" an appalling blow, and have given to feed the raven the remains of the most gifted and dashing cavalry leader that "the great plains" shall know for many a bitter day. Our camp still mourns the youthful hero, whose dauntless bearing shall ever be associated with the closing hours of the great civil war. In reading the many accounts of the battle of Five Forks, more than 11 years ago, one passage descriptive of Sheridan and his boy-general remains fixed in my memory. "Beside him (Sheridan) rose and fell, like yellow foam upon the waves of war, the long locks of Custer." Who, then, could have dreamt that "the yellow foam" would yet mingle with his heart's best blood on the fatal slopes of the Big Horn? It was, indeed, a soldier's death, but with grim surroundings that dimmed its sun of glory. His doom recalls the lines of Lord Byron on the Death of Murat—the Napoleon of cavalry:

> Little didst thou dream when dashing
> On thy war-horse thro' the ranks,
> Like a stream that bursts its banks,
> White helmets cleft and sabres clashing
> Shone and shivered fast around thee,
> Of the fate at last which found thee,
> Was that haughty plume laid low
> By a slave's dishonest blow?
> Once, as the moon sways o'er the tide,
> It rolled in air, the warrior's guide,
> Thro' the smoke-created night
> Of the dark and sulphurous flight,
> The soldier raised his socking eye
> To catch the crest's ascendency;
> And as it onward, rolling rose,
> So moved his heart upon our foes—
> There, where death's brief pang was quickest,
> And the battle's wreck lay thickest,
> Strewed beneath the advancing banner
> Of the eagle's burning crest,
> There, with thunder-clouds to fan her,
> (Who could *then* her wing arrest,
> Victory beaming from her breast?)
> While the broken line enlarging
> Fell or fled along the plain,

> There, be sure, was *Custer* charging,
> There he'll never charge again.[27]

True, he led his soldiers into the valley of death, and they never emerged from its shadow; but with the rank and file, the famed and hapless leader nobly died. Peace to his gallant spirit. He has paid the penalty of a glorious rashness. War must have its victims, and in choosing George Custer, "The Giant" has done its worst.

Wherever his bones may be laid, whether in Montana or in Michigan, the man of the future will say, as he bends above the final resting place of that fearless horseman:

> His honored grave
> Contains the bravest of the brave.[28]

The soldiers and chiefs who died with Custer divide with him the honor and the grief of the army and the nation.

Four Crow Indians came through via the Big Horn mountains and Ash creek, from Terry's command two days ago. They report the Sioux still in the neighborhood of the Little Big Horn river, with hunting parties down on Tongue river and among the mountains. The savages must stick to the game country, where the buffalo is not scarce. Therefore, their present stronghold is in the famous buffalo range, between Tongue River and the Yellowstone. In my earlier letters I told you that game had almost ceased between Fort Phil Kearny and Fetterman. This explains why the Sioux have left that part of the country comparatively free from their ravages. It is of no possible use to them. While the buffalo lasts, Sitting Bull will last. When the bison is exterminated, good bye to Indian resistance. The redskin's commissariat marches on the hoof. Moral—exterminate the buffalo, and give Longfellow a chance to write a newer and a truer "Hiawatha." We may have, according to some theories, more grasshoppers, but we shall have less Sioux. The daring raider of to-day will be the starving beggar of to-morrow. The stomach is a better civilizer than the sword. (I use the latter word metaphorically, for there is not one weapon of the latter kind in the whole command.) The Indian heart is bold and defiant, but the Indian belly is, like the abdominal apparatus of all men and beasts, a weak vessel, which, like a bad conscience, "doth make cowards of us all." Some philanthropist may call this suggestion shocking and barbaric. Not at all. "The most civilized" of European nations not long since resorted to some such measure to re-establish its control over a remote island in the Atlantic. The plan succeeded most admirably. After a war which lasted the better part of seven centuries, "the most civilized" of nations gave up the idea of shooting down its rebels. Starving them was much cheaper and much more effective. A "civilized" statesman went systematically to work, and, taking advantage of a temporary vegetable blight, he, in three years, killed off 1,500,000 rebels, and the women and children of rebels; and behold, a people renowned for fighting sank quelled like poltroons before the withering breath of famine.

The American nation is much in the habit, especially around Boston, of copying the fashions set by "the most civilized" country alluded to. Therefore, I humbly suggest to THE TIMES, and, through it, to the American people, that, instead of fighting Sitting Bull, we all set to work and kill off his meat supply. If a highly moral and thoroughly Christly country of Europe succeeded, years ago, in subduing white and Christian rebels by the simple starvation process, surely we, who are only middling moral and not over-Christianly, can afford to dispose of our red, heathen rebels in the same way. The trouble with us is, that before we can slaughter the bison, we must do battle with the Indian. The latter has neither "the moral force," nor the "humility," nor the requisite love of God and horror of blood-letting to be politely starved out of existence.

Further of the Crows: They report numerous Sioux dead in the country through which they passed—the savages who, doubtless, fell before the rifles of Maj. Reno and his men. Judging by such reports as we have seen, Custer's troops could not have done much slaughter, hemmed in and confused as they were. Besides, the cavalry carbine, in many cases, proved a treacherous arm. It appears that the ejector often failed to throw out the shell of the exploded cartridge, and, being unprovided with ramrods, the soldiers were virtually disarmed. A word on this subject: The government cavalry carbine is a very delicate weapon, easily injured, and once damaged, hard to repair. It has but one shell ejector, which often fails to work and leaves the soldier at the mercy of his enemy. The official dolts who got up the arm failed to have rammers provided, a great oversight. Even if the shell of the infantry soldier should stick, he has still his iron wand wherewith to punch it out. Furthermore, short arms in Indian warfare are extremely inefficient.

The long infantry rifle is the thing to lift the Indian off his feet, wherefore the Sioux dread the "walk-a-heaps"—terribly armed and unembarrassed by scary horses—much more than they do our showy cavalry. Had the latter "the long rifle," they would be twice more effective than they are. It is objected that the infantry gun would be "unhandy." I don't think so. Gen. Crook always carries one on his saddle, and surely any trooper can do the same. The carbine is a pretty weapon, but compared with the musket of the foot, it is a mere military toy, excellent for dress parade, but damnable for active service. A double ejector would much improve the arm and save trouble from inextricable shells.

I saw, at Rosebud fight, not less than half a dozen soldiers in my immediate neighborhood punching and swearing at their carbines, all of which had "stuck." Is not this a nice time to be finding out the weak points of our firearms? Our enemy discovered the defect long ago. No Sioux will carry anything but a long rifle, if he can help it. The carbine is generally regarded as a make-shift.

"Why have we not artillery?" is a question very frequently asked here of late days. In the slang vernacular, "I give it up." The country is practicable for light or "flying" artillery, and, in the roughest parts, mules can carry mountain howitzers that would make the defenders of Indian villages sick. But, unless we join Terry, there will be no guns, heavy or light, for this command. This unfortunate omission is due to estimating, in the first place, the Sioux as being of Apache calibre.

By the way, the Crow runners assert that Terry's command is only four days' march from us. Crook sent out a courier named Kelley, a half-insane kind of person, with dispatches for Terry the other day. He turned back twice—once because the cactus pierced his moccasins, and once because he was seen by an Indian.

Two days ago he made a third attempt and has not since been heard from. He may get through all right, but if he does it will be miraculous.[29]

Crook's dispatch invited Terry to form a junction with him at the head of North Tongue river. The meeting *may* take place, but, like many others here I should be much better satisfied if the Crow scouts were sent back with the dispatches. Should evil betide Kelley, who is a brave fellow, although semi-crazy—there will be no junction, and, without being a croaker, I predict a hard time for this command should the Sioux give battle in force.

They will fight if it suits their convenience, but if they do we may be assured that they feel their over-mastering strength. It is not their policy to make war at a disadvantage.

A courier arrived from Fort Fetterman last evening with a very slim mail. This is our greatest annoyance. All couriers ride as light as they can, and no newspapers or any account ever reach us. This, under the circumstances in which we are placed, is a great deprivation. The few journals I have seen appear to be discussing Gen. Crook. A flashy New York sheet calls for his removal, because he did not please that paper's reporter on the day of Rosebud. *The Herald's* warrior must have been awfully excited if he calls [the] Rosebud fight a defeat. Another correspondent, too, enthusiastically, calls the affair a victory—a brilliant victory, I believe. With all due respect for these great ink-bottle generals, THE TIMES correspondent would mildly venture to opine that neither is correct. Crook set out from Goose Creek to thrash Sitting Bull, and allowed himself four days in which to do the job. Sitting Bull swooped down on Rosebud to meet Crook and, to all appearances, gave himself only an hour or so to finish the whole command, *a la* Custer. There was a fight—that much I am sure of—the Indians were repulsed at every point. An unlucky blunder in retiring a battalion for a strategic purpose exposed us to unnecessary loss, but the Indians were even then driven back. Crook did not use his entire command in the battle. Sitting Bull brought up most of his men, and, judging by recent reports, moved his village while he engaged Crook. Then he "lit out," bag and baggage. We were short of rations and ammunition, and could not, with any degree of sanity, have followed him up. He frustrated Crook's object, the capture of the village. Crook cooked his coffee on Rosebud creek that night, buried his dead, and regaled his eyes on the scalps of slain Sioux. Technically he was victorious. Judged by the standard of *results*, he was baffled, and had to retire on his base.

Where did his mistake begin? Not on the Rosebud, but on Goose creek. He ought to have carried his base along with him. His fine pack-train would have provisioned and ammunitioned his men for at least 15 days. We could have carried the wounded with us. Crook could then have "stayed with" Sitting Bull, and five days later, Custer would have found us in the neighborhood of the village, where he met his doom, investing it, or else laid out stark and stiff after having done all that men could do.

In view of more recent developments I am forced to conclude that misguided by the *then* headquarters estimate of the Sioux nation, a part of our brigade would have been led into the Indian trap and slaughtered wholesale. In that case for "Custer" you would substitute the name of "Crook" or "Royall," or "Evans" or "Mills," or "Noyes" or "Chambers," before the scarlet word "massacre." When all his reinforcements shall have arrived, Crook's command will be a very fine one. I do not say it by way of disparagement when I observe that it will be Crook's last chance. Should we be checked or defeated, there will be a cry raised against our present leader, and every eye will turn to Phil Sheridan. *He* will be called upon to meet the conquering Indian, and renew, among the Montana hills, the laurels which have had no bloody nurture since Lee converted his sword into the traditional plow-share under the Appomattox apple tree. Gen. Sheridan's presence in the field would. And all jealousy among military men of subordinate rank, for "the green-eyed monster" is potent both in war and in love.[30] I observe that Gen. Sherman is in favor of raising volunteers. Tecumseh's head is level. Sheridan wants to give "the regulars" another chance. Very well, let them have it by all means. Judging by doings in congress, the popular mind is in favor of reducing the army. Sitting Bull as a mustering out officer has no rival on this continent.

Crook's pet regiment, the 5th cavalry, are now en route from Fetterman to join us. Sheridan says that the eight companies muster over 500 men. He ought to know, but it is a fact disgraceful to the war department that our companies are shams and our regiments skeletons for the most part. Only think of our infantry averaging 35 men to a company! Our cavalry average about 10 men more. Will not any unprejudiced person remark that this state of things is simply damnable? They are sending us out some recruits from Carlisle [Barracks], we hear. What good are they? Half of them cannot ride, and not one in ten could hit a hay-stack at 100 yards. They may be useful for holding horses while the veterans go on the skirmish line. However, we must do the best we can with such material as we can get. The next scout will be decisive one way or the other as regards the face of this summer's campaign; but this Sioux war will not be terminated this year. The Indians are not going to give up the struggle so speedily. They have been expecting the conflict for years, and have made preparations accordingly. Their magazine is well supplied, and, so far, their course has been one of triumph.

Half a dozen big defeats will be necessary to inflict upon them before they come to terms, if, indeed, the nation, incensed by the late butchery, will accord them in their downfall—which sooner or later must come—any terms save those of utter extermination. In the grim horizon of the war we can see the black flag, with its skull and cross-bones, on both sides.

Our Indians report that a strong party of miners is being organized in Montana to hunt for gold down here. Graves' expedition had been entirely unsuccessful, and most people now believe that if an El Dorado exists in the Big Horn region it must be on the western slope of the mountains. This slope has been pretty thoroughly explored with no result except that of finding nothing, as I have stated in former correspondence.

If I am asked how stands the morale of Crook's command, notwithstanding the discouraging news from the 7th cavalry, I can safely aver that I have not yet seen "a man dismayed"; on the contrary, a spirit of vengeance has grown in the breasts of the soldiery, and, should the day go against Sitting Bull, Custer and his men will be suddenly and terribly avenged. Crook has been taught a useful lesson—not to divide his command. The Indians can scatter and re-concentrate twice as fast as can our troops, under the most favorable auspices, which gives them the advantage, when we separate our columns too far apart, of bringing their heaviest masses against our weak detachments, just as Bonaparte scooped out the slow Austrians in his first wonderful Italian campaign, commencing with Montenotte.

We are impatient for the coming fray as we are heartily sick of the camp. The 5th cavalry cannot be far off now. Sheridan ordered them up more than a week ago, but they switched off near Powder river after a straggling party of Cheyennes. Crook is much displeased with Merritt for not coming right on.[31] We ought to have fought one battle more by this time, but I predict an engagement before ten days. The 5th will have a very short breathing spell after they arrive.

To illustrate the spirit of the soldiers, I transcribe two verses from a song which I heard sung in one of the larger tents last night. It breathes the proper admixture of saltpetre, gore and tenderness—matters that generally go together in all emergencies of this kind. Here are the stanzas:

>Boys, fill your glasses,
>Each hour that passes,
>Steals, it may be, from our last night's cheer.
>The day soon shall come, boys,
>With life and drum, boys,
>Breaking shrilly on the soldier's ear.
>Drink the faithful hearts that love us,
>'Mid to-morrow's thickest fight,
>While the old flag floats above us,
>Think, boys, 'tis for them we smite!
>And if at eve, boys,
>Comrades may grieve, boys,
>O'er our corpses, let it be with pride,
>When thinking that each, boys,
>On that red beach, boys,
>Lies the flood-mark of the battle's tide.
>See! the first faint ray of morning

> Gilds the east with golden light.
> Hark! the bugle notes give warning,
> One full bumper to old friends to-night.[32]

As the singers were chiefly Celts, and as their refrain bore entirely on Irish affairs, I have omitted the chorus, only selecting from the ballad, which has a most spirited air, such words as have a cosmopolitan application.

I sincerely hope that my next communication to THE TIMES may convey the assurance of this command having obtained a substantial victory.

John F. Finerty

CHAPTER 6

The Trail Leads to Terry

In Finerty's late-summer letters he foremost rejoiced in the mustering of Crook's Big Horn and Yellowstone Expedition and its advance, finally, from its Goose Creek camp. In attempting to explain the delay, he shook a finger at the tardy arrival of Colonel Wesley Merritt and the Fifth Cavalry, a primary contingent of reinforcements that had diverted to intercept a band of Northern Cheyenne Indians fleeing Red Cloud Agency in mid-July. Finerty at the moment merely echoed a commonly held sentiment in Crook's camp that Merritt's chase was unnecessary and unduly delayed the resumption of the general's own operation. In the days and years since, that conclusion has been much debated, when even from the start Merritt and Sheridan justified the action, and Sheridan separately repeatedly implored Crook to renew the campaign on his own, irrespective of the Fifth. In *War-Path and Bivouac*, Finerty altered his view, allowing that Merritt's diversion served a meaningful purpose in the larger scope of the war.

Without knowing any of the particulars, Finerty grasped that Sitting Bull's village was again on the move, having departed the headwaters countryside of the Little Big Horn River in mid-summer and apparently ambling its way northeastward into the open country between Rosebud Creek and Powder River. This likely was simple gossip running the camp. An abundance of buffalo in those eastern drainages proved the lure. That Sitting Bull's village moved on its own volition and without apparent fear of Crook on Goose Creek or Gibbon or Terry on the Yellowstone speaks plainly to a conceit evident in the Indian camp. After having defeated Crook at Rosebud Creek and Custer at the Little Big Horn, and so readily

The Trail Leads to Terry 143

and repeatedly harassing Crook on Goose Creek, these people remained proud and resolute. Even then, of course, circumstances were changing for Sitting Bull's adherents, but the generals had no way of knowing this. As one reads in the accounts of reporters like Finerty, the ascendant village remained an unvanquished, intimidating foe.

In these letters Finerty said much about Terry, the decimated Seventh Cavalry, and the embarrassing surfeit of rations, canvas, clothing, and grain carried by the Dakota column, points juxtaposed against the impoverishment of Crook's command. The combined Montana and Dakota columns were immediately supported with wagons and behind them by steamboats on the Yellowstone. As well, Terry's operation featured a sutler enterprise providing practical clothing, tobacco, canned fruits, other comestibles, and even alcohol. This dichotomy of orchestration was odd from the start—Crook's measly outfitted and supplied command sourced dozens to hundreds of miles from his forward base on Goose Creek, and that base some 160 miles from Fort Fetterman, itself an island in Wyoming. Terry's command on the other hand was never far removed from massive supply caches on the Yellowstone that were delivered, forwarded, and ceaselessly supplemented by boats in perpetual motion from Fort Abraham Lincoln on the Missouri River and Camp Hancock, the department's quartermaster depot at the Northern Pacific railhead in Bismarck. Crook's men groaned with envy when encountering Terry's infantry and cavalry. When comparing the physical toughness of the respective commands, Finerty was convinced that Crook's men were a superior stock. But when considering the healthfulness of horses and the general wherewithal of support, Terry's command was a veritable cornucopia and model of humane field service. The nature of the Great Sioux War quickly changed after the Little Big Horn. The generals could not yet know it, but the time for massive commands, wagons, steamboats, and sutlers had all but passed.[1]

Finerty's August 18 letter closes on a critical note, doubtless a reflection of the disappointment and malaise permeating the massive soldier camp then sprawling over the confluence of the Powder and Yellowstone Rivers at mid-month. Finerty's own entrée to the campaign was courtesy of General Sheridan, who provided a letter of introduction to General Crook. And yet in his final summer letter to the *Chicago Times* Finerty lambasts the "official imbecility" that sent an insufficient force to fight a powerful enemy and supported it with green infantry and cavalry horses fit only for the purposes of a glue factory. Those were harsh words coming from a Chicago-based reporter, appearing in the city's foremost newspaper, and directed straight at a downtown Chicago audience fixed in the headquarters of the Division of the Missouri. In Finerty's eyes, this Indian war for the moment seemed unwinnable.

Chicago Times, August 9, 1876

IN AT THE DEATH
THE BOYS ARE MARCHING
[*From Our Own Reporter*]

CROOK'S EXPEDITION, IN CAMP ON THE MAIN TONGUE RIVER, Montana, Aug. 2, via FORT FETTERMAN, Wyoming, Aug. 8. Owing to the slow arrival of reinforcements the whole aspect of this campaign has been altered within the last few days. The Indians, after firing the country and a portion of the mountains all around us, have abandoned their village on the Little Big Horn, and changing their purpose of going into the hills and Wind river valley, have moved north-eastward toward the mouth of the Tongue river and doubtless to the hunting range lying between this stream and the Powder river. This unexpected change of base is attributed to two causes: First, the possible seizure of Kelly, Gen. Crook's first courier to Gen. Terry with dispatches, advising the latter officer to meet Crook at this point on Aug. 2, together with news from the Red Cloud agency of Merritt's march to gain us, and second, the exhaustion of the chief meat resources of the combined hostile tribes of Sioux, Cheyennes, and Arapahoes, compelling them to go into some region where they could kill buffalo for subsistence. The first theory is regarded as the most likely, the Indian leader being too cautious to risk a battle with Crook and Terry on both his flanks.

Frank Grouard and some of his scouts returned from the deserted Indian village on the Little Big Horn, about 15 miles from here, this afternoon. Louis Richard and some Snakes were there the previous day and found a bugle belonging to the 7th cavalry, and several saddles, etc., the property of the same regiment. All the relics are in possession of the headquarters. Two dead Indians, one a chief, was [*sic*] found near the village. Grouard thinks they were killed in Sibley's fight, on July 7. The Indian trail, an immense one, leads directly from the mountains to the northeast. Our experienced men say that it will find Sitting Bull on Powder river or else the Little Missouri.

Just at nightfall scouts from Gen. Merritt arrived, announcing the arrival of the 5th cavalry on Goose creek. He has, including recruits for our regiments in the field, about 700 effectives. Crook has just issued an order for this command to move northeast for the purpose of forming a junction with Merritt.

[*From Our Own Reporter*]

IN CAMP ON MAIN GOOSE CREEK, Wyoming, Aug. 4. We arrived at this point, after a march of nearly 20 miles through a country entirely burned up by Indian fires, at noon on yesterday. Gen. Merritt, with 10 companies of his splendid corps, joined us at 5 o'clock. His arrival has put everybody in good humor, as his military reputation stands high, and the 5th cavalry are a tried regiment. Gen. Carr, Majs. Upham, Sumner, and "Buffalo Bill" are also with the command.[2] We are packing up for an immediate movement against the Indians, and will march to-morrow morning. The Snakes have been reinforced by 30 fresh warriors bringing their strength up to 250 fighting men, including a score of half-breeds. Crook is very much annoyed at the slow advance made by the reinforcing column, as he would have fallen on Sitting Bull in his village had all been up in time.

There is hardly a blade of grass left between this stream and the Big Horn mountains. The Indian chief is acknowledged on all hands to be the ablest general America has produced. So far he has fought and marched all around us. His rear guard passed within easy reach of our camp about a week ago and challenged the Snake scouts to come up and fight. The Snakes came back to camp for their friends and went after the Sioux, but the latter had cleared out and a sea of fire intervened between them and pursuit. Nothing can defeat Sitting Bull in this country, as long as he pursues the fabian policy unless it be the failure of his food and ammunition supplies.³ The order to march has just been promulgated. We take on our horses four days' rations, 100 rounds of ammunition, a blanket, and an overcoat. The mule-pack train, escorted by 10 companies of infantry, will follow to supply what we need should we get run ashore.

We now have a fighting force of 1,300 cavalry, 407 foot, 250 Indian scouts and half-breeds, in all about 2,000 men. One-fourth of the horsemen must hold the animals in a battle, and the infantry cannot keep up with the mounted column. Thus we shall have when the fight begins only a little over 1,000 effective men, exclusive of Indians, in the line of battle.

We have no artillery of any kind. The Crow scouts who recently came from Terry were sent back with a dispatch to his command several days ago. So far as I can learn we are going down the Tongue river toward the Yellowstone. Gen. Merritt is chief of the cavalry, Col. Carr commands the right, and Col. Royall the 3d and 5th [*sic*, five] companies of the 2d horse.⁴ Maj. Chambers commands the 10 companies of infantry. The latter march at 4 o'clock in the morning. We expect to be gone 15 days. The wagon train goes into permanent camp near this point. There are 146 mule wagons including Merritt's, and 200 men will guard them. We expect to strike Sitting Bull, if he means to fight this time, within three days.

J. F. F.

Chicago Times, August 19, 1876

THE HUNT FOR HAIR
THE JUNCTION OF THE TROOPS
[*From Our Own Reporter*]

CROOK'S EXPEDITION, IN CAMP ON ROSEBUD CREEK, 30 Miles from the Yellowstone, Aug. 10, via BISMARCK, Aug. 18. Our column marched from Goose Creek camp at 6 o'clock on the morning of the 5th and moved down Tongue river 40 miles. Finding no fresh Indian trail we struck west to the Rosebud on the morning of the 7th. The hills were on fire all around us and we could see nothing. On the 8th, on account of the smoke we halted till night and made 20 miles northward, striking a fresh Indian trail about half way down. We followed the trail 20 miles further on the 9th, and again halted till this morning, when we moved northward 15 miles and discovered a cloud of dust which Buffalo Bill said was caused by troops marching. He went forward with some scouts and found Gen. Terry's entire command with a wagon train. We formed a junction immediately amid every demonstration of joy. The Indian trail shows the savages breaking up and moving on Powder and Tongue rivers. It is supposed they have crossed the Yellowstone, in which case we may bid adieu to much chance of catching them. We move in the morning. Four companies of infantry under Gen. Miles with artillery are going to the fort[s] at the mouth[s] of Rosebud and Tongue rivers to prevent the Indians from crossing at those points. The rest of the command will swing around in their rear, and if possible cut them off. Great doubts as to the success of the enterprise are entertained. If the Indians with their stock and baggage are on this side of the Yellowstone their capture is inevitable. Otherwise this campaign will have come to a lame and impotent conclusion. We have now 1,900 cavalry, 1,300 infantry, and a battery of artillery. Gens. Terry and Crook have agreed to act in concert. Terry's wagon-train will remain at this point for the present.

Chicago Times, September 22, 1876

THE WAYS OF WAR
THE MISERY OF THE MARCH
[*From Our Own Reporter*]

BIG HORN AND YELLOWSTONE EXPEDITION, COMMANDED NOT BY THE GREAT JEHOVAH, BUT BY CROOK AND TERRY, IN THE FIELD ON PUMPKIN CREEK, Montana, Aug. 12. "Oh, blood and thunder, and oh, blood and 'ounds (the quotation is Byronic and therefore classical).[5] It is now nearly middle August and we of the above armament have smelt no gore since our sad encounters with Gen. Sitting Bull. For 10 days after my last letter was sent to THE TIMES, Crook, nervous and unhappy, kept vibrating like a pendulum between the divers branches of Tongue river and Goose creek. He felt instinctively that the Indians were playing him a trick, and he was puzzled what to do. To attack them with an inferior force, after the tragedy on the lower [Little] Big Horn, was too much risk, and to wait for the promised reinforcement was both tedious and unheroic. Half a dozen times while awaiting the slow advance of Merritt, the unlucky general made up his mind to march on the Indian village, posted in the foot-hills of the mountain range, on the head waters of the Little Big Horn, but the memory of Custer held him back. Finally patience forsook him and he moved to the main branch of Tongue river, one march from the Sioux, on Aug. 1, for the double purpose of keeping his appointment with Terry and of making a charge on Sitting Bull. He got there only to find the Indians gone, and the man of Fort Fisher fame absent from the place of rendezvous. Meanwhile the Sioux had hovered all around us for days. They fired the mountains and the plains, obscuring the country with smoke and maneuvering in a manner which made it very difficult to determine whether they had retired into the Big Horn valley or retreated toward the British possessions. The scouts, after due examination, declared the latter to be the case, although many held to the opinion (and I am included to concur therewith) that the reds had separated, sending the bulk of their ponies, their old men, squaws, and papooses, under strong guard, north, and

The Trail Leads to Terry

leaving a powerful war party in and around the mountains to chase the buffalo and harass our communications. Anyway, we were sure of one well-defined, gigantic trail leading toward the Yellowstone, but the question was which of the tributary valleys it descended after getting away from the mountain foot.

On the evening of Aug. 2, the long-expected couriers from Merritt, announcing his arrival on Goose creek, came into camp. Crook moved north next morning, making a 20 mile march to join him. The forces did not unite until that evening, and the next day was consumed in getting ready for the road. I have already sent you by telegraph the organization of the force, consisting of about 2,000 fighting men, horse, foot, and irregulars. This Crook deemed sufficient to punish any body of Indians in the country.

Our wagon train, comprising 160 wagons, including those of Gen. Merritt, was parked on Goose creek under command of Quartermaster Furey, not a soldier being left to guard it. The teamsters, discharged soldiers, and other hangers-on of the expedition, to the number of 200 men, were deemed sufficient to protect it from all attacks. At 6 o'clock on the evening of Aug. 4 the order to march at daybreak next morning was issued. Each man was allowed four days' rations, a blanket, and 100 rounds of ammunition on his saddle or on his back, according as he was mounted or on foot; while the pack train, commanded by Commissary Bubb, carried for each soldier 15 days' rations and 50 rounds of cartridge additional. That night it blew great guns. It was our last chance under canvas for some time, and Old Boreas[6] determined that we shouldn't enjoy it. Three-fourths of the tents were blown down, and so terrible were the clouds of dust and smoke blown from the burning prairies and wooded hills that suffocation was imminent with those who had the philosophy, or the necessary weariness, to sleep.

Daylight came at last, accompanied by the usual shrill bugle call, and the hoarse harangue of the Snake "head-soldier" as he roused the sleeping savages from their lairs to look after their neighing ponies. Clouds partially obscured the sun as we tightened our horse girths, or swallowed our scanty allowance of ration coffee, bacon, and hard-tack. All our superfluous baggage was rolled into bundles and turned over to Maj. Furey, while we, like the highwaymen of old, had nothing except what we had on our frames and what we could impose on our sorry looking steeds. The poor horses looked supremely miserable. Even those of the newly arrived 5th were completely played out by that senseless scout in pursuit of a few Cheyennes—the very thing that allowed the main body of the enemy to escape from the Big Horn without a battle. As for the animals of the 2d and 3d cavalry, they had no grain or corn since the beginning of June, and at least a third of them looked well fitted for the bone-yard.

The infantry, under Col. Chambers, appeared stout and soldierly and moved off at a swinging step three hours ahead of us. Gen. Merritt became chief of cavalry. Royall retained his old command of the 2d and 3d, and Carr led the 5th. The 25 companies were formed into five battalions, the 3d and 5th being strongest, having two each and the 2d one. At 7 o'clock we were all in the saddle and moved in three columns via Prairie Dog creek to Tongue river, following the track of the guides and the infantry. Frank Grouard and William F. Cody ("Buffalo Bill"), who came up with Merritt, were in advance with a select body of scouts. Col. Stanton, paymaster,[7] has chief command of the irregulars, while Maj. Randall, with the Chief Washakee, directed the Snake Indians. We made about 20 miles that day, passing over the old campground of June 9, where the Sioux gave us that first salute. Everything around the place looked desolate, and it seemed to me as if years had elapsed since I saw it last. Since Merritt joined we adopted the plan of forming a circular camp, with our horses picketed in the centre during the night, so that in case of attack no stampede of our stock could be effected.

To detail all the incidents of a march would be very tiresome both to me and to your readers, so I will only glance at the chief features of our second northward pilgrimage. We marched 45 miles further down Tongue river on Aug. 6, crossing that sinuous stream—perhaps "the crookedest" in the world—no less than 17 times, which made the march tell severely on our admirable infantry, who, nevertheless, got into camp just as soon as we did. Our course lay through "Tongue river canon," one of the most rugged and dangerous passes

The Trail Leads to Terry

in this land of difficult and interminable defiles. The sun was hotter than on any march during the campaign, and the thermometer must have ranged at 105 in the shade from 8 A.M. to sundown. The men crossed Tongue river into a bathing reservoir, for our soldiers lose no opportunity in the way of keeping their bodies clean, especially when they march without even a change of underclothing.

Failing to cut across the Sioux trail at that distance down the Tongue, Crook determined to move westward, through a dry canon to Rosebud creek, and move down that rivulet some distance, as the southern part of that valley is a favorite Indian resort. This gave us another 25-mile march over a very broken country, full of rocky bluffs and clumps of pine trees, and having hardly sufficient water to refresh our already used-up horseflesh. Finally, after halting innumerable times because of the intolerable heat and dust, which nearly asphyxiated man and beast, we reached the famous Rosebud, some ten miles north of our fighting ground of June 17, and about a mile and a half from the point in the canon to which Mills' battalion of the 3d cavalry penetrated on the day of the conflict. Subsequent investigation showed what a dreadful fate we escaped by obeying Crook's order to countermarch. Immense piles of felled trees in our path and on the sides of that savage ravine showed where the Sioux had lain in ambush for our approach. Half a mile further on and not a man of our battalion would have come out alive. The five companies of the 2d, following to support us, would have been massacred without fail, for there was no room to deploy or rally. The Indians held the timber barricades in front and flank. They would have closed upon our unguarded rear, and another horror would have been added to the long and ghastly catalog of Indian-American warfare.[8]

However, a miss is as good as a mile, and we feel duly thankful that we escaped being the awful example of this unfortunate campaign. We camped in a most beautiful valley, hemmed in by thickly timbered hills, which were blazing like so many volcanoes, the Indians having fired the woods either by accident or design. This portion of the Rosebud vale is called "the Indian paradise," and truly, for many miles it deserves that heavenly name. Two miles north of where we bivouacked we found the site of the mammoth Indian village to protect which Sitting Bull fought on the 17th of June. It was situated in an expanse of the valley two miles square, and protected by steep, rock-guarded eminences on every side. Crook's force could never have captured and held such a position, defended as it must have been, judging by the number of lodges, by at least 3,500 fierce, desperate, and well-armed warriors.

The scouts went down the Rosebud 15 miles and returned in the evening with intelligence of a fresh Indian trail, leading diagonally from the Little Big Horn river toward the Yellowstone. This cheered us up somewhat, and we lay down to sleep with the hope of a speedy encounter and a quick return, victorious of course, to civilized existence. But, as usual, "man proposes and God disposes." When the reveille sounded on the morning of the 8th, no man could see his neighbor, owing to an abominable alliance between the fog and smoke. We felt our way down through the old Indian village for a few hours, and then Crook ordered a halt, hoping for a gale to clear away the atmospheric obscurity. We lay by until 6 o'clock that evening when an obliging breeze sprang up and everything came out of the gloom smiling and picturesque. We knew that we had a night's march before us to make up for the lost time; so when the orderlies came galloping along the lines with orders to saddle up we were not taken by surprise.

Still following the Rosebud, we marched at dark, the cavalry on the flanks and the infantry and pack train in the centre, but not far in advance, so that all might be within supporting distance. The moon did not rise for some hours, and the evening was dark as Erebus.[9] Intense silence pervaded the line of march, and not a sound was heard but the solemn tramp of the cavalry columns advancing through the gloom, except when a solitary jackass, attached to the pack-train, gave vent to his perturbed feelings in a bray which, amid the mountain echoes, sounded like the laughter of a legion of mocking devils. The lonesome donkey repeated his performance so often and so loudly that he had to be muzzled, as he appeared determined to apprise the Sioux, if any were hearing, of our approach. The mules were heard from occasionally, but on the whole, their conduct was decorous and patriotic. Does any reader of THE TIMES remember his experience during a night march in total darkness? Of course thousands of your readers marched with Sherman and Thomas and know all about it. But a night march in the Indian wilderness of the north is one of the most impressive incidents of war. It is weird, *outre*, awe-inspiring. The vastness of untamed nature is around you and its influence is insensibly felt. You are on the track of a mysterious enemy. The country over which you are marching is to you an unread chapter. You see something like a black shadow moving in advance. You are conscious that men and animals are moving within a few paces, and yet you cannot define any particular object, nor even your horse's head. But you hear the steady, perpetual, "tramp—tramp—tramp" of the iron-hoofed cavalry broken by an occasional stumble and the half-smothered imprecation of an irate trooper; the jingle of carbines and sling-belts; and the snorting of the horses as they grope their way through the eternal dust, which the rider can feel in his throat, like the thick, stinking vapor of a champion London fog.

Once in a while a match struck by a soldier to light his pipe would flash in the gloom, like a huge fire-fly, and darkness would again assert itself. In this manner we proceeded for quite a time, when, all of a sudden, a tremendous illumination sprang up from behind us and lit almost the whole line of the valley. Reflected in it we could see the arms glistening as our battalion moved steadily along, and the bluffs, left and right, seemed like giants keeping watch and ward upon the pass. We turned in our saddles to observe the phenomenon and beheld a flood of flame, rushing like a charging battle-line storming some fated town, bursting over the mountain crest behind us, 20 miles away, flinging its lurid banner to the very arch of the firmament, almost as if the gates of hell had been flung wide to allow "the demons down under the sea"[10] to throw defiance at the power which parted them from the heavens during the apocryphal battle which the genius of a Milton has portrayed in immortal words. I have seen some magnificent freaks of fire in my time (including the Chicago disaster and the conflagrations in the

Big Horn range) but that sudden outburst of flame in the Plutonian gloom of Rosebud valley surpassed in lurid splendor anything that I have ever imagined or beheld. It was something to be witnessed only once in a lifetime. Soon afterward the moon rose on our right and its chaste luster tamed down the infernal glow on the southward hills. We pressed forward until 2 o'clock, when we halted and lay down with our single blanket to catch the hasty sleep of Indian campaigners.

Next day we made 20 miles through one of the roughest countries I ever traveled over, still following the Rosebud. It looked like a bottom of an extinct lake. We were pursuing the Indian trail, but the Sioux had burned almost every blade of grass behind, so that our horses were nearly starved. That entire section of the valley is a huge coal-bed—one of the most extensive in America, and this accounts for the peculiar sterility of the surface sod. We saw huge lumps of coal sticking out of the sides of the canon, while the ground in many places was black as ink from genuine coal dust. Some day, when the Sioux are all in the happy hunting grounds, this valley will rival the Lehigh of Pennsylvania. But my observations of coal did not blind me to the fact that the weather had taken a change for the worse. A cold, disagreeable rain, accompanied by a chilling north wind, set in, and, after a tramp of 22 miles, we halted in a cross canon, where, fortunately, some grass remained, limited amid the gigantic rocks, cut into fantastic columns and corners by the action of waters which subsided countless ages ago, and made ourselves as comfortable as it was possible to be in the most inhospitable looking country outside of Iceland or Siberia. Honestly, this part of the world looks utterly unfinished, just like a half-built house, raw, dirty, and cheerless. Tyndall might be able to find that "missing line" somewhere along the Rosebud.[11]

Soon after we halted, Capt. Jack Crawford ("Buffalo Bill's" friend) and Capt. Graves,[12] of Montana, rode up to our dismal, smoky camp-fire, and handed me some private letters, for which I was duly grateful. The gallant fellows left Fort Fetterman with dispatches for Crook on July 28, reached our wagon train four days later, and, despite every warning, had followed our tortuous trail by Prairie

Dog, Tongue river, the dry canon and Rosebud, until they came up with us in that home of storms.

The night came on, cold as midwinter, and we, provided with only summer outfit, shivered like palsy patients. It seemed to me as if the combined winds from "a' the airts"[13] had concentrated on that wretched spot, to give us sinners a foretaste of the inferno. Heat and dust are bad; but cold and mud take the vim out of a fellow, and make him think of houses and stoves. We have seen neither since May 29. Nevertheless, the morning of Aug. 10 dawned on a comparatively happy set of mortals, for we were nearing the famed Yellowstone river, and that would, at least, be a change of scene. We had marched only 12 miles, however, when some of the scouts rode back to inform the general that the Sioux trail had suddenly diverged toward Tongue river. We were then marching over a portion of the route followed by Custer on his last fatal scout. We halted on some high, grassy ground above the creek, at the point where it turns due north, where we allowed the horses to have a lunch. Then we moved northward, and had not proceeded more than a mile when we observed a mighty column of dust indicating a large body of men and animals in motion, in our front, about three miles down the Rosebud.

"They are Sioux!" explained some of our officers. "If so, you will immediately hear music," others replied. Just then "a solitary horseman" separated himself from our vanguard and rode like the devil in a gale of wind down the river. It was "Buffalo Bill," the most reckless, and the handsomest, of all frontiersmen. "He's going to reconnoitre," remarked Col. Royall. "That's Bill's style, you know." At this point a handsome young Shoshone Indian—the only one of the reds for whom I entertain a shadow of liking—rode up and ejaculated "How?" He looked down the road and his piercing eyes glittered like jet in the sunbeams. "What's that?" I asked, pointing to the pillar of dust. "Heap pony-soldier (cavalry). No Sioux—Sioux far off—run when pony-soldier and good Indian come strong—heap strong now. Sioux no good—run away. Ugh!" and the young savage with a ferocious grin distorting his comely features, lashed up his pony and disappeared over the ridge. Within a few minutes "Buffalo

Bill," his long hair streaming on the wind, came galloping madly back to our lines. "What is it, Bill?" asked Col. Royall. "Terry and his outfit," replied the scout. "He's got wagons enough to do an army corps. Were we to catch Indians with such lumber as that," and he dashed off to see Crook.

It was true. Terry has been three days marching from the Yellowstone 30 miles from where we halted. Crook immediately ordered us into camp and Terry, who mistaking us for Sioux because of the panic of his Crow scouts who saw some Snake Indians in our van had formed line of battle, continued to advance. The general and his staff rode up first and joined Crook and his officers. It appeared to be a cordial meeting, although I am convinced that Crook intended to operate alone and met Terry by accident. Gen. Terry is a fine looking man, about 50 years of age. He has a genial face and looks like a fighter. Whether Indian warfare is his forte has not been so far fully demonstrated.

The principal thing that attracted my attention and that of all of our force was the remnant of the 7th cavalry. It came in, formed into eight small companies, led by Maj. Reno—a short, stout man, about 50 years old, with a determined visage, his face showing intimate acquaintance with the sun and wind. The horses were all in splendid condition, having been grain-fed all along; but many of the officers and men looked tired, dirty, and disgusted—just as most of Crook's column have appeared for many weeks. The 2d cavalry (four companies) and a crowd of rather green infantry—most of them recently from Detroit[14]—followed, and after them came a light field battery of four guns, and a huge wagon train. The men of the respective commands saluted each other cordially but there was no cheering or undue excitement of any kind. Every one felt that there was naught to cheer about. When you have seen one regiment of our cavalry in the field you have seen all. There is hardly any difference in the caliber of the men, and, as for uniform, the absence thereof is a leading characteristic of the service. Perhaps this is all the better, for a more disfiguring costume than the fatigue dress of the United States army the imagination of the most diabolically inclined of existing tailors could not conceive.

Our Indian allies, on the other hand, with their beautiful, glossy, abundant hair, their ornamented "leggings," and flowing richly-colored blankets, together with their slick, fat forms, present a most picturesque aspect. To be sure they are more or less troubled with parasites, but so shall we be in a few weeks, without a change of under-clothes. It is a comfort to reflect that, probably, Julius Caesar, Pompey, and Mark Antony picked "grab-backs" off their togas in olden times, that "the Little Corporal" certainly amused himself in driving the crawling enemy from his shirt about the morning of "Lodi's murderous bridge," and that Gen. Grant, with characteristic phlegm, routed them from his body, by all of blue ointment, when he started "the Rebs" out of Vicksburg. As a correspondent, I am doubly consoled to know that only one insect got into Washington from Manassas before "Bull Run Russel," and that was the louse which occupied his hat when it was blown off his head while crossing the celebrated Long bridge.[15] Excuse this chapter on vermin, but Scotia's favorite bard devoted one of his neatest sonnets to the same subject.[16] When a young lady, full of romance, is inclined to fall in love with a dashing soldier, let her conjure up this picture: A summer morning in the wilderness. A hero with a single shirt, 300 miles from a laundress. A willow tree and the warrior depopulating said garment in the shade thereof.

The Crows, Snakes, and Rees, when they met, had a grand howl in concert, their enthusiasm being in striking contrast with our indifference. In fact, the shadow of a coming fizzle was already upon us. Terry and Crook had a "big talk" that evening. The former did not wish to deprive Crook of command. The latter insisted that the senior should take his proper place. Finally he of Fort Fisher agreed to accept "the glory" thrust upon his councils. The commander of our column looked the picture of disgust. "This command is now too large," he observed to a friend. "We shall find no Indians while such a force sticks together." I am afraid he's right. Sitting Bull has licked us out of our boots. He has done enough for glory, and he'll devote the rest of this fall (it is that already here) to leading us on wild goose chases, until we have neither horses nor spirit left to pursue him further. Truly the general who undertakes to fight the Sioux has a hard contract. This country is so immense—the enemy are so rapacious, and our base of supplies is either so distant or so precarious that the prospect of catching the Indians at a disadvantage—or even on equal terms—is very poor indeed.

The combined columns, about 4,000 effective men, horse and foot, were ordered to march eastward to Tongue river, on the Indian trail, at daybreak. We marched, accordingly, about 15 miles, reached the river, and went into camp in one of the beautiful valleys that abound in this region. We found the skeleton of a murdered miner—a bullet hole through his skull and shoulder bone—and buried it. The man had been killed about the beginning of June, and coyotes had eaten the body, the clothing being quite fresh, and the hair on the head showing the mark made by the Sioux scalping knife. The hapless man's dead pony, which had been shot also, lay near him in a state of most offensive putrefaction. Such is the fate of him who seeks fortune in this demon-peopled land.[17]

That night a terrific storm of wind and rain came up. We had no tents and had to sleep in the puddles. You can imagine how we passed the night. Water saturated us at every point, and the rain kept pouring down until the afternoon of the succeeding day, retarding our march, and making every man of the command feel as if possessed of a devil. We have been wet in the same manner every day and night since, and have, no doubt, laid the deep foundations of future rheumatism. This, however, is "glory," and no one must complain. Notwithstanding, I am tempted to remember a passage in the book of M. M. Eckmann-Coatrian on "Waterloo," describing the sufferings of the French army the night before that historic butchery: "Was it for *this* God created and placed men in the world?"[18] Evidently—and all for $13 a month "and found,"[19] so far as the rank and file are concerned.

The officers fare not a whit better on the scout. All sleep in the rain and dirt, drink coarse coffee, eat hardtack and chew raw bacon. All this is the concomitant of war and fame. The rays of the star of "glory" are made up of filth, hardship, and disappointments.

Fighting is the least of the evils attendant on a military career. And yet, the worst feature of a summer campaign is paradise itself compared with the untold miseries suffered by our troops when engaged in a winter hunt after Indians. But, after all, the best time to strike the Sioux is when snows are deep and pony locomotion almost impossible. To give some idea of the severity of the fall and winter in this region, let me recall the fact that Gen. Connor, when operating against the Sioux in this same territory, in 1866, had 300 horses frozen to death on the picket lines, the night of Sept. 7.[20]

On Aug. 12 and 13, we continued our northward march on the Tongue, losing horses every mile of the way. When we reached Pumpkin creek this morning, about 40 miles from the Yellowstone, we switched eastward toward Powder river. The rain and mud made the marching terrible and Gibbon's young infantry lay down exhausted in the dirt. Many of them had to be placed on pack-mules or carried on travois. Every company almost of the 2d, 3d, and 5th cavalry had to abandon or shoot used up horses. We made fully 30 miles over a most infernal country before halting. Chambers' "astonishing infantry" (as Napier would have called them[21]) made the full march and not a man fell out of the ranks. In fact they reached camp and were in bivouac before ourselves. The Roman legions or the army of Austerlitz[22] never made better time than the splendid detachment of the 4th, 14th, and 9th infantry. They and their gallant officers deserve unstinted praise for their magnificent foot-work.

This so-called creek is a miserable stream, full of alkali and about the color of the mud on Clark street crossings after a rainy spell.[23] There is very little wood and we have to sleep to-night in pools of water and are thankful to get a chance to lie down even in that way. A heavy rain coming down at this moment compels me to wind up this letter. As a German friend of mine puts it—"Sioux, dear Sioux, where the devil you are?"

J. F. F.

A God-Forsaken Land
[From Our Own Reporter.]

CAMP OF JOINT EXPEDITION, CONFLUENCE OF YELLOWSTONE AND POWDER RIVERS, Montana, Aug. 18. We marched all day Tuesday, Aug. 15, along Pumpkin creek through a terrible section. The soil looks like the surface of a non-atmospheric planet, hard, repulsive, sterile. It made one's heart sick to look at the place. But there were strong marks of mineral wealth, especially iron and coal, along the route. I am convinced that all this part of Montana is a tremendous coal region, which, one day, will yield untold wealth to some enterprising corporations. This kind of land continued until we struck the Powder river valley, which, like all the valleys of the larger streams, is extremely fertile. But our animals were so exhausted that we hardly made more than a couple of miles an hour on the average. The horses staggered in the columns by scores, and most of the men had to lead during three-fourths of the march. Very frequently a played-out horse would fall, as if shot, and the rider was compelled either to abandon the equipments or pack them on a mule. All the led horses were in use, owing to frequent deaths of the line animals, and dozens of dismounted cavalrymen toiled painfully along, over steep, rugged hills in the rear of the column. Our whole line of march from the Rosebud to this point is dotted with dead or abandoned horses. Some of the newly enlisted infantry grew desperate, their feet bleeding and their legs swollen from the continuous tramp, and refused to move a step. They had to be mounted on the ponies of the friendly Indians and carried along. One man, Gen. Terry's cook, without saying a word to anyone, lay back under a tree to die. He was not missed for 12 hours, when the general, who is very kind-hearted, sent back the Crow Indians and some cavalry to see what had become of the poor wretch. They found him a raving maniac and bore him into camp strapped to an extra pony.[24]

Many of the young foot soldiers are injured for life. Terry's foot could not keep up at all. They are more of a hindrance than a help. Chambers' men rival O'Leary and Watson. Taken all in all, Crook's column has the better material, except as regards horses. What chance have we of catching Indians with such beasts? The animal I ride is a fair specimen. His shoulder is a mass of scabs and blood. He stumbles at every step, and I have to lead him more than half the time. When I get on his back I make a bargain with him—he carries me and I keep him from falling and breaking both our necks. Yet this poor devil of a horse is a superb, prancing, fiery, and most untamed steed compared with the ghostly skeletons that disfigure most of our cavalry companies. Such is war in the wilderness. Our government ought to have a supply of fresh horses here, so that we might follow hot on Sitting Bull's trail, which leads direct to the Little Missouri river.

The reds are scattering and running into the agencies. Why the devil should we have agencies at all? Why not let the savages live on their own resources, if they can, when they accept rations and other government allowances, under the belief that we are bribing them for mercy? Every post-trader, frontiersman, or half-breed that sells the Sioux et al. arms and ammunition ought, upon conviction, to be hanged drawn and quartered, according to the ancient barbaric law.

All Wednesday and Thursday we kept moving at snail's pace north along the glorious valley of Powder river, thickly timbered and covered with grass knee high. It has a uniform width of about four miles—the country on either side being sterile, except as regards mineral products. Finally, at 8 o'clock yesterday afternoon, we sighted the famed Yellowstone, a majestic stream, wide and deep, and camped on the angle made by the junction of Powder river (the dexter bank) with the new inland inter-thoroughfare.[25] From this grand river the part of Montana and Wyoming good for anything will, undoubtedly, be settled. At 5 o'clock the steamboat *Far West* came from Tongue river and the soldiers ran, like a flock of overgrown children, to see it. The poor fellows had not seen steam since May 18, and this glimpse of civilization reminded them of home. Some fresh, well-dressed infantry were on board, together with a couple of cannon. Also there was a colored cabin girl—another reminder of "the States." Dinah modestly covered her eyes when she saw all of the soldiers who were not on picket or on the river bank, about half the command, naked in the water. Lieut. Von Leuttwitz, of the 3d cavalry, had just got on his shirt and was standing with his stern toward the boat, when the waves caused by the motion of the vessel flew over him, swept away half his clothing and wet him thoroughly. He received a thundering cheer from "the boys," and ran up the bank *a la Adam* before the fig leaves, swearing German oaths and damning the Yellowstone from the bottom of his heart. Every man that marched from Rosebud and Goose creek washed his shirt, etc., yesterday, allowed the garment to dry in the sun and put them back on without ironing. There was one great drawback to the common laundry—a dearth of soap. Despite of this, I feel comfort in knowing that I am a little less like a ground-hog to-day. Why do not the gallant Chicago 1st go down to Calumet and practice the noble art of washing without soap for a few days?

I think I mentioned the fact that Crook insisted on Terry assuming command while the two expeditions hung together. Terry is therefore responsible. Crook feels awfully disgusted. Sitting Bull has played all of us a shabby trick. Like a greedy gambler, he has won a large stake and then, when the chances are about equalized, he draws out and leaves us in the lurch. Probably I am disappointed in Mr. Bull, but he knows his own business best. I went to see Crook and his staff last night. Having no tents it is rather difficult to discover the whereabouts of any one. After a long chase, I finally came upon a group of seedy-looking fellows—having all the appearance of brigands—sitting on the wet grass under a cotton-wood tree. There were Crook and his staff. I interviewed them, but could not obtain much information. The general idea was to follow the trail to the Little Missouri, and then nobody knew where. This makes the affair extremely unpleasant for all concerned. I think the game is up, and that there will be little, if any, fighting.

I close this letter with a feeling of disgust and disappointment. Incertitude is the order of the day at present. Many camp followers, including some of the correspondents, are leaving the expedition. I have not yet made up my mind what is best for me to do. I hate to leave at this stage of the futile campaign, and, yet by remaining I shall see very little else than mud, misery, and tough country. One good battle and a decent wind up to this wretched business would just suit me now. But I fear very much that the last shot of this section of the campaign has been fired. This comes of the official imbecility which, at the outset, sent an insufficient force to fight a powerful enemy, and, in the end, sent green infantry to impede our movements, and left us cavalry horses fit only for the purposes of a glue factory.

John F. Finerty

CHAPTER 7

Mud, Mules, and Blood

"I T RAINS AGAIN." Finerty's rain-soaked, soppy setup to General Crook's horrific mud march, so often called the Starvation March, is sublime. Montana and the Dakotas have a predictable cool, wet cycle each late summer or early fall, then as now. That peculiar weather pattern is normally short, lasting but a few days or maybe a week. But in August and September 1876 Finerty related how the men of the Big Horn and Yellowstone Expedition endured twenty-four wet days in a span of forty-two. Exposed on the open prairie, the men and animals of Crook's command were drenched and chilled to the bone. Adding to the misery, wood was scarce and cooking and warming fires hard to source, ignite, and maintain. Feet and hooves balled with mud and each day's advance was a pure torture. Many soldiers were so physically drained by the interminable day-to-day slog that they simply collapsed in the mud and could move no more. The lucky ones rode mules when possible; the rest were left to their own devices and were invariably late arrivals in the nightly camps. The torment was nearly unbearable and no one was immune: officers, enlisted men, packers, and newsmen suffered alike.[1]

Compounding the drear of the weather was Crook's fateful decision after crossing the Little Missouri River to turn his command south toward Deadwood rather than continue east to Fort Abraham Lincoln, despite by then the near exhaustion of all rations and the prospect of eating horses and mules. Finerty cross-examined Crook about this. The general's justification at the front end of the ordeal seemed reasonably plausible. He noted that it was a five-day march to Fort Lincoln and a seven-day march to the Black Hills. Either way the command would run out of food but Crook preferred to be nearer his own department instead of at Lincoln, in Terry's department. Aiming for Fort Lincoln would also have meant a doubleback march another day. A week later Crook's rationalizations read as sheer lunacy. Out of simple necessity, Finerty too ate the flesh of worn-out cavalry horses and pack mules, and Indian ponies, and his assessment of that lowly fare, variously "bad beef," "stringy," "leatherish," "fat and rank," and some of it a "combination all of the foregoing, with pork thrown in," is riveting if nauseating reading.[2]

In the midst of this march, selected men from Crook's command chanced onto and attacked a small Sioux village in the Slim Buttes, some seventy-five miles north of the Black Hills. The detachment, led by Captain Mills of the Third Cavalry, had been forwarded to purchase beef and other foodstuffs in the mining camps. Finerty intended on accompanying Mills, but his horse gave way at the very start of the advance and he came onto the Slim Buttes scene some hours after the fighting began. He immediately sought out Mills, however, who provided him with a firsthand overview of the action to that point. Mills, it will be remembered, commanded troops in the opening action of the Rosebud fight on June 17, and Finerty was almost always at his side.

Finerty's several accounts of the Slim Buttes fight, including the telegrams he forwarded via Fort Laramie and Cheyenne and his lengthy day-to-day campaign narrative appearing in his newspaper some weeks later, are among the finest of the many prepared by reporters and officers that day. In the scheme of things, Slim Buttes was a small fight, and yet some moments were exceedingly dramatic, and the setting, as always, was extraordinarily picturesque. Finerty reported it vividly and also acknowledged but did not harp on Crook's great missed opportunity that day and the next. Warriors from afar renewed the battle later that afternoon and again the next morning. In other circumstances Crook almost certainly would have chased those warriors home, harassing and destroying their village or villages, and serving a doctrinal lesson. In simple numbers, he had sufficient men for such a task. But by now this command—both men and animals—was fully used up. Like Rosebud, Crook won and lost the Slim Buttes battle too.

In his letters Finerty drops names incessantly but then usually (and regrettably) adds little more about this sizeable cast of interesting, sometimes compelling characters. Crook and Mills were among his exceptions. Through Finerty's eyes one sees Crook as the ever-stoic, invariably evasive, and deeply complex individual that history has come to know. To be sure, the general was savvy and proud, but also sometimes seemingly in over his head on the northern plains, where its vast openness and its haughty Sioux and Northern Cheyenne inhabitants were enormously challenging and quite apart from his experiences and successes in Arizona and elsewhere. Still, from time to time Crook was approachable and Finerty seized such moments, affording opportunities to collect and share insights into the man and his views and management of this campaign.

Another of the reporters accompanying the command, Reuben Davenport of the *New York Herald*, showed none of Finerty's deference to Crook. Davenport was exceedingly critical of almost every Crook decision at Rosebud and Slim Buttes. He rode all the while with Royall of the Third Cavalry, a regiment that had endured much in the early course of the war, some of it less than sterling, and Davenport plainly chose a side. Finerty's criticism of Crook was much more nuanced, except at the close of this long summer campaign, where he found the suffering of men and animals utterly inexcusable.

While Finerty's criticisms of Crook were calculated, he was strikingly candid about Mills, with whom he had spent so much time during the campaign. Mills was the senior captain of the Third Cavalry and by many measures a soldier and Indian fighter with an indelible reputation. Already in the Sioux war Mills had demonstrated highly visible and commendable conduct at Powder River, Rosebud, and again at Slim Buttes. Oddly, Finerty outwardly saw Mills, at age forty-one, too old and seasoned a soldier to need much special mention. But he then scorned him repeatedly in print, at one point noting, "If he were half as popular personally as he is energetic and fearless in the field he would be the idol of the brigade. But Mills is peculiar, and occasionally the reverse of unselfish, which to some extent neutralizes his undeniable ability as an officer." Those words and others in these late letters were uncharacteristically harsh. Perhaps Finerty presumed that he would never cross paths with Mills again. Mills, on the other hand, had commended Finerty in his Rosebud battle report, embracing his coolness and courage in the fight. He lived until 1924, authoring a notable autobiography, *My Story*, in 1918 (in which he says nothing about Finerty), and died in Washington, D.C., a wealthy man. Finerty lived into 1908, mostly residing in Chicago except for a couple of years when he too resided in Washington. His characterizations of Mills are puzzling. Apparently, something in Mills's personality caused Finerty to squirm.[3]

Chicago Times, September 30, 1876

The Hungry Heroes
The Deluges on the Powder
[*From Our Own Reporter*]

Crook's Expedition, Powder River Camp, Montana, Aug. 24. We are here drying our saturated clothes on the banks of the filthiest river in America or elsewhere. For a wonder, it has not rained during the last half hour. Thunder and "everlasting wet" have pursued us since the date of my last letter, but last night, on the Yellowstone, was the most utterly miserable that we have so far experienced. Unfortunately, our camp had to be moved in order to give the horses fresh grass, and the temporary bivouac had to be abandoned in the midst of a perfect tornado of rain. There was no very dire necessity for this, as Gen. Terry had supplied "the stock" with grain for a few days, but the soldiers had to obey orders all the same. The movement was countermanded when too late, and we went into our new camp, hardly 200 yards from the old one, in a lowland under a sand-hill range, flooded with water, and fully a mile from wood. Clothing and blankets were soaked thoroughly, and, having neither tents nor camp-fires, some of the companies were in a most unenviable condition. To keep dry was impossible, and to keep warm was equally so; for a cold north wind set in at nightfall to drive the water more mercilessly into our bones.

The officer with whom I mess and myself made a desperate effort to sleep, but met with almost utter failure. Our one army blanket and leaky ponchos were no protection against a solid sheet of rain falling from the opaque clouds, and the eternal, infernal rat-tat-tat, growing faster and heavier each second, on the gum covering made us think that the devil was beating his famous tattoo for our especial benefit. Cold may be warded off. Heat can be modified in some way, but, without canvas, it is impossible to combat the terrible rain-storms of this region. The oldest of the soldiers, men who served all through our great war and some of the wars of Europe, declared that they had experienced nothing more distressing, either under Havelock in India, Von Moltke in France and Germany, or Sherman in Georgia and the Carolinas. Vivid flashes of lightning, followed by tremendous peals of thunder, added satanic grandeur to the misery. All the artillery in the world could hardly have produced such an indescribable uproar. The horses drew their picket-pins from the sodden soil and stampeded, plunging helplessly around in the swamps. Something that felt like an elephant walked over my "bunk." I punched the creature with my carbine, and by the vigorous kick which it gave my saddle in return, I became aware of the presence of a scared pack-mule. The lightning percaled [revealed] the wretched troops gathered on the sheltered side of the low hills, huddled in groups and vainly trying to keep up some animal heat. A few of their remarks came fitfully to my ears, and served to amuse me in some measure. One fellow had had enough of glory, and would either desert or secure his discharge before coming on another Indian campaign. Another damned whiskey for leading him into the army.

"Now, George," said an Irish soldier, "wouldn't you just wish you had a little drop to mix with all this water?"

"No fear of you mixing it, Tim," George replied, "you always take it straight in Ireland."

"Bad luck to the ship that bought me over thin," Tim replied, "if I had taken my poor owld mother's advice and remained in Cashel it isn't like a drowned rat I'd be this night."

"Och, be J——, this is the most G—damnablest outfit I ever struck in my 25 years of service," said a Milesian veteran, in disgusted tones. "Devil shoot the ginerals and the shoulder sthraps all around. Shure they have no more compassion on a poor crayture of a soldier than a wolf has on a lamb!"

"A tough old lamb you are, Jerry, sure enough," said another warrior. "A wolf would have to howld his head a long way from the wall afore he could eat you."

"We can't even have coffee, and must eat all our bacon raw tonight," lamented a native American. "The confounded sage-brush won't burn, and the d—n rain won't let it."

In the midst of these flying remarks, I suddenly fell asleep, and awoke perhaps an hour later to find water running over, under, and all around me. To get up was useless, so I lay and soaked in my clothes until morning came, gray, cold, and cheerless. Then I looked at Lieut. L——, bundled up in his blanket beside me. He was just as badly off as I was, so we rose with great unanimity and made a break for Capt. Meinhold's camp-fire, where we wrestled with the rain fiend for more than an hour. Everybody looked tired and haggard, but the situation was not without its ludicrous features. At about 7 o'clock the weather cleared a little, and then, seated on a stone a captain could be seen wringing out his shirt-tail; a lieutenant wrestling with his one pair of stockings, and the non-commissioned officers and privates helping each other to dry their overcoats and saddle-blankets. As for under-clothing and shoes being wet, they were too well used to that to mind it much. I have slept in the rain several times on this trip, but the experience of last night was the nearest approach to hell upon earth that I have ever known. There may be worse before us, however.

At 10 o'clock, our 15 days' rations being all packed, the order to march came, and Crook's column turned their backs upon the Yellowstone. We marched up the west bank of Powder river, through unending coal-fields, about 10 miles, and went into camp on high ground. I have just been informed that we have cut loose from Terry, and are going to follow up the Sioux trail to the Little Missouri river. Our halt on the Yellowstone has, I think, destroyed all chance of hitting an effective blow, as, most likely, by the time we reach the stream indicated, the Indians will have broken up. My dispatches have already told you that the Snake and Crow Indians, disgusted with our tardiness, quit our command some days ago.[4] Only one full-blooded red man remains with us now. He is known as "Ute John," can talk English perfectly, and is said to be quite an accomplished barbarian.[5] "Buffalo Bill" has given up all hope of a fight, and is going down the river on the steamboat. Three newspaper correspondents followed his example, and only four of the fraternity now accompany this brigade. Despite the inevitable hardship which I foresee, I am determined to go with the main column until the campaign is definitely wound up. The finale cannot be very far off now.

In a Land of Promise

Beaver Creek, Dakota Territory, Aug. 31. Since my last essay at writing I have been tormented by neuralgic fever and the blue devils.[6] My hated enemy, the rain, has pursued us like a plague, making officers, soldiers, packers, and journalists alike moody and disagreeable. We are following the Indian trail which we struck on Rosebud and which Gen. Terry's junction prevented us from pursuing with sufficient alacrity. To do Crook justice, although he is a hard officer to serve under as regards personal comfort, he has more energy than most of our generals, even if his judgment may not always be correct. He will dare anything to get a fight out of the Sioux or destroy their villages. His terrible disregard for shelter and other human necessaries makes him many enemies both in the upper and lower strata of this army. He is by no means popular with the rank and file, and the officers do not seem to like him, unless in exceptional cases. Crook is a singular man, and one impossible to estimate at a glance or even on long acquaintance. It is, however, a complimentary matter to him individually that the officers and men who have served with him longest seem to like him most. From what I know of the general, I think he resembles Grant in bull-dog tenacity and is far more indifferent to the filth and misery of war. He accepts the situation, and from his long residence among the Indians, and white men who in some sort have imbibed Indian ways and ideas, has become a good deal of an Indian himself. I don't think that Crook is a hard-hearted man, but he is stoical, and, to carry his point, would not hesitate at any sacrifice of either himself or his command. While urbane in manner and easily approached, he has a certain amount of military hauteur, when necessary, that keeps intruders at a distance. Whenever you see Crook standing alone, his hands in his pockets and his heels stamping the ground, while his eyes appear absorbed in contemplation of his boots, don't go near him. But when you see him seated on a log chatting with his officers, then you may ask him any question relative to his plans and prospects which may suggest itself. I think the general is somewhat mystical, but a man of strong character withal.

To resume my unavoidably hasty and disjointed narrative: On Aug. 25 we made another short march up the left bank of the Powder, and were visited by a very severe frost that night. I was told that Crook would march direct for the Little Missouri next day, and he did so, making 20 miles, and halting on a branch of O'Fallon creek, a rivulet scarcely defined on any of the maps. On the 27th we made the same number of miles, and went into camp on O'Fallon creek proper. Our march on the succeeding day brought us to Cabin creek, why so called nobody can tell, as nothing more substantial than an Indian tepee was ever erected thereon. That night we had thunder, lightning, and a deluge. We gave up the idea of rest, and were glad to keep even moderately warm. The horses sunk in the mud to their knee-joints, and soldiers' shoes were pulled off in trying to drag their feet through the sticky slime. "Can hell be much worse than this?" said an officer to me next morning. He was cleaning about twenty pounds of wet clay from his boots with a butcher knife. His clothes were dripping, his teeth chattering, and his nose a cross between purple and indigo. If looking like the devil could make a man fit for the region he inquired about, that young lieutenant was a most eligible candidate.

The scouts reported the Indian trail growing fresher, so we moved 10 miles further east, and encamped among a detached section of bluffs, chiefly cone-shaped, which were very picturesque. We found that the Indians were following the Sully trail of 1864, which leads at this point direct to the Missouri. Gen. Crook thought that the point might be on the headwaters of either the Glendive or Beaver creeks, and sent out scouts, who remained absent over 30 hours, which compelled us to lie over for one day. On the morning of Aug. 31 they reported no Indians at the points designated, so we marched to this creek, about a dozen miles, so that the troops might have their bi-monthly muster for pay. Beaver creek is called the Indian branch of the lesser Missouri, and runs through a lovely champagne country. How Gen. Hazen, in his famous report, could call the section of territory from Powder River to this stream "a desert" passes comprehension and excites general surprise.[7] A finer locality for either grazing or tillage purposes can hardly be imagined. With few exceptions the tract indicated is an unbroken meadow-land. Timber is scarce, but coal abounds in miraculous quantities. Every cut made by the water, and the sides of every bluff, large or small, show immense blocks or veins of that mineral, thus settling the fuel supply question beyond cavil. Our troops lit some fires made of this material and found them admirable. We saw two burning coal ledges. The coal is bituminous on the surface, but, doubtless, all the other varieties can be found when mines are opened here, which must be the case in the not remote future.

If inexhaustible supplies of coal, water, and grass cannot make a country rich, the Americans have lost their renowned enterprise and the pioneer spirit which, more even than the words of the continentals "Made a gigantic nation spring from the waters of the Atlantic, and converted a fettered colony into a proud republic, prosperous, limitless, and invincible," is no more. We expected to find a Sahara and we entered a land of promise. Our animals appreciated this fact as much as we did, for the starved creatures filled themselves to satiety with the succulent grasses of the Montana plains.

The March for Life

Heart River, Dakota, Sept. 5. We made two marches north on Beaver creek, about 32 miles, and, finding no Sioux, moved up Andrew's creek, nearly due east, about 20 miles. Crook became satisfied that the Indians had crossed to the Little Missouri, and, on Sept. 4, we marched to that river on Custer's trail of 1874, perhaps 18 miles east, and crossed it at 2 o'clock in the afternoon.[8] The stream is sullen and muddy, like its large namesake, and has tremendous bluffs or "buttes," which are filled with coal and iron veins on both sides. Wild cherries, plums, and "buffalo berries" grow in profusion on the banks, so our soldiers had quite a feast that evening. Many men were suffering from internal ailments, and this timely fruit supply checked sickness of that nature to a great extent. It rained all day, as usual, and made night a thing of horror. We camped where Sully camped in 1862, and where Custer did ten years later, and on some of his later scouts. It was an amphitheatrical valley, "rock enchaliced," as it were, and would have been an excellent thing for some artist to sketch. By the way, our artistic brethren have not been very enterprising on this occasion. A man capable of producing good sketches could have made a small fortune since this campaign opened. But hard campaigning, on very coarse food and sometimes insufficient, would hardly enliven the genius of a city man gifted with the artists' magic skill. On the whole, I think the artists were sensible to remain in the land of the civilized. I never appreciated the force of the lines,

> O solitude! where are the charms that sages have seen in thy face?[9]

until I "struck" George Crook's Indian hunting "outfit." "The wild freedom of the plains" sounds well in a comfortable parlor, but does not feel quite as well when your ride is wet and clammy with rain, like the skin of a frog, when you have as much mud on your person as would disgrace a Bridgeport pig.

I have seen an English regiment after returning from the Crimean war, hairy, patched up, and tanned, but so ragged, filthy, forlorn-looking a set of men as the soldiers of this expedition I have never beheld. That they are not vermin-eaten is to me a bewildering mystery. That they will be so is inevitable before many days. Let civilization scratch itself all over when it hears that we have not three pounds of washing-soap in this entire command, and that no man, not even Gen. Crook himself, has a second shirt to his back! I have seen that officer wash his own under-clothes in the Yellowstone and sit on the bank to let them dry.

Gen. Gibbon cried out to our column when he passed us the day the junction was effected, "Why, soldiers, you're even dirtier than my men!" I should think they were. Terry's men moved with 205 wagons, "Sibley" and "A" tents, together with a pack-train, while Crook's command had only rations on their mules, and all the clothing they possessed on their frames. Terry's troops applied to Crook's a nickname unfit for ears polite, but which unmistakably referred to the dilapidated condition of the rear portion of their pantaloons. If any reader considers this picture overdrawn, I call upon any man in this column, from Gen. Crook to the humblest private, to contradict me. I wish to let the American people know what their gallant army has to undergo in fighting those red scoundrels who have too long been treated as chiefs and equals. Crook is severe, and I'd rather be with Terry, as regards food, shelter, and clean flannel, but he goes for the Indians as one of themselves would do, and has shown that an American army can stand, without much growling or the slightest approach to mutiny, more than any other troops upon this earth. At the same time, I hope that the general, should he ever repeat this experiment, will allow a little more soap and an additional pair of stockings to each man.

In referring to the army as American, I do not wish it understood in the native sense, for the larger proportion of the rank and file is made up of the material that covered the British arms with glory in the Peninsula—the never war-absent Irish—and of Germans, whose slow bravery solidified the Celtic ardor with Yankee coolness, and makes the three combined a military body that, to use the words of a dashing American officer who has accompanied this column from the onset, "which would go with the Balaklava 'six hundred' into the mouth of hell and then brandish their carbines and call upon the 'Light Brigade' to follow them and fight their way out at the other end." Such are the soldiers what congress threatens with pay reductions whenever a politician desires to make cheap capital. If the pay is to be cut down at all, let the patriots apply the pruning-knife to the higher branches. For my part, I think an American private soldier on an Indian scout is a condemned soul passing through the torments of hell, and that his officer is very little better than a boss devil, hardly less wretched than the mortal he commands.

A word about officers. Most of them are high-bred, manly, learned, good-humored, hospitable gentlemen, while a very few are narrow-minded, jealous, punctilious, "swell-headed," irritable, excitable, and generally unfit for anything but retirement into private life. I am glad to say that the percentage of the latter grade is insignificant, and the sooner the army is rid of them the better. The high-toned, chivalric class of officers almost extinguish the others, but one disagreeable "shoulder-strap" is enough to disgust an entire regiment. As for bravery, the quality is so universal in the American army, that no officer gets credit for fearlessness, which is regarded as a matter of course. Judgment, skill, and dignified firmness are far more necessary. A hectoring, bullying officer never gains the respect and confidence of his men, were he as bold as Ajax,[10] while the quiet, determined yet courteous commander wins the hearts of his subordinates, and, because of his moral influence, is obeyed with all the more alacrity. Personally, I have nothing to complain of; but were I an officer serving under certain other officers, I think I'd feel like occasioning a special court-martial. Nothing appears so unmanly and uncalled for in any soldier as an insulting, snappish tone toward his inferiors, knowing, as he must know, how utterly helpless, according to the humiliating military code, they are. If an inferior officer resents the impertinence of his superior he may obtain temporary satisfaction, but, in the end, he will be made to suffer. In regard to the privates they count for so many serfs, and have no right to question orders good or bad.

> Theirs not to reason why
> Theirs but to do and die,[11]

without resisting the higher power. Their only recourse is the disgraceful one of desertion, and no wonder that some of them adopt even that vile mode of breaking their fetters. How a man of spirit, brought to enlist through intemperance or other folly, must burn and long to tear the wind-pipe out of some official bully, who talks to him as though he were a dog. I admit some of the soldiers are roughs and blackguards, just fit to be kicked around, but the greater number are good men enough, some of them men who "have seen better days," and some who, in soldiering, have learned a lesson that will reform their lives.

We marched some 30 miles from the Little Missouri to this stream, called Heart river, today. We are within 160 miles of Fort Lincoln, and are about 200 from the northern edge of the Black Hills. To accomplish either march we have rations for two and a half days only. I interviewed Gen. Crook on the subject half an hour ago. This was what occurred:

"You are sending in a courier, general?"

"Yes, to Fort Lincoln. He will carry some mail and telegrams for the command," Crook answered.

"What do you propose to do now, general?"

He paused for a moment and, pulling his peculiar beard, said very slowly—"We are five full marches from Fort Abraham Lincoln. We are seven, at least, from the Black Hills. By going to the Missouri we lose two weeks' time. By marching on the Hills we gain so much. I march on the Black Hills to-morrow. Between going to and coming from Fort Lincoln we should lose more than half our horses."

"How much rations do you have left?"

"Only two days and a half, but we must make them last for seven, at least. It must be done. The Indians have gone to the Hills and to the agencies. The miners must be protected, and we must punish the Sioux on our way to the south, or leave this campaign entirely unfinished."

I looked at him in undisguised amazement, and could not help saying: "You will march 200 miles in a wilderness with used-up horses and tired infantry, on 2½ days rations?"

"I know it looks hard," said Crook, "but we have to do it and it shall be done. I have sent a telegram for supplies to Gen. Sheridan. They will meet us at Custer City or Deadwood. If not, the settlements must supply our wants. Nobody knows this country, but it looks fair. We'll kill game en route to make up for the short supplies. Half rations will be issued after to-night. You and the rest will be glad of the movement after the march is accomplished."

That was all he said, but I looked at the worn horses and tired men with some foreboding, and visions of devouring the hind-quarter of a government mule was [sic] before us. Crook's resolve was bold and even rash. Cold weather would kill our animals, and freeze half of us to death. In this region winter often steps in where summer has just been basking in the sun-rays. Fortunately this season is not prematurely cold. Crook's resolve has been surmised, and the camp feels gloomy. We are in *terra incognita*, and have a weary march before us. The plains are heavy and the hills steep, the streams swollen and the army discouraged, but human endurance has ere now vanquished greater difficulties. Many soldiers and some officers are very sick, but there is nothing for it except march as directed. I'd give something this minute to be drinking Crook's health at Wolford's, or devouring "a square meal" at Burke's or Thompson's. The very idea makes me both dry and hungry, so I'll substitute soft water and a "hard tack" for the far-away luxuries alluded to. When I was coming on this trip, some of my friends said it would be a picnic. I had my misgivings then, but now I'd give any one of them eager for "glory" in exchange for their city life this 200 mile ride on a sore-back horse, with the prospect of being dismounted before going one-tenth of the way. This may be appropriately named the devil's own picnic. The worst we have gone through was pleasure compared with what I feel to be coming. But, croaking will do no good, so I'll swallow the dose and make my journalistic pilgrimage, like the Irish magistrate, "with a gun in one hand and a pistol in the other while I write." Who knows but I may have to eat my horse before getting through. Well, he's a tough-looking mortal, and the most ingenious butcher could hardly scrape enough flesh off him to feed a cat. There is, after all, a diabolical ludicrousness about this business, so I find myself feeling diabolically jovial and ready to face the worst. "What can't be cured must be endured," and so your correspondent, seeing that he has no means of escaping, "accepts the situation." It rains again.

The First Horse-Steak

MENAMED CREEK,[12] 86 miles from Heart River, Dakota Territory, Sept. 8. The skies are pouring still, and I write this in the shade of a blanket kept up by a few willow poles. Since we left Heart river we have made 86 miles, nearly due south, and did not see a stick of wood all the way to this point, where we have had the good fortune to find some brush. The "washes" and "aroyas" are all filled with water, and nearly impassable. This, together with the soft ground, has ruined our stock, and fully 200 cavalrymen are walking with the wonderful infantry column, which still holds the palm for military pedestrianism. Some of the younger men give evidence of playing out, and will have to be mounted on pack mules. Our bread (hard tack) and bacon rations are exhausted, and we have been eating horse meat since yesterday morning. Coffee and sugar will not last another day, so you may imagine our condition. Last night Gen. Crook detached 150 men, picked, 15 from each of the 10 companies of the 3d cavalry, under command of Col. Anson Mills and Lieut.'s Crawford, Von Luettwitz, and Schwatka, to ride ahead to the Black Hills settlements and procure rations. Lieut. Bubb, our commissary, and Mr. Thomas Moore, the chief packer, with 50 pack-mules and some drivers, accompanies the military. They have orders to return at once and meet us on the Belle Fourche, about 100 miles from here. I'd have gone, too, only I had nothing to ride, my horse being "dead-beat," and it being impossible to procure another. However, they'll have a hard ride—they must go at the top of their speed—and we who remain here will be just as well off as they are. Many people in the column doubt whether supplies can be had in the Hills. If not, then "the crack of doom" will have come for us in earnest. Gen. Crook appears to feel confident as ever. He talks of whipping the Indians around the mining districts, and forcing them in to Red Cloud and Spotted Tail. We left 50 horses on the road to-day. The infantry cut steaks from the carcasses and are now roasting them at their camp-fires.

The Battles of the Buttes

Clay Ridge Creek, 17 miles from Slim Buttes, Dakota, Sept. 10. Some stirring events have transpired within the last 48 hours. As we were about breaking camp on the morning of the 9th, George Hermann, a packer, accompanied by a soldier, rode up to Gen. Crook with a dispatch from Col. Mills, which stated that his detachment had captured that morning an Indian village of 41 lodges, a large herd of ponies, and some supplies. The Sioux were still fighting to secure what they had lost, and the colonel requested reinforcements. He was then 17 miles south, at Slim Buttes, on a tributary of Grand river. Gen. Crook at once selected 100 men, with the best horses, from the 3d cavalry, 50 from Noyes' battalion of the 2d, and the 5th cavalry, and, accompanied by his staff and the commanding officers of the different regiments, rode forward to the assistance of his subordinate.

Mills, not anticipating an Indian fight, had allowed his men only 50 rounds of ammunition each, and Crook was alarmed lest the Sioux should compel him to expend his last cartridge before assistance would reach him. I accompanied the advance, but my infernal beast broke down completely two or three miles from camp, and I had to lead him the rest of the way. The road was so bad that the cavalry could not go at a very fast pace, so I was lucky enough to reach the captured village very soon after Crook got in. All was quiet then, for the Sioux had withdrawn to procure reinforcements before Crook arrived and, as subsequently appeared, did not know of his arrival at all. They fancied that Mills, like Custer, was all alone.

Approaching the scene of the fight I saw a small ravine, between gentle hills, in which the captured pony herd was corralled, while our cavalry horses were picketed along the slopes. Several large Indian tepees, covered with canvas or buckskin, were pitched on the east side of the northern slope, and showed the location of the village. A solitary tepee on the north side of the hill was used as a hospital, and there the wounded were placed.

I met Mills as I led in my jaded hack, and he showed me the position. He was surrounded by high, very steep bluffs on all sides but the east, and, consequently, the defeated Indians had a full chance to annoy him. It was noon when I met him, and the fight had closed about 10 o'clock. The capture of the village was but the work of a few minutes, and my telegram, if received, will give you a full account of the affair. The Indian trail had been struck the previous afternoon, and was followed up to within four miles of the village when Mills went into camp. He reconnoitered, with Grouard, and found the location, determining to attack next morning. Of course it rained all night, and, while yet dark, the colonel moved forward his detachment, together with the pack mules, for two miles. Here he halted the packers, fearing their beasts' braying would alarm the Indians, dismounted all his cavalry except 25 men under Schwatka, and moved forward to "fall on." Capt. Jack Crawford, of Omaha, a well-known scout, and some other guides,[13] went with Grouard, and joined in the subsequent charge. Mills arriving in the edge of the ravine where the redskins slept securely, as they thought, sent Lieut. Schwatka with his 25 mounted men, to drive off the pony herd. The ponies were stampeded at once, but rushed for the village and alarmed the Indians. Von Luettwitz and Crawford, with 50 men each on foot, surrounded the lodges and charged. There was a ripping of canvas and buffalo hide, as the Sioux had no time to untie the strings of the lodges and cut the tents with their knives. The soldiers fired a volley, which the Indians returned in a desultory way. Almost at the first shot Lieut. A. H. Von Luettwitz, of "E" company, 3d cavalry, fell with a bullet through his right knee joint. This gentleman had served in the Austrian and Prussian armies, had fought at Montebello, Magenta, Solferino, all through the Italian campaign of '59, had distinguished himself at Gettysburg and other great battles of our war, and had escaped comparatively unscathed. Yet his hour had come, and he fell wounded in a miserable Indian skirmish, the very first man. If he does not lose his life he has surely lost his limb, which is nearly as bad. Lieut. Crawford and Col. Mills then led on the soldiers and made short work of the village, although the Indians kept up a scattering fire from the bluffs.

When daylight came the Sioux made matters much hotter, and the soldiers being much exposed on that bare bluff were almost at their mercy. Mills sent back for his train, which came up with Moore and Bubb and Messrs R. B. Davenport and R. A. Strahorn, all of whom behaved in a gallant manner during the skirmishing which followed. Lieut. Crawford acted with fine judgment, and is spoken highly of by the soldiers who participated in the affair. Schwatka did his work in a thorough manner and made a mark of which he may be well proud. Mills is too old a soldier to need much special mention. If he were half as popular personally as he is energetic and fearless in the field he would be the idol of the brigade. But Mills is peculiar, and occasionally the reverse of unselfish, which to some extent neutralizes his undeniable ability as an officer. But, for all that, Crook's column can never forget his brilliant dash on Sept. 9, which saved us from actual famine. He captured a large amount of dried provisions, 2,500 buffalo robes, and many other campaign luxuries which Indians appreciate as much as white men.

One of gallant Custer's guidons, Col. [Myles W.] Keogh's[14] gauntlets, and several other relics of the fated 7th cavalry were among the prizes secured. A party of Sioux, unable to make their escape, took refuge in a sort of deep, brush-covered gully, just above the site of the village, on the eastern slope, dug entrenchments with their hands and knives, and could not be dislodged by Mills' detachment. In an attempt to drive them out nearly all the casualties occurred. Private John Wenzel, of "A" company, [was killed,] and Sergt. Ed Glass, of "E" company, one of the boldest non-commissioned officers in the army, was shot through the right fore-arm. Six other soldiers were wounded in attempting to carry this fatal den. The names have been furnished by telegraph. The firing of the Indians from the bluffs compelled the soldiers to throw up temporary breastworks, which saved them from particularly serious damage. The riding mule of Mr. Moore and a horse belonging to "I" company were shot from the "lava-bed" arrangement.

Mills, when he sent back for his train in the morning, had the good sense to send for re-enforcements at the same time. Crook arrived a little after 11 o'clock, and immediately attacked the Indian burrow in the gully. In that affair he displayed to the fullest his eccentric contempt for danger. No private soldier could more expose himself than did the general and the officers of his staff. I expected to see him shot down every moment, for Charley White, the well-known scout, was shot through the heart just across the ravine, not 10 paces from Crook. [Edward] Kennedy, of the 5th cavalry, and [John M.] Stevenson of the 2nd, were wounded, the one mortally and the other dangerously, beside him, while many other soldiers had hair-breadth escapes. The boys in blue, although unquestionably brave, did not relish the idea of being shot in the digestive organs by an unseen and "ungetatable" enemy, but the officers rallied them without any difficulty, leading the assault, musket in hand. Besides Crook and his staff, Maj [Samuel] Munson, of the infantry, Maj. [Daniel W.] Burke, of the same branch of the service, Lieut. [Captain Calbraith P.] Rogers and Lieut. W. P. Clark of the 2d cavalry, took desperate chances in true "forlorn hope" fashion. The guide, Baptiste Pourier (not Custer's) fought his way right into the cavern, and killed one of the Sioux, ingeniously using a captive squaw as a barricade between himself and the fire of the other warriors. He took the scalp in a manner that showed perfect workmanship. Scalping is an artistic process, and, when neatly done, may be called a satanic accomplishment.[15]

Crook formed a cordon of infantry and dismounted horsemen around the den and opened upon it an incessant fire, which made the hills echo back a terrific music. The imprisoned Indians distributed their shots liberally among the crowd, but the shower of close-range bullets horrified the unhappy squaws and they commenced singing their death-chant. The papooses wailed piteously and Crook ordered the firing to cease immediately. Then Grouard and Pourier, both of whom talk Sioux, by the general's order, offered the women and children quarter. The brigadier, in person, went to the mouth of the cavern and handed out one fine looking woman, who had a baby strapped to her back. She trembled all over and would not let go of the general's hand. Eleven of the squaws and six papooses were then taken out, but the surviving warriors refused to surrender and savagely recommenced the fight. Then our men reopened a very "rain of hell" upon the infatuated Indians who, nevertheless, fought it out against such desperate odds for nearly two hours. Such matchless courage electrified the enraged soldiers into chivalry, and Crook, recognizing the fact that the unfortunate savages had fought like fiends in defense of wife and child, ordered another suspension of hostilities and called upon the dusky heroes to surrender. Then the chief, American Horse, a fine, broad-chested Sioux, with a handsome face and a neck like a bull, showed himself with the butt-end of his musket turned to the general. He had just been shot through the bowels, and, in his native language, said he would yield if the lives of his warriors with him were spared. Some of the soldiers shouted "no quarter," but not a man was coward enough to shoot down the disabled chief. Crook hesitated for a moment and said: "Two Sioux more or less can make no difference. I can use them to good advantage. Tell the chief," he said to Grouard, "that he and his young men shall not be harmed further."

This being interpreted to American Horse, he beckoned to his young men, and two strapping Indians, with their long, graceful stride, followed him out of the gully. Over two feet of the chieftain's bowels protruded from his wound. A squaw tied her shawl around him, and, never uttering a complaint, the poor, fearless warrior walked slowly to a little camp-fire about 30 yards off and sat down among his children. Crook took the entire party under his protection and ordered the dead to be taken from the late stronghold. Let the country praise or blame the general for his clemency, I simply record the affair as it occurred.

Some soldiers jumped into the ravine and bore out the corpses. The buck killed by Pourier was a grim-looking old fellow, covered with scars, and loaded down with jewelry. The other dead were three squaws (one was at first supposed to be a man) and a tiny child. The captive women, with their papooses, came up to view the corpses. They appeared quite unmoved, although a crowd of half-savage miners, unkempt scouts, and infuriated soldiers surged around them—a living tide. The entire upper skull of one squaw was blown to atoms, revealing the upper roof of the palate. Another of the dead females, a middle-aged woman, was so thoroughly riddled with bullets that there appeared to be no unwounded part in her. The third squaw was young, plump, and light-colored. She had a magnificent physique, and, for an Indian, a most attractive set of features. She was shot in the left breast, and was not in the least disfigured. "Ute John," our friendly Indian, unknown to the general, scalped them all, and I regret to be compelled to state that a few brutal soldiers bore a hand in the revolting business. The unfortunates ought to have been respected, even in death. In that affair, at least, the army were the assailants, and the Sioux acted in self-defense. I must say, in justice to all concerned, that neither Gen. Crook nor the soldiers suspected that any women or children were in the ravine until the cries were heard in the short intervals of the volleys.

A dead cavalry horse lay on his side on the western side of the burrow and Moore's mule, his feet sticking up in the air, lay on his back thirty yards beyond. On the southern slope of the embankment, face downward, resting on his forehead and knees, the stiff, dead hands still gripping the full-cocked carbine, two empty cartridge shells lying beside him, was the body of the soldier John Wenzel. He was shot through the brain by American Horse, after he had fired twice into the gully, and never realized that he had been hit. Poor fellow! He knew more about a horse than any man in "A" company of the Third cavalry, and used to attend to my animal before he was sent, for the reason of his being well mounted, quite unexpectedly, on the fatal detail. Diagonally opposite, on the northern descent, lay the stalwart remains of Charley White, "Buffalo Chip," as he was called—the champion harmless liar and most genial scout "upon the plains." I saw him fall. He crept over the slope to fire on the Indians. The crowd shouted, "Charley, get away from there," Just then a shot was fired from the den, and White raised himself up to locate the spot it came from. Just as he did so, quick as lightning, one of the Indians took his range and shot him square through the left nipple. White threw up his hands, crying out loud enough for all of us to hear him, "My God, my God, boys, I'm done for this time!" One mighty convulsion doubled up his body; then he relaxed all over, and rolled like a log three or four feet down the slope. His face expressed astonishment rather than agony, when I looked at him some hours later. The wind blew the long locks over his cold face, and his eyes were almost perfectly closed. The slain hunter looked as if he was taking a rest after a toilsome buffalo chase. Last and least, the slaughtered Indian papoose, only some two months old, lay in a small basket. Had its hair been long enough, doubtless "Ute John" would have scalped it, too.

With all this mutilated mortality before them, the hungry soldiers tore dried Indian meat into eatable pieces, and marched away as unconcerned as if they were at a holiday picnic. It was a ghastly charnel group—one which properly painted would, more than any I have heard described, give the civilized world a faithful picture of the diabolism of an Indian war. Our dead were hastily buried by their comrades, but the Indians were left on the field, as they were, until their friends took charge of the bodies after we left. The Sioux never, so far as known, place their defunct in the earth, so that leaving the bodies above ground was of no particular consequence in their case. American Horse and the squaws told Gen. Crook that he would be attacked by Crazy Horse and his band without much delay. Accordingly no one was surprised when, at 4 o'clock yesterday afternoon, we were fired upon from the bluffs surrounding us everywhere except to the eastward. To occupy them thoroughly would have required an army corps, so that nobody is to blame for the second Indian attempt at rescuing the ponies and recapturing the tents and other property.

The "buttes" called "Slim" are of an extraordinary shape, very lofty, and strongly resemble a series of mammoth Norman castles, or a semi-circular range of exposition buildings. They have tier upon tier of rocks, with the hardy northern pine growing in every crevice, contrasting the green with the gray, and clothing the bare, stern, granite crags with savage beauty. Along the ledges and among the pines the Sioux led their war ponies and commenced operations. No time was lost in meeting their assault. Quick as an exploded shell the brigade, which had all arrived, with the exception of a small rear guard, broke into a tremendous line of skirmishers, forming a cordon around the cavalry horses, pack-mules, and captured ponies. Gen. Merritt was Crook's second in command, but the latter-named general gave the order of battle. The Indian fire whizzed into us for a few minutes, and the voices of our officers could be heard shouting: "Steady, men! Take your proper intervals! Don't fire until you get the range! Forward! Double-quick time! Up in the centre! D—n it, Reilly, are you firing at the Black Hills? Never waste a shot, boys," as the infantry and dismounted dragoons trotted on to meet the enemy.

Col. Chambers and his officers went straight for the southern bluff, while Col. Carr, with the 5th cavalry, pushed toward the hills on the southwest. The 3d cavalry, under Col. Royall, took charge of the northern and northwestern heights, while the 2d cavalry, under Maj. Noyes, protected the eastern flank, and, being mounted, cut around the north end of the bluffs to checkmate an attempt made by Crazy Horse to cut off the rear guard, which was driving the stragglers and used-up horses in before it. The bloodiest battles are not always the most picturesque. The evening fight at Slim Buttes was not sanguinary, as regarded our side, but it was the prettiest battle scene—so acknowledged by men who have seen a hundred fights—that ever an Indian war correspondent was called upon to describe. When our men got within range, their fire opened steadily. First it was pop-pop-pop slow and sure, while the incessant ring of the Winchester rifle in reply, and the screaming of bullets, fired from too elevated a position, indicated that Crazy Horse was neither "dead nor deaf nor dumb." On the infantry front the rattle soon swelled into a roar. The 5th cavalry caught the infection and it spread nearly around the line. Our men had plenty of ammunition and resolved to drown out the Indian enemy. Long wreathes of smoke, which showed all the more as the evening advanced, encircled the skirmish line, crept up the height, and shrouded the combatants in the sulfurous gloom.

Through this martial uproar you could observe the vivid flashing of the guns—our boys creeping steadily from ledge to ledge, and the Indians, bold as ever, but utterly confounded, stunned, shattered, and deafened by that unending fusillade, retiring before them, fighting every foot they retreated. It has been a matter of astonishment to nearly every one on this trip how our men came off so safely in every engagement with the Indians. The latter nearly always fire from the backs of their ponies, which, in some degree, accounts for their general inaccuracy. Besides this, firing down hill, unless there is a clear slope, cannot be very effective, while on the contrary, the party advancing upward, can see every object clearly defined against the sky.

Every time an Indian got killed or disabled his comrades picked him up and bore him off. The infantry must have done terrible execution, their "long toms" reaching the enemy far beyond the range of the carbine. The 5th cavalry were also warmly engaged, and enfiladed the Sioux with great enthusiasm. Driven by the forces named from their original positions, the defeated Indians came through the ravine in the northwestern angle of the bluffs and charged the position of the 3d cavalry. Like the cuirassiers at Mont St. Jean,[16] they rode around the line, looking for a gap through which to reach the pony herd. They kept in perpetual motion, apparently encouraged by the presence of one warrior, doubtless the chief himself, who, mounted on a fleet, white horse, galloped along the line and seemed to possess the power of ubiquity. He was blazed at by every soldier that saw him, without effect. Failing to break in that formidable circle, the Indians, after firing several scattered volleys, their original order of battle being completely broken, and recognizing the folly of fighting such an opposing force longer, glided away from our front with all possible speed, and, as the shadows came down into the valley, the last shots were fired and the affair of "Slim Buttes" was over.

It was the first occasion during the campaign on which our side had the undoubted advantage. We had only five soldiers badly wounded and about a dozen slightly hurt in the evening combat, while the Sioux must have lost quite heavily. Infantry officers—men who are above the meanness of a falsehood—have assured me that, in their front, the Sioux were terribly shattered. Several of their ponies, riderless, were captured during the evening. Indians never leave their war-horses, unless surprised or killed, which shows that many saddles, to use the Caucasian term, were emptied. Pools of blood were also found on some of the ledges, showing the places where some of Crazy Horse's men paid for their valor with their lives. I have heard the Sioux numbers variously estimated, but I cannot attempt to verify any estimate made. There could not have been more than six or eight hundred of their fighting men opposed to us. Had they had equal numbers, notwithstanding the unquestioned courage of our troops, it is hard to say how the fight would have terminated. I am prone to believe, however, that 2,000 good white men, such as compose Crook's brigade, could not be beaten by the same number of Indians even though more warlike—if that were possible—than the fiery and ferocious Sioux nation.

American Horse died at 6 o'clock this morning. Dr. [Valentine] McGillycuddy examined his wound and told him, through the interpreter, that he must go to the happy hunting grounds. He appeared quite cheerful, and, before breathing his last, spoke freely about the present war with the whites, as recorded in my telegram to THE TIMES from the scene of action. His squaw, two wounded women, and a few children were left with the body of the dead chief. He was not subjected to the scalping process.

The rear guard of the column, Capts. [Samuel S.] Sumner and [Robert H.] Montgomery's companies of the 5th cavalry, were attacked by a party of Indians shortly after leaving camp. The "reds" were again unfortunate, losing five men killed and "counted," while the 5th had two men wounded. Crazy Horse, evidently sick of the business, made no further demonstration and has not been heard from since.

Food for the Famished

Belle Fourche River, Dakota, Sept. 13. We turned Clay ridge through a winding and tedious defile amid a pelting shower, on the 11th. It ought to be termed "Church-spire range," for the rocks are shaped into fantastic pinnacles, resembling those which "pierce the clouds" from the summit of sacred edifices. The number of steeples reminded me of Brooklyn, Beecher, and "nest-hiding."[17] Mills, with a swift-riding party mounted on Indian ponies, set out for the Black Hills, visible from Clay ridge, at noon. He was accompanied by Lieuts. Bubb and [George F.] Chase. "Capt. Jack" Crawford and Frank Grouard went in as couriers. We had a beef-herd sent to meet us from Crook city. It arrived in our camp on Willow creek, five miles back, this morning. We were all having our breakfasts on Indian pony steaks when we heard the lowing of the steers. How cheerful everybody became, and how soon the fatigues and privations of the march were forgotten by the light-hearted and easily-pleased soldiers. "Hurrah for old Crook! Hurrah for old Mills!" they shouted, like a pack of school-boys who get an afternoon "off." Neither of the officers named are very venerable, but when a soldier speaks of his superior as "The Old Man," be sure he is in good humor with him.

Our march from Owl creek to Willow creek on the 12th was the most tedious made during the campaign. We were "on the go" from day-light until dark and made only 35 miles. We tumbled into our bivouacs and picketed our horses in Egyptian darkness,[18] our signal-light from afar being the fire kindled by headquarters staff, which got in ahead. On the road we deserted some 70 horses, and buried over 60 saddles and other equipments. I omitted to state that Gen. Crook burnt up all the Indian property captured, except what the soldiers carried with them. The wearied troops straggled in, brought up by the rear guard, all through the night. With the exception of the dried meat taken from the Sioux—poor diet for white men—the command, general and all, lived on horseflesh and pony-meat from the morning of the 7th until to-day. I have tried both articles, and also tasted mule steak. Here is my opinion in brief: Horseflesh, "played-out" animals, fried without salt, "stringy," leatherish, and nauseating; horseflesh, young animal, not over thin, resembles bad beef; Indian pony (colt) tastes like antelope; Indian pony (adult) has the flavor of elk; mule meat (fat and rank) is a combination of all the foregoing, with pork thrown in. Some soldiers were fortunate enough to shoot a few antelope while on the march, but, as there was no bread, hunger was general, and the horses and ponies were killed by men regularly detailed for the purpose. Indians and whites have, before now, seen American armies that could do any amount of fighting, but neither red nor white man has ever before seen an American army march 200 miles on two and one-half days *half* rations (for beans, etc., were not included) through a country utterly strange and barren of food; over bottomless swamps and sticky soil, in obedience to a general who, before his late success, was regarded as brave but unlucky, rather than as adventurous and fortunate. Gen. Crook calculated correctly, except as regards bad weather, which no mortal could foresee, and no previous mistake should rob him of whatever credit attaches to his latest experiment. At the same time it might be as well for Gen. Crook to study the personal comfort of his troops a little more. If a winter campaign is contemplated, they should have enough clothing to keep them from being frozen, and sufficient food to make them cheerful and well disposed for rough duty.

It is difficult to carry much on an Indian scout, but men, being like most other animals, sensitive to cold and hunger, cannot be called upon to endure too much. Bread rations, brought in wagons from Crook city, where they were purchased by Col. Mills, arrived this afternoon. We are to lie over here for some days, and, meanwhile, I shall take the opportunity of visiting Deadwood and the other mining centres. What I may observe in those places shall be reserved for a future letter. Meanwhile I shall send all important news, through the medium of couriers, by telegraph. I have succeeded in getting a decent horse and can ride with "the advance" once more.

John F. Finerty

Chicago Times, September 9, 1876

SKEDADDLE OR STARVE
THE RETREAT OF CROOK
[*From Our Own Reporter*]

CROOK'S EXPEDITION IN CAMP ON HEART RIVER, Dakota, Sept. 5, via BISMARCK, Dakota, Sept. 8. Since Aug. 24 this command has been employed to march to Powder river and across the country over O'Fallons, Cabin, and Beaver creeks, to the Little Missouri river, which we crossed on yesterday. This camp is about 26 miles eastward from that stream. Wet weather has caused much sickness and suffering among the men. Excellent pasturage has somewhat restored our horses, but many of them are in a deplorable condition and must inevitably break down. Crook followed the Indian trail all the way and is not convinced that the redskins have broken up, some heading toward the British possessions, but the main body moving toward the Black Hills and the agencies. At this point we are about 150 miles from Deadwood in the hills, and have only two and a half days rations left. Fort Lincoln is nearly the same distance from us, so Gen. Crook has decided to march on Deadwood at once. We hope to find rations at that point. Otherwise we must eat our spare mules in order to get in. Winter already begins to show itself in this region, and cold drenching rains harass us continually. Not a man of the command is prepared for bad weather, so that should cold overtake us the suffering will be intense.

It will take us at least eight days to make Deadwood. To-day Col. [Thaddeus H.] Stanton and some of the scouts came upon a small party of Sioux, but the latter got away without loss. As a matter of fact this column is in an unserviceable condition, utterly unfit to do more than act as infantry. The horses are too poor and broken down for active pursuit of the enemy. Gen. Terry's column is living in comparative luxury, while we have marched almost continuously for a month on the poorest kind of rations and without so much as a shelter-tent to keep the men dry during this rainy season. This may be Bonapartean policy, but there is a vast deal of difference between campaigning minus shelter in Italy and doing the same in Montana or Dakota.

Dysentery, rheumatism, and fever are spreading fast among the soldiers, and the sick have to be borne all the way from here to the railroad posts, a distance of about 500 miles, in mule litters. All we need is a few snow-storms to make this column parallel, on the small scale with the horrible retreat from Moscow. We have all else to make us as miserable as were the French—short rations, used-up horses, a vast wilderness, and a discouraged soldiery. As for the Indians, we have no chance of making them fight unless they wish it. Marching on Fort Lincoln would hardly improve our condition, and might tie us up there all winter. No more news can be had from Crook's brigade until it passes the Black Hills.

John F. Finerty

Chicago Times, September 17, 1876

Squaw Scalps
A Siouxprise
[*From Our Own Reporter*]

Crook's Expedition, on Fork Grand River or Slim Buttes, Dakota, Sept. 9, via Fort Laramie, Sept. 15. It is pleasant to be able to record a genuine victory for this command at last. We reached a lagoon, 30 miles from our camp on Heart river, on the evening of Sept. 6, and made 30 additional miles the succeeding day. On the evening of Sept. 7, Gen. Crook detached Col. Anson Mills with 150 picked men and the best horses of the 3d cavalry, to march on Deadwood by forced marches, in order to procure rations at the place named, the expedition being already reduced to the necessity of eating horses.

Fifty pack-mules accompanied the party. The colonel set out that night and made 18 miles. It rained all day on Sept. 8, but he made 30 miles and struck an Indian trail leading south. He resolved to follow the trail and attack the Indians, if possible. At 5:30 on the afternoon of yesterday the party observed a herd of ponies grazing on some bluffs about five miles ahead. Col. Mills and Frank Grouard went forward to reconnoitre, and they became satisfied of the existence of a village. Mills told his officers, Lieuts. Schwatka, Von Luettwitz, and [Emmett] Crawford, that he would attack in the morning, and arrangements were made accordingly. The detachment went into camp in a ravine, but being unable to sleep because of the pouring rain kept vigil until the dawn of day. With the first light the command was in the saddle, and at 4 o'clock came upon an Indian village, situated in a small valley which was commanded by bluffs on the south side. Some bluffs were also on the west, but not in close proximity. Mills ordered Lieut. Schwatka to take 25 mounted men and charge the pony herd, so as to cut it off. Schwatka obeyed his orders in a most dashing manner, surprised the Indian herders, drove them pell mell before him, and captured about 200 first-class ponies. He charged right through the village, and produced a regular stampede, the Sioux being completely surprised.

Meanwhile Crawford and Von Luettwitz dismounted, charged into the village on the flank, and captured tepees, 5,500 pounds of dried meat, an immense number of buffalo robes and other Indian fineries, and, lastly, 200 dogs. They also took a large quantity of dried fruits and other eatables, quite a God-send to the soldiers. The men displayed heroic bravery, and reflected credit on the American army. Nothing could have been more gallant than the conduct of the officers engaged in the fight. Taken altogether, it was a bright page in the history of this expedition. Taken by surprise, the Indians cut themselves out of their tepees and managed to escape for the most part through the ravine. They gave our men two volleys before they cleared their village, and then the darkness of the morning (it was still raining) enabled them to get away.

Von Luettwitz, of company E, of the 3d cavalry, was shot through the knee joint at the first volley. Lieut. Crawford showed excellent judgment as well as soldiery daring. Col. Mills is much congratulated because of the success of his dashing venture, for the Sioux, although taken unawares, fought as usual with consummate courage. They rallied in the hills and soon made matters warm for our boys, keeping up an incessant fire and making desperate efforts to recover their captured ponies. A party then took up position in a kind of burrow down in a small rut between two cliffs, covered with brush and protected by rocks, and with a kind of lava beds. The troops made desperate efforts to dislodge the savages, but the latter, although very few, fought with the desperation of despair.

During the morning the following of ours were killed or wounded: Third Cavalry—A company, killed, John Wenzel, of Frederick, Md. Wounded, E company, Lieut. A. H. Von Luettwitz, severely; Sergt. Edward Glass, severely, right arm; Corporal Edward McKeeon [McKiernan], severely, body and head. D company, Private Augustus Dorn, slightly. B company, Private Charles Forster [Foster], severely. M company, Sergt. [John A.] Kirkwood, severely. C company, Private Charles Dubois, slightly.[19]

Col. Mills, having taken too much property to guard, and being harassed by the Indian fire, sent couriers to Crook, 17 miles back, with the main column, for reinforcements. Crook immediately took 100 selected men from the 3d, 50 from the 2nd, and the entire 5th cavalry, and arrived on the field as the last Indian shots were being fired. He ordered the savages in the ravine to be dislodged, and led the attack in person. He displayed splendid pluck, and captured a dozen squaws and half a dozen papooses right at the mouth of the Indian burrow. Lieut. John G. Bourke, of his staff; Lieut. Rogers, Lieut. W. P. Clark, of the 2d cavalry, the guide Baptiste Pourier, Col. Royall, of the 3d cavalry, and Capt. Munson, of the infantry, also exposed themselves with conspicuous gallantry. The Indians, however, although some were shot, kept up a deadly fire, and killed the scout Charles White, alias "Buffalo Chip," a friend of Buffalo Bill's, shooting him through the heart. Private Edward Kennedy, of E company, of the 5th cavalry, and Private [John M.] Stevenson, of I company, of the 2d cavalry, were dangerously wounded at the same time. The squaws, who were placed under guards, state that the defeated Sioux are Brules, from the Spotted Tail agency, and that their chief is Roman Nose.[20]

Among the trophies secured by Mills are one of the guidons of Custer's regiment, and an officer's under and over coat, blouse, several saddles, and a pair of gauntlets marked "Col. Keogh," also some horses which belonged to the same unfortunate command. We expect to fall on more Indians as we advance, and, having plenty of rations now, can make matters hot for them. Our horses are falling off by the score, which is the worst feature of our present situation.

Sept. 9, 4 P.M. The Indians, strongly reinforced, have recommenced the battle to recover their ponies. American Horse, a celebrated chief, and two young warriors have just surrendered out of the burrow to Gen. Crook, on condition of sparing their lives. They went in with their women and children, who were unable to escape, in the morning, preferring to die rather than desert them, expecting no quarter. They fought with a tigerish ferocity never excelled. Three hundred soldiers volleyed them for half an hour, and they never budged until the squaws got scared, and Gen Crook and Baptiste Pourier handed the women out of the den at the point of their lives. Pourier shot and scalped a buck after the women were rescued. American Horse and his young men held out for two hours, until the chief was shot through the bowels. The Sioux say that it is Crazy Horse's men who are now peppering us all around the horizon. The fight is getting so warm that I must suspend writing for the present.

Sept. 9, 7 P.M. The fight has just closed. It was beautiful to look at, from a military standpoint. Crook entirely redeemed himself and made things move like clock-work. The dauntless Sioux, although much fewer than ours, came down on the front and flank like men. They rode around us and fired into us, still striking for the captured ponies. It is impossible to estimate how many Indians attacked. They are supposed to have numbered from 800 to 1,000 warriors. They evidently expected to find Mills with his small party, but struck our whole brigade, which was in bloody humor, being hungry and tired. The infantry, under Col. Chambers, and Majs. Burt, Burke, Munson, and Capt. Luhn, charged the southern bluffs and dislodged the Indians who occupied them.[21] The 5th cavalry, on foot, stormed the heights on the southwest. The 3d cavalry drove the northern hills, and the 2d cavalry entirely defeated a bold effort made by the Sioux to cut off a portion of our rear guard, which was driving in used-up horses, and consequently was delayed on the march. Our eastern flank was on a plain, so that it escaped serious annoyance. The infantry fire was particularly galling, and the Sioux opposed to it melted away like snow, carrying off their wounded, as usual. The bluffs are very high, and as the shades of evening fell it was magnificent to see our skirmish line, lighting up the mountain sides with their volleys. The Indian return fire was well sustained, but they were completely routed before night fell upon us. They must have suffered very heavily as many riderless ponies were captured, and blood stains along the height they occupied at the commencement of the fight showed where many warriors had fallen. Crook's command may well be proud of today's work.

The following casualties are reported from the hospital: Private [Robert] Fitzhenry, H company, 9th infantry, dangerously wounded; private Daniel Ford, F company, 5th cavalry, severely; Edmund Schreiber, corporal, K company, 5th cavalry, dangerously; Geo. Cloutier, private, D company, 5th cavalry, seriously. The number of men slightly wounded but not incapacitated is too large to be recorded just now. Lieut. Von Luettwitz' right leg has just been amputated above the knee. He is in a precarious condition. Private Kennedy, of the 5th cavalry, died of the wound received in the afternoon. Private Stevenson, of the 2d cavalry, has lock-jaw, and will not live many hours.[22]

Four dead Indians have been taken from the burrow. Unfortunately, two were squaws. They were armed and fought with their men. One child was accidently killed. All is quiet now.

UNKNOWN CREEK, ABOUT 45 MILES NORTH OF THE BELLE FOURCHE RIVER,[23] Dakota, Sep. 10. We marched 20 miles this morning. Our rear guard, Capt. Summer's company of the 5th cavalry, had a fight with the Sioux at 10 o'clock and killed five, who rode at them out of the ravine. Private [William] Madden was severely and another soldier slightly wounded.

The famous chief American Horse died in our camp at 6 o'clock this morning. Before dying he said that the Indians are scattering, and did not suppose that Crook would dare to pursue them into this region. It was a bold adventure, the chief said, and might have resulted like Custer's attempt had it been three weeks earlier. He said, also, that the Sioux were pretty well tired of the war, and were discouraged by the immense columns of soldiers thrown into their country. If they were to be disarmed at the agencies, he thought they would fight to the last. Neither Crazy Horse nor Sitting Bull, nor the other wild chiefs, would give in, but the tribes for the most part would. He appeared satisfied that the lives of his squaws and children were spared.

The Sioux prisoners, men, women, and children, 22 in all, are with our column, and talk freely to the guides. They are treated like our own people. So far they have told us the truth about the lay of this unknown land. We may have some more fighting before we reach Camp Robinson, Red Cloud agency. We have suffered very much from the constant rain, and the number of sick is daily increasing.[24]

Gen. Sheridan is now at Fort Laramie, awaiting the arrival of Gen. Crook or advices from him as to what point he may meet him for counsel.

John F. Finerty

Chicago Times, September 21, 1876

Mule-Masticators
Crook and his Command
[*From Our Own Reporter*]

Crook's Expedition in Camp on the Belle Fourche, Sept. 15, via Fort Laramie, Sept. 20. A portion of Mills' advance guard are in Crook City, 20 miles from here, with Lieut. Bubb, commissary, and Lieut. Chase, adjutant of the 3d cavalry, sending out supplies. Col. Mills himself, owing to exposure and overexertion, is quite ill, and will remain in the mining town for some days. This command will be within a dozen miles of Crook City to-night, as we are now moving by easy marches in order to give man and beast some chance to recuperate. The brigade, officers and men, lived almost exclusively on horse and pony meat from the evening of the 7th to the morning of the 14th. We have lost between 300 and 400 horses since we marched from Powder river on Aug. 26, and as many more are in so weak a state as to be unfit for service this season. We made in our exhausted condition a march of 35 miles, reaching Willow creek at dark on the 13th. The next morning supplies reached us from Crook City, and we marched eight miles to our encampment on the Belle Fourche river. We rested on the 14th and got in all our detachments, including the 150 men detailed from the 5th cavalry on the 13th to follow a fresh Indian trail leading to the northeast, under command of Maj. [John J.] Upham. The major was unable to overtake the redskins, but the latter killed a soldier named Milner, who went out hunting too far from the column.[25]

Gen. Crook said to your correspondent yesterday that Crazy Horse was the head and front of the trouble in the Hills, and that he would crush him this fall if allowed to go ahead. To this end he had ordered 800 ponies from Laramie plains [the cattle and horse country around Laramie] to remount the cavalry, and last night issued an order for supplying the troops with such clothing and equipage as were needed for a two month's vigorous campaign. All this is changed by an order from Gen. Sheridan requesting or commanding Gen. Crook to meet him at Fort Laramie, in order that they may have a consultation. The general will leave immediately, and the command will follow by easy stages. It is impossible to say when all the troops will reach their forts or where they may be ordered.

Regarding the Black Hills mines, most of the people living around them are enthusiastic as to their wealth. They say that new settlements are springing up in all directions and that the gold yield is very abundant. Your correspondent prefers going slow on giving an opinion until further investigation is made, and there will be ample opportunity for that.

All our wounded are doing well, and since we struck fresh supplies the number of sick has decreased to less than 50. We had to bury some government property on the road, but it will most likely be all recovered. The command has made 186 miles on about two days' rations since leaving Heart river on the morning of the 6th. Since we left our wagon train, 42 days ago, we have had 24 wet days and nights, which made the bivouacs miserable and the marching terrible. A considerable number of infantry and cavalrymen had to be mounted on mules. Our only vegetables on the march were wild onions and roasted cactus. Scurvy is pretty general among the soldiers, and everybody with us expects the prospect of a winter campaign. The country over which we have marched [illegible] but our first 80 miles from Heart river [illegible] purposes, through a region in which there was no wood.

The prospect of getting back to their posts has put the soldiers in good humor. We have seen no Indians since the fight at Slim Buttes on the 9th, but detached parties of the devils are creating terror in the Black Hills.

John F. Finerty

CHAPTER 8

Deadwood Gold and the End of the Trail

VERY EARLY IN JOHN FINERTY's correspondence from the Sioux war he expressed a reluctance to pass judgment on the intrigue and worth of the Black Hills and its gold, a landscape and prospect stirring enormous national attention but which he had not seen for himself, despite having encountered the smothering gold rush bustle of Cheyenne and prospectors on the trail to Fort Laramie. He may well have presumed, of course, that such an opportunity might one day present itself, and that occurred at the conclusion of Crook's summer campaign. Crook's combat trail had taken Finerty to Fort Fetterman, Goose Creek, the Rosebud battlefield, the Yellowstone River, Slim Buttes in Dakota, and now the gold country. Evincing a veteran reporter's knack, when Crook advanced ahead of his column to meet Lieutenant General Philip Sheridan at Fort Laramie in mid-September, Finerty tagged along, knowing perfectly well that the general's route would take him straight through the Black Hills from Crook City and Deadwood in the north to Custer City in the south. Why it was, however, that Crook opted to travel from Custer City to Fort Laramie southeastward via Buffalo Gap, Red Cloud Agency, and Camp Robinson, is not altogether clear, aside perhaps from the simple want to assess conditions at that tempestuous Indian agency ahead of his visit with Sheridan. The alternative route by way of Red Cañon and Hat Creek would have shortened Crook's travel by at least a day. Regardless, Finerty tagged along through all of it.

If Finerty's letters from June, July, and August were filled with news from the Indian war, these final letters in mid-September were nearly all about gold. Already Deadwood had its own newspaper, *The Black Hills Pioneer*, a sheet warmly acknowledged by Finerty as having good local news, if not much from the national scene. By now, of course, the nation's newspapers had brimmed with gold news for months. Finerty's accounting of the new El Dorado was frank and in some ways unique. He sought out and interviewed keen-eyed local observers, individuals like William R. Keithly of Salt Lake City and William H. Parenteau of Central City, Colorado, men familiar with gold country elsewhere and candid in their assessments now. Finerty's informants were positive that this was good gold country although the well-paying placer claims were taken. They acknowledged that problems existed, however. Throughout the Hills there was a perpetual need for water, and Indian treachery jeopardized the margins of the diggings and the vital plains beyond. Finerty's informants already sensed that the Black Hills gold rush had reached a pivotal turn when, as happens in gold country everywhere, the placer rush had about run its course and would yield to industrial mining, characterized by massive machinery, high finance, and outside control. The era of the great Homestake gold mine loomed on the not too distant horizon.

Finerty also found occasion to socialize in Deadwood and provided his readers with a candid, almost charming glimpse at that boisterous gold rush town. When Crook and his entourage reached the city, they headed first to the bath house and marveled when its waters flowed with their own dust and grime, a veritable Powder River in color, Finerty thought. To Finerty's surprise, decent clothing establishments abounded. For raw gaming, Chicago had nothing on Deadwood, aside perhaps for the caliber of its faro dealers, many of them women exuding the danger of vipers. The camp's variety houses were disappointments, the miners, he thought, having little or no artistic sense and the performers scarcely more than run-down hacks. Frontier camp-town luminaries like Banjo Dick Brown, Jack Langrishe, and Fannie Garrettson were playing in Deadwood by then and one might presume that Finerty never saw them perform (or that he grouped them with the hacks).¹

Finerty's summer with Crook was foremost a campaign assignment, of course, and he brought his season of telegrams and letters to a close with a foretelling of yet another campaign in the offing, Crook's third against the Sioux in 1876. En route to Fort Laramie he encountered elements of that new effort, including Colonel Ranald Mackenzie and the Fourth Cavalry, newly arrived from the south. At Fort Laramie Crook put his best spin on the forthcoming wintertime campaign, but a wizened Finerty knew that Jack Frost was a more troublesome enemy than the Sioux. "Crook's brigade dread Boreas more than Sitting Bull."² But that was a tale for another reporter. John Finerty went home.

Chicago Times, September 23, 1876

The Boys in Blankets
The Movements of Crook
[From Our Own Reporter]

CUSTER CITY, Black Hills, Sept. 18, via FORT LARAMIE, Sept. 22. Gen. Crook and escort, proceeding to Fort Laramie to meet Lieut. Gen. Sheridan, have reached this point, being their second day's march from Deadwood. Gen. Merritt is in command of the brigade encamped on Whitewood creek. The citizens of Crook City and Deadwood gave Crook quite an ovation. He had dinner at the first-named place, and then proceeded to the great centre of the gold region, 14 miles further south. Deadwood turned out en masse. A public meeting was held in front of the Grand Central hotel, and another in the theater. Both were overcrowded gatherings, and much feeling was displayed on the Indian question.

Deadwood has been organized into a municipality. At the election held a few days ago Judge [Ethan B.] Farnum, formerly of Wisconsin, was elected mayor, 1,200 votes or very nearly that number, being cast. He introduced Crook to the street mass-meeting, and Judge [Joseph] Miller introduced him at the theater. Gen. [Andrew R. Z.]

Dawson, United States inspector of internal revenue, presented a numerously signed petition, addressed to Gen. Crook, requesting him to have a military post established at the northern point of the Hills, which the Indians were constantly harassing.[3] Gen. Crook, in response, made the following remarks:

> CITIZENS OF DEADWOOD AND AMERICAN CITIZENS: My sympathies, as you know, have ever been with the mining interest of the continent, wherever situated. There is no need for me to make mention of a matter which many old miners whose faces I can recognize as being from the Pacific slope can attest. The sympathies of the lieutenant general are, I know, also with you. I am not aware of any lukewarmness in your cases on the part of the country in general. I see before me an immense number of stalwart men who ought not to fear any force the Indians can bring to bear.
> A VOICE—But we can't fight and do mining at the same time. There was a man killed by Indians not a mile from here to-day.
> GEN. CROOK—Very true. I can understand all that; but the Black Hills, unless a very small corner, are not in my department. Gen. Terry commands here. To the secretary of war your petition should be presented, not to me. In order to show you, however, that I am willing to use such influence as I may possess for your benefit, I promise to deliver the document into the hands of Gen. Sheridan. (Applause.) My command have had a hard and almost unapproached march from Powder river to the Belle Fourche. They had to live on horse meat. So had I; but I know that the Indians had retired northward, as after events at Slim Buttes amply proved; but, citizens, while you welcome me and my personal staff as the representatives of the soldiers who are here encamped upon the Whitewood, let me ask you, when the rank and file pass through here, to show that you appreciate their admirable fortitude in bearing the sufferings of a terrible march almost without a murmur, and to show them that they are not fighting for $13 per month, but for the cause—the proper development of our gold and other mineral resources, and of

humanity. This exhibition of your gratitude need not be expensive. Let the private soldier feel that he is remembered by our people as the real defender of his country. (Applause.) I thank you, gentlemen, for your very cordial reception.

All along the line of march and here Gen. Crook has been heartily received. The miners turn out in force everywhere. He will reach Fort Laramie within five days, and then future measures will be decided upon. Everybody expects a winter campaign. We met the supply train from Camp Robinson for the brigade under escort of Maj. [Captain Frank G.] Smith, and three companies of the 4th artillery on Box Elder creek yesterday. He is corralled there awaiting Merritt's advance.[4] Capt. Egan with a supply train from Fort Laramie is encamped here to-night. It is doubtful whether he will proceed further, as we are given to understand that all our forces in the rear are moving on the agencies. This gold fever at Deadwood is furious, but in other sections it is not over enthusiastic.

The Arrival at Red Cloud

RED CLOUD AGENCY, Neb., Sept. 20, via FORT LARAMIE, Sept. 22. Gen. Crook and escort, together with all the newspaper correspondents, left Custer City at 8 o'clock yesterday morning. A dispatch from Gen. Sheridan made Crook change his line of march. Being remounted by Capt. Egan, he, in company with Cols. Chambers and Stanton, Majs. Burt and Powell, Lieuts. Bourke, [W. P.] Clark, and Schuyler, and Messrs. Wasson, Strahorn, Davenport, your correspondent, and one orderly, in all a party of 13, cut across the Black Hills to the Cheyenne river, and from thence to this agency, a distance of at least 90 miles.[5] We started at 8 o'clock yesterday forenoon and arrived here at 9:30 this morning. No Indians showed themselves on the route. The treaty council is being held here, but as the mail leaves in an hour, and as you are already represented here, I need not go into the matter.[6] I will proceed to Fort Laramie, whither Gen. Crook will go immediately, as soon as practicable. Maj. Randall and Lieut. Sibley are marching by this route with the main escort, their horses not having been in condition to keep with the advance.

John F. Finerty

Chicago Times, September 25, 1876

After the Sioux
The Winter Campaign
[*Special Telegram*]

FORT LARAMIE, Sept. 21. Gens. Sheridan, Crook, and [Ranald] Mackenzie had their conference in this place on Friday evening. Nothing was divulged to outsiders, but your special correspondent with Crook's column, arriving here to-day with the general's staff, succeeded in gleaning the following information: Gen. Crook will remain at this post until the winter campaign, to be inaugurated within 30 days, is completed. It will probably conclude about Christmas. Meanwhile, Gen. Merritt, with his 5th cavalry, will scout along the head of the Little Missouri river, while the main column of the brigade will march straight south to this post and to Fort Fetterman, there to recuperate for the approaching winter operations. It is probable, however, that the 4th cavalry will relieve the weaker companies of the 2d, 3d, and 5th, and that few if any infantry, unless those detailed to guard the pack-trains, will be used. Crazy Horse is regarded as the head of the Black Hills trouble, and to crush him will be the main object of the contemplated movement. A depot of supplies will be established on Powder River, within easy distance of the Black Hills settlements, and Deadwood will also be drawn upon in case of necessity. Before recommencing active operations fresh horses will have to be supplied, and all the men must be clothed for winter work. This may take much longer than is now anticipated. Gen. Crook hopes to wind up the Sioux war before the new year comes. The only thing to prevent such a consummation, he thinks, is the fact that the Indians are much split up. It is well known that the savages have sent all their mules and spare ponies into the British possessions for the purpose of procuring ammunition and arms. They are on a friendly footing with the half-breeds, etc., of that region, and can doubtless become quite formidable within a short period. Merritt's movement on the Little Missouri will be, it is supposed, of no particular importance. The 5th cavalry will follow the arc of a bow, while the main column will march along the cord.

Chicago Times, October 7, 1876

The Last of Lo

[*From Our Own Reporter*]

Cheyenne, Sept. 27. The order of the lieutenant general to Gen. Crook, which reached the latter on the Belle Fourche, Sept. 14, commanded the brigade to march southward, via the Black Hills, and directed the brigadier to meet Sheridan at Fort Laramie without loss of time. The column was turned over to Gen. Merritt, and on the night of the 15th—the expedition being then encamped on Whitewood creek—Crook and his staff, around a huge fire, drank farewell to their comrades in champagne procured from Deadwood and served in tin cups. Some Black Hillers of the prominent type assisted at the ceremony, Gen. Dawson, United States inspector of internal revenue, being the principal person. Next morning Crook's party, consisting of himself and his personal staff, some infantry officers going home on leave, an escort of 20 men under Lieut. Sibley, and the newspaper correspondents, whose mission ended with the cessation of "war's alarms," and the "Hillers" turned their faces southward, and, seeing that the fogs and damps had cleared away, like the idolaters of the Orient, worshiped the sun. Crook City, the northernmost picket of the Hills, was distant 10 miles, and Deadwood lay about the same distance beyond.

We met a regular caravan from the settlements proceeding to the camp, bringing with them onions, turnips, potatoes, and other vegetables, all of which were grown in the neighborhood of the "cities" already named. Oak groves and gentle uplands, watered fairly, were the chief features of the nearer landscape. Herds of cattle, guarded by grim-looking herders, "armed to the teeth," of course, grazed with bovine tranquility among the pretty dells of this northern Arcadia. Behind rose the irregular and far from imposing wall of the Black Hills proper—pastoral in their singular beauty, but entirely, at their first view, destitute of that imperial grandeur which makes the mighty range of the Big Horn mountains monarch of the northwestern mountains. Covered thick with pine and fir trees, the hills have a sable appearance, which, for a wonder, makes their title a misnomer. They are a ring-worm formation on the face of this earth—independent and eccentric in formation—separated by hundreds of miles of prairie or bad lands from all other eminences—and neither the parents of lesser eminences nor the children of greater. Prof. [Walter P.] Jenney has expended the harsh vocabulary of science in his report upon these highlands, and I, having a horror of technical verbiage, and a profound belief that too much indulgence in the same leads to thorough mystification and final softening of the brain, refer the geologically curious to that person's documents, if they desire more thorough information.[7]

We were not long in reaching Crook City, a rough-and-tumble place, situated in the opening of a wooded ravine, on the Whitewood. It contained about 250 houses, all frame or log—the latter style of architecture predominating. An explosion stirred the atmosphere and made the hills shiver with sound as we approached. It was a cannon which some enthusiastic parties fired in honor of the general's visit. This performance was repeated several times, and a fair-sized crowd of hairy men and bilious women thronged around the little cavalcade, and indulged in stentorian or shrill shouts of welcome. We were all forcibly dismounted and led to an attack on Black Hills whisky, which we found more formidable than either Sitting Bull or Crazy Horse. Subsequently dinner was served in the nearest approach to a hotel that place could furnish, and if Crook City failed in many of the delicacies of the season, it certainly did not fail in warmth of hospitality. There was an appearance of depression about the settlement which showed a lack of prosperity, and some of the houses appeared untenanted. The mining gulches were either deserted or worked in a slow, unsatisfactory manner. The men loafing around with their hands in their pockets did not carry upon their faces the light of success. I made some inquiries and found that Crook City was on the wane. It started up, mushroom like, last May, but the main gulch having been "washed out," it was found impossible to utilize the water in Whitewood creek any further and the energies of the populace are directed toward the work of running the water-power of Spearfish creek—one of the finest streams in the Hills—into the first-named stream so as to create the proper sluicing facilities for mining such gold as may exist in that district. I asked several men, who did not know I was a newspaper correspondent, how the place was doing. Hardly one of them felt cheerful, but all spoke hopefully of the sluicing enterprise already alluded to. They had no doubt of success if they only had the water. Plenty of gold had been taken out there in the spring and early summer, but of late very few good claims had been discovered. Those that promised well could not be thoroughly worked because water was scarce, and the quartz ledges could not be utilized at all, because there were no mills wherewith to pound the mineral.

Gen. Dawson, the government revenue inspector, is a man of intelligence, and not being, so far as I could discover, very deeply interested in any of the mining claims, was likely to give impartial information. We had a conversation somewhat of this kind:

"Do you think, general, that the settlements around here can exist independent of the mining interest when that is used up?"

Gen. Dawson. Not to any extent. You have seen a good country between here and Belle Fourche. It is magnificent along Spearfish valley, but right among the hills a population cannot exist except as a mining settlement. When the gold yield is over, the people will leave here for some more promising country in an agricultural sense.

Correspondent. What is your opinion of the gold supply in this region?

Gen. D. I am convinced—I cannot help being convinced that this section is rich in gold. But we want more water, and we must have quartz mills. Also, we must be protected by the army, as the miners cannot prospect while parties of Indians are lying loose around here watching to cut off any adventurous men who seek to make further discoveries. No less than 60 miners have been murdered by the Indians since last spring. This cannot fail to prevent the development of the gold districts—a man cannot dig for gold and fight Indians at the same time. I am convinced, however, that the weightier part of the gold yield is along Whitewood and Deadwood creeks and the gulches that open upon them. Had we the water-power in this region that I have seen in other mining countries, I think the Black Hills would have twice the celebrity they have now.

COR. What do you estimate the present population of the mining districts at?

GEN. D. It cannot be less than 10,000, everything included. You will see for yourself as you proceed toward Custer City, which is nearly 100 miles from here. Between this place and that point all the mining settlements of any consequence are established.

COR. Has not your population diminished rather than increased lately?

GEN. D. I think not. True, quite a number of men who expected to find gold lying around here in heaps, turned back and produced a temporary stampede, but the bolder spirits remained and encouraged their friends to come. Crook City is not a fair criterion by which to judge the Black Hills. Wait until you have seen Deadwood.

By this time Gen. Crook was ready to proceed, and, followed by the usual mob of cheering, we rode on to Deadwood city, over a well-defined and "improved" wagon-road, through a wooded tract, just enough undulating to escape being called a timbered prairie. On the right and left, however, rose some lofty pinnacles of rock, and ledges of quartz showing themselves at every step. Heaps of the mineral, thrown around promiscuously as it were, appeared in the most unexpected places, looking like deposits of petrified snow. Quartz being the concomitant of gold, its presence always indicated the strong probability of the presence of that precious metal, and, as regards quartz, the Black Hills appear to be an irregular mass of that material. We encountered a number of horsemen and several wagons on our way to Deadwood. Everybody was armed and the men all wore huge spurs, which jingled like some sleigh-bells after the first snow-fall. Some "ranches" appeared at intervals, bearing the legend "saloon" on their dingy fronts. As a rule, it would be better for the traveler to have some Indian lead in his carcass than have a glass of ranch rot-gut in his stomach.

About three miles from "the city" we met a group of equestrians who were well mounted and dressed in civilized fashion. Their clean, civilized, respectable aspect made us, by way of contrast, look like white savages—veritable Goths and Vandals. I am free to say that a seedier, more tattered and generally disreputable-looking group of cavaliers, from the general downward, than we were, never rode into any town, ancient or modern. The gentlemen who came to meet us were introduced by Gen. Dawson as Mayor Farnum and the aldermen of Deadwood. Half an hour's ride brought us to the suburbs of the mountain municipality.

We passed by several groups of miners hard at work, "panning out" gold dust, which, they told us, ranged from 3 cents to 85 per pan, the latter being very much in the minority. I had always looked with some degree of suspicion on the Black Hills business and was considerably astonished to find a settlement of such proportions as we were riding through. First we "struck" Montana "City" and then lower Deadwood and then Deadwood "City"—an artillery salute of 13 guns being fired as Crook's figurehead appeared in the latter place. The general acknowledged the universal enthusiasm, nearly all the population being in the main street cheering, yelling and prancing around as if the day of jubilee had come, by lifting his unduly ventilated hat and bowing right and left, after the manner of public men.

We drew up in front of "The Grand Central Hotel"—a wooden hash-temple kept by a sturdy Teuton—and "threw ourselves from our saddles"—*a la* the knights of old returning from a crusade against Turks and fleas in the Holy Land. Mayor Farnum did not say to Crook what Colvin said to Kalakaua, "Now, your majesty, we'll take our leave until you put on a shirt and clean yourself up," but he pointed significantly to the public bath-house—for such a luxury exists in Deadwood—and pointed out the best ready-made clothing establishment in town.[8] The general took the hint, as did all of his companions, who were not any better off than himself, and, half an hour later, the sluice leading from that bath-house looked as if Powder river—of muddy memory—had been emptied into it. When we appeared in public that afternoon, our persons were not quite as revolting to the public as they must have been in the morning, but there was still considerable room for improvement.

I devoted the rest of the day to visiting mining claims in the vicinity and to interviewing every miner with whom I came in contact. Deadwood takes its name from a rivulet which flows into Whitewood creek at the point where the city is located and which, up to the present, has been the grand centre of the gold-fields. Judging by the amount of gold which was taken out during the summer—all on the placer principal—it must be equal to any of the famous California "runs." But, unfortunately, for the enthusiasts, the formation of the Black Hills defies all former experience of mineral regions, and the unevenness of the claims in any section of the mining district is a thing of mystery to the oldest miners. One man purchases a claim and suddenly becomes wealthy. A dozen neighbors may purchase claims along the self-same "gulch" or "run" and find hardly enough to pay expenses. A great many enterprising corporations and individuals have, undoubtedly, "fallen on their feet," while a very large number met nothing but drudgery and disappointment.

To obtain a fair statement from any man directly interested in Black Hills mining is, naturally, very difficult; but there are some gentlemen in Deadwood who do not desire to delude the people of the United States and who conscientiously gave their views according to their lights. Among these it was my fortune to meet that brave old explorer who has traversed a great part of British Columbia and most of our own territories—Judge W. R. Keithly, of Utah.[9] He has been among the Hills since May, and has done as much "prospecting" as any man in the whole "outfit." Taking advantage of a favorable opportunity, I subjected the judge to the interviewing process, and he "panned out" as follows:

> CORRESPONDENT. Have you any objection, judge, to giving me some idea of what you think of this region, as regards the gold-yield of the present and the future prospect?
>
> JUDGE KEITHLY. Not in the least. I have come here as much for the purpose of satisfying myself respecting the country and its resources as for speculation. Regarding the gold-yield in this neighborhood, of that there can be no doubt. It is wonderful—very wonderful, but the good claims are all occupied, and there is hardly any chance for new-comers.
>
> COR. Do you believe that this yield will continue on Deadwood creek?
>
> JUDGE K. For some time, undoubtedly. The chief supply will be found on these two creeks, Whitewood and Deadwood. I have done some "prospecting" outside of them, but, although I had the experience of a lifetime in mining, this country puzzles me. Placer mining here is limited to a very small proportion of the creeks called gold-bearing runs. The districts are discouragingly circumscribed. I have never observed so singular a geographical formation as these hills present. They are not a chain or a range, but appear to have been thrown up by some extraordinary effort of nature like so many potato hills. Gold here is in a state as primitive as nature, after the lapse of many ages, will permit. It is found in all kinds of shapes, crude and undeveloped, just as it fell from its mother, or handmaiden, quartz.
>
> COR. Then you hold that no former experience in mining can safely guide a man in the Black Hills.
>
> JUDGE K. That is it precisely. Even here in Deadwood, the portion of the run that pays prolifically does not extend over half a mile, and so it is in all cases that I have observed. I have been in the gold fields of Australia, of California, of Oregon, New Zealand, British Columbia, everywhere in fact that gold has been spoken of or found, and I never before met quartz ledges thrown up as they are here.

Cor. How do you mean?

Judge K. In the other countries to which I have referred, the ledges are placed perpendicularly, while here they are both perpendicular and horizontal—something I have never known before. In addition to this, I find other eccentricities of nature, which go to prove that this gold region is eccentric and cannot be judged by scientific principles as hitherto applied.

Cor. But apart from this eccentricity of which you speak, Judge, what is your opinion as to the gold-bearing properties of the Black Hills quartz?

Judge K. I have seen much free gold in some of the specimens, especially around what they call the Golden Gate, but there has been, thus far, no opportunity of working it. When the new mills are brought here, I have no doubt that the quartz will be found quite rich. In its singularly detached forms, I think the amount of quartz in the Black Hills is fully equal to that of any other gold-bearing country that I have been over.

Cor. What do you think of the water resources here for working the gulches?

Judge K. That is the main, and, I fear, the insurmountable obstacle. This is, without exception, the worst and most irregularly watered country I have ever come across. As the geological formation is eccentric, so the water courses are almost useless for sluicing purposes. They have little force, and there is next to no fall. There are no regular defiles, but, as I have before remarked, the whole country is chopped up like a series of potato hills. Throughout the summer and fall there is a discouraging scarcity of water, and the periodical rains do not help us much. Another singularity about our runs is this: You will find gold below where the quartz ledges cross the defiles, and none above, and *vice versa*. You will find gold where there are no indications to lead you, and you will find none whatever where the common indications are plenty.

Cor. Do you take much stock in this Indian scare, which some of the miners say, prevents prospecting?

Judge K. There is something in it. Men cannot go a mile from the settlements without great risk. One young man was killed this morning, making four citizens of this place within a week. The Indians come in small parties, and hang around until they get a favorable opportunity to murder or to plunder, or both. Naturally this checks adventure, and without adventurousness there cannot be much discovery. No doubt there are "runs" as prolific as Deadwood—but there are not many—yet undeveloped, and so they will remain until the Sioux trouble is over.

Cor. Now, judge, will you answer me a question fairly and squarely, which I am going to put you not for any private or professional reason, but for the benefit of our fellow citizens?

Judge K. Certainly, sir. I always try to be fair, and never intend to mislead anybody, so far as my experience goes.

Cor. Very well. Would you as an honest American citizen advise your fellow-men, who have neither capital nor mining experience, to come here on speculation and try their fortunes?

Judge K. I unhesitatingly say "No." Let no "green-horn" or "tender-foot" come here to speculate. He would surely starve, or, at best, make a scanty living inferior to what he makes in the states. Even an experienced miner, used to roughing it, has a hard time here occasionally. Men from the states can make a living here as peddlers or petty traders, while the gold harvest is still good, but apart from that only mining corporations and miners who have had the good fortune to locate their claims early, can make it pay here now. I advise all people who have neither money nor time to waste to stay where they are just now.

Cor. Do you think there are enough people here now for what the country produces?

Judge K. I do—quite enough. No community is bettered by a surplus population which is utterly non-productive. Besides it would be madness for tender-feet to come here in fall or winter, when placer-work is suspended, because the streams are frozen.

Cor. What is the average wages paid to men experienced in mining by your mining firms?

Judge K. From $4 to $6 per day and not much chance of increase. Only picked miners, or "bosses" get the higher figure. A "tenderfoot" is virtually useless in the mines. The firms working claims here now will make them pay, but new-comers must take the most desperate risks.

Cor. What are the chief mining firms operating in this neighborhood?

Judge K. In quartz mining, or preparing for it, there are Nicholas Haven & Co., who own the Golden Gate and the Beecher and Father De Smet ledges. They are putting up machinery and are importing a mill to be put up with smelting furnace attached. They have the richest quartz "take" of any in this place. Their mill will be located about three miles from here. Then there is the mine known as the Chief of the Hills, principally owned by Cheyenne or Denver men, such as French, Chase, Gardner & Co. They are on Black Tail creek, which is a tributary of Deadwood. They also are putting up machinery and will be ready to pound quartz very soon. Judge Whitehead, of Cheyenne, is at the head of Whitehead Creek Hydraulic Mining company and is making great effort to reap a golden harvest.[10] So far as I know the results have been profitable with most of the larger firms. The Wheeler Brothers took away a large amount of gold from here the other day. You know how much things are exaggerated, but I don't swallow all I hear worth a cent. In fact I have been too much among gold diggers to trust to hearsay.

Cor. I have heard a good deal of talk about that Wheeler matter. How much did they realize to the best of your knowledge?

Judge K. To be honest, I cannot say. Some put it at $400,000, but that is manifestly absurd. From the best authority I have heard, the amount may be placed at $150,000, which is to be divided among a whole crowd of those concerned. They employed a squad of 20 well-armed men, all more or less interested, to guard that precious load while en route eastward.[11]

This about ended my interview with the judge, who bears a high reputation even among those who do not like his plain-spoken policy.

Deadwood city in appearance is a cross between Braidwood, Ill., Cheyenne, Wyoming, and McGregor, Iowa, as the latter appeared a dozen years ago. Like Braidwood, it has a long, straight frame or log street—just as is popularly believed a snipe has one straight intestine destitute of ramifications. Like Cheyenne, it has a multitude of "varieties" and a crowd of bedizened and brazen harlots, intermingled with Jews and one-horse Gentiles; gambling halls galore and drunk-factories that smell like the vapor from "armory" vomits on a Sunday morning, when floors are strewn with the wrecks of humanity, male and female, brought low by drink and debauchery. Like Cheyenne, it has also got a few good hotels and restaurants and some unexpectedly decent clothing establishments. It has the same air of grasping enterprise which everybody feels who has ever passed through the most impudent and thriving town in Wyoming territory. There are other similarities which need not be recorded here. Like McGregor, Deadwood is shut in by wooded hills, which appear to choke off air currents and to massively protest against any extension of the city's width—the tendency being to force the place along the ravine and make it as narrow and as long as possible. But Deadwood has no grand river, like McGregor, in front of it, and is watered only by the two rivulets whose names are now forever associated with the latest discovered of American gold regions. Walking along this municipal intestine before sun-down, I encountered half the population, about, that I met in Cheyenne last May. I recognized Dr. Whitehead, who is quite an enthusiast, and, for ought I knew, may be the Yankee Monte Christo.[12] I also met Mr. French, a most intelligent and agreeable gentleman, who spoke of the plans and prospects of the mining region in a very rational manner, not too much exaggerating, but still sufficiently sanguine to show his great interest in the success of the mines. Judge McCutchin, who looks after such law as Deadwood possesses, was also quite dispassionate and instructive. All these gentlemen, and many others showed me specimens of free gold in quartz and nuggets out of quartz, until I felt like a man with the jaundice—everything I looked at turned yellow and I thought of Midas and the damnable fix that gentleman got himself into, and speculated as to whether some such fate might not befall myself. For four mortal hours I heard nothing but gold, quartz, sluices, dust, nuggets, mills, pans, and the other paraphernalia which make the stock in trade of a mining camp.

I also became impressed with the opinion, judging by the general amount of "conglomerate" material on exhibition, that lead and silver are very prominent feature[s] of Black Hills mining, but the rush for the more precious metal places everything else completely in the shade. I heard a good deal—nearly all over-gushing—relative to the mines from those directly interested, but as the special organs in Chicago and elsewhere do their "puffing" *ad nauseam*, I have concluded to omit their brilliant passages and to give the public only such opinions as, in my judgment, are unprejudiced—at least as much so as the conformation of the human mind will permit. Let the Black Hills, as the patriot once said who forgot the anatomical structure of mankind, "stand on their own bottom" and appeal to the country on their merits. Judge Keithly, whose sentiments I have given pretty nearly in full, is about the ablest authority that can be quoted on the subject. His clear and concise view of the situation will best enlighten all who are interested in the matter.

After dark, all Deadwood and the surrounding settlements, over 2,000, people, turned out and gave Crook an "ovation."

It was very noisy. The general had to address the crowd from the hotel balcony. He made an off-hand speech which showed intimate acquaintance with the habits and sentiments of the mining fraternity. Neither did he hesitate to crack a few rough jokes about the Indian troubles which, as the phrase goes, were "well received." Afterward he was ushered to the Deadwood theatre, where he was formally addressed and presented with the "freedom of the city." His sentiments have already been published per telegram. When that much was disposed of, Crook, who abhors hand-shaking, was subjected to the pump-handle nuisance at the front door of the dramatic temple. He survived it all, not without some wry faces, I imagine. The general appears to be very much liked by the miners. His long residence on the Pacific coast having familiarized him with hundreds of the brotherhood.

In the evening I took a stroll around the city and visited everything of interest. Wearing cavalry pants, and looking altogether like one of Uncle Sam's boys out of repair, the hardy and hearty miners took it for granted that I was earning $13 per month fighting "Injuns." As I wished to "post" myself on the country I did not undeceive them, but was compelled to swallow enough "forty-rod" to kill an ordinary alderman. The effects of that accursed "beverage" were apparent for a week later, and I was not the only awful example. But as I am now making my own confession I'll say nothing about other people's follies. As Mickey Free would poetically observe,

"Their failin's is nothin' to me."[13]

I visited half a dozen "hells" where I noticed some Chicago "mugs," all engaged in the noble art of faro or some other thimble-rigging devilment. It must be a strong temptation that keeps such worthies away from Cook county during election times. However the chances of their getting speedily shot or scalped around Deadwood are infinitely better than if they were here. In the lively season Deadwood "sports" kill off a man or two every night. Between them and the Sioux it is a hard matter to keep the population of the place up to the maximum standard. Women, as in Cheyenne, act as "dealers" at many of the tables, and more resemble incarnate fiends than do their vulture-like male associates. I observe that decided brunettes or decided blonds are more engaged in evil works than their negative fellow women. Most of the miners would prefer playing "faro" or "monte" with men, for the women are generally old and unscrupulous hands, whose female subtlety makes them paramount in all the devices of cheating and theft. I observed one of them, a brunette, either French or Italian—something of the Latin order anyway—with some attention. She had a once-handsome face, which crime had hardened into an expression of cruelty. Her eye glittered like that of a rattlesnake and she raked in the gold-dust or "chips" with hands whose long white fingers, sharp at the ends, reminded one of a harpy's talons.

Every gambler appeared to play for gold-dust. Nobody took greenbacks, and the gold scales were in constant requisition. They allow

$20 for every ounce of gold, and place greenbacks at the regular discount. Not alone in gaming but also in commercial transactions is "dust" used. A miner swaggers up to the bar with five or six others and calls for "the drinks." They are supplied, and he tosses his buckskin wallet to the bar-tender who weighs out the requisite amount of "dust" and hands back the balance. I am inclined to believe that this display of crude bullion is done a good deal for effect, to make people believe that gold is as plentiful in Deadwood as are sands on the sea-shore.

In one of those gambling shops, run by parties from Chicago, I met an honest looking miner who did not appear to take any personal interest in the exciting pastime of the place. I learned that his name was W. H. Parenteau, of Central City, Col., foreman for Lee & Williams, of Deadwood, who own gold claim 22.[14] This gentleman, not knowing I was a correspondent, told me that the claim he was working about paid, but that there was no fortune in it, and that this was the rule in the great majority of cases. Some claims did not pay at all, and were being abandoned from day to day. Very few new discoveries had been made, and taken altogether, he considered that the summer passed would prove more prosperous than those which were to come. Like Judge Keithly, he found fault with the water-power, but had some faith in the richness of yet unexplored gulches and quartz-ledges. He was of the opinion that the northern edge of the hills was the chief gold bed, and that outside of it the product would be very meagre. In regard to a further influx of people, Mr. Parenteau thought there were enough settlers there now, and said that distress would surely follow any late fall or winter rush into the hills. If men were bent on trying rash experiments, early summer would be the best time. Even now men were often completely idle for weeks at a time. The arrival of Crook's starving and half-naked army in the neighborhood had been a god-send to the storekeepers, who found trade, especially in Crook City, extremely dull.

From other miners I gleaned information, all more or less like the foregoing. I talked to an immense number of persons, and, supposing me a soldier with no direct interest in the matter, they talked without restraint, not as they felt. Of course, I had to drink with them, and all seemed anxious that the army might be quartered among them until the Indian trouble was over. They found it impossible, they said, to act in the double capacity of miners and soldiers. Crazy Horse was, they thought, the head-center of the Black Hills Sioux.

Later that night I witnessed a variety performance, and concluded that the average miner's theatrical taste was not of a high artistic order. The male performers were chiefly broken-down hacks, and the women had skinny arms, wrinkled necks, burnt hair, red eyes, sawdust calves, and splay feet. To this rule there was, as to nearly every rule, an exception or two.

Nearly every horse-shoer in town happened to be on a spree, and Lieut. [William P.] Clark, our acting quartermaster, had to go around with a posse of soldiers and sober up sufficient of the gang to get our horses shod. This operation consumed several hours, and it was nearly daylight before we got to bed. We did not start very early next morning, and, at breakfast, I read a copy of *The Black Hills Pioneer*—a neat little sheet, which contained a very good account of our recent campaign, and of Crook's oratorical effort on the preceding night. It "blew" a little about the Hills, and advertised the Cheyenne and Sidney routes in sensational style. I did not notice any politics in its pages.

At 8 o'clock that morning we were in the saddle, and en route for Custer City. We moved on through a forest road, meeting "ranches" every mile or two, and encountering or overtaking wagon-trains coming to and fro between Deadwood and the railroad settlements. We passed by several mining camps, most of which reported fair progress. We met a wagon-train from Red Cloud, loaded with supplies for the expedition, on Box Elder creek, escorted by three companies of the 4th artillery under Maj. Smith. It seemed strange to meet that branch of the service—nearly always on coast duty—so far inland. Like nearly all soldiers, they were hospitable, and we had a pleasant time for an hour or two. I had not come in contact with the 4th artillery since June 3, 1866, when I saw them at Buffalo patrolling the Niagara river in order to save Canada from the Fenian invasion. Their sincerity may be somewhat questioned when it is related that nearly an entire company crossed with O'Neill from Black Rock and aided that commander in winning [the] Ridgeway fight, wherein the "Queen's Own" were "run away with by their legs," covering the ground with overcoats, blankets, muskets, knapsacks, colors, cartridge-boxes, and other accompaniments of a first-class military panic. I wondered whether any of the artillerymen before me witnessed that incomparable foot-race.[15]

Gen. Crook is a regular "path-finder," and when we started on Monday, the 16th, after making Castleton, about 42 miles from Deadwood, we took another "cut-off," marching in the direction of Harney's peak. At Castleton we found great preparations being made both for gulch and ledge mining, but matters were in too undeveloped a condition to glean much important information. It was evident, however, that something had been discovered there or people would not be going to so much trouble. The inhabitants of Castleton number about 200, mostly practiced miners. They have some strips of cultivated ground and several herds of cattle. They were people of "great expectations," like nearly all of their class.

Our "cut-off" lay through a superbly parked country, resembling the Big Horn foot hills, over which towered in craggy sublimity the haughty crest of Harney's peak. We followed the course of Castle creek and its tributaries—streams that are as transparent as the air on a sweet May morning. The grass and the leaves were green and nature was clothed in loveliness. Birds sang amid the shady groves and trout leaped in the rivulets. The squirrels frisked from tree to tree and there was an exhilaration in the atmosphere which made us triumph over time and recall the days of happy youth, when every leaf and flower charmed us into many a wildwood ramble. How gloriously the sympathetic genius of Burns would have sung that lovely scene. Perhaps Moore interpreted some of our emotion in the well-known lines:

> When in foreign climes we meet
> Some isle or vale enchanting—
> There all looks flowery, wild, and sweet,
> And naught but love is wanting;

> We think how great had been our bliss
> If heaven had but assigned us,
> To live and die 'mid scenes like this
> With some we've left behind us.[16]

At noon we had reached the plateau above "Hill City," a "deserted village," not indeed like "sweet Auburn,"[17] but a rough-hewn affair of 200 shanties inhabited by one solitary mortal who keeps a "ranch" for the benefit of travelers. We asked this stout-hearted hermit why the place was abandoned, and he answered contentiously, "Indian scare and no gold." We continued our ride to the south, having ascertained that Custer City was about a dozen miles further. The same romantic beauty which had smiled on us since reaching Castle creek accompanied our course all through the day. I have seen more sublime but never more charming scenery. The hand of man has never shaped anything so beautiful as the groves and paddocks that ornament almost every foot of that enchanting wood. The soil is not rich, but the Queen of Beauty might fix her throne forever there—at least while the summer lasted. Half a dozen azure lakes would make the place an American Killarney.

When the sun was dipping into the western cloud-banks, on the evening of Sept. 18, we reached Custer City and had quite a friendly greeting. There we met another supply train from Fort Laramie, escorted by Capt. "Teddy" Egan, of the 2d cavalry—a fighting officer who is a general favorite on the frontier. We stopped at the City hotel, a thinly-partitioned edifice through which every sound penetrated. That night a sick infant roared right lustily, and its fond mother wasted the dictionary of material nonsense in trying to soothe the screeching "darling" into slumber, without effect. I have slept with the infernal chorus of the Snakes, Crows, and Rees making night and our camp hideous with their horrid yells. I have slept with the cayote—or the Sioux imitating the cayote—howling around the bivouac; but that Custer City baby was more terrible than the untutored savage or the ravening wolf. He annihilated Morpheus and made the undersigned depart from the moral principles and swear profoundly.

I found Custer City in quite a sickly condition—from a gold-finding stand-point—but hoping to "pick up." The population has greatly decreased since it was the centre of excitement. It has now about 450 inhabitants, and does a fair huckstering business as a half-way house between Red Canon and Deadwood. Very little gold is now found in that once-famous mining-camp. The usual complaint "want of water" and "Injuns" also apply to this locality.

The couriers from Sheridan to Crook arrived during the night, and found the general resolved to go to Fort Laramie *via* Buffalo Gap and Red Cloud, as Philip was impatiently awaiting him. On the morning of the 19th Crook said to Capt. Egan: "I must reach Red Cloud in 24 hours. Can you give me a mount that will carry me through?" Egan said that he could not mount the whole party, but could manage a dozen or so. Accordingly Crook determined to leave his escort and pack-mules behind with Lieut. Sibley and Maj. Randall, and proceed with a dozen or so of his companions to the agency, having to make a forced ride of about 95 miles.

It was a splendid morning and the fortunate few who were to accompany the brigadier felt a thrill of pleasure as they sprang upon the backs of Egan's gallant grays, and galloped off southeasterly in the direction of Buffalo Gap. Sibley and Randall were ordered to follow by easy marches. The remounted party consisted of Gen. Crook, Col. Chambers, Col. Stanton, Surgeon Hartsuff, Maj. Powell, Maj. Burt, Lieuts. Bourke, Clark, Schuyler, four journalists, and an orderly. How soul-stirring it is to ride at full speed on a swift, strong horse, in the invigorating morning breeze, after lumbering along for weeks on some jaded, sorry hack! It is like changing from a stagecoach to a lightning express. We made first-class time until the general tired of the road and resolved to strike a new trail to the Cheyenne river on the south. This led us into a handsome but rugged country, which retarded our progress to a great extent.

Custer City "civilization" told on some of our party, and Dr. Hartsuff's hands were full in attending the sick. About 2 o'clock we arrived on the bank of a charming mountain stream, where the general shot a deer and we had a hunter's dinner. The sun was low in the west when we emerged from the southern boundary of the Hills, as we found great difficulty in getting our horses safely across the marshy bottom-land running along the handsome stream whose course we followed to the peat-plains. As we cleared the last eminence, we beheld not a quarter of a mile in our front the waters of the South Cheyenne, and felt recompensed for our long and rugged journey. Fording the famous river we found ourselves on an unbroken prairie, and soon struck the main wagon-road leading to Red Cloud. We increased our pace to a round trot and then broke into a gallop which we kept up for a number of miles. In all my experience on the plains, I have never so heartily enjoyed anything as that wild ride, in the evening shadows, along the Cheyenne plains. I wished for a horse that could gallop without ever tiring; and every rider, unless the unimpassioned Crook, felt, I am sure, all the mad ardor of the chase or the charge. Egan's grays did credit to the 2d dragoons, and covered the ground at a swinging stride that showed good blood and good grooming. We continued our ride until 10 o'clock that night, when we reached a branch of Hat creek, where we halted to water and graze the horses. Gen. Crook took a vote of the party as to whether we should go into bivouac or ride ahead. An overwhelming majority—11 against 3—voted to go on. Our ride was resumed, and we did not halt until we reached within 10 miles of the edge of "the bad lands" at 2 o'clock on the morning of the 20th. We lay down, after picketing our horses on the frosty ground, and threw our saddle-blankets over us for shelter. We were tired, and slept soundly until 4 o'clock, when the general called us, and we were soon on the road again. The early streaks of dawn revealed a box-like rock at the southern angle of a low range of bluffs some 20 miles ahead. That, the general said, was Red Cloud.[18]

The country over which we were passing was rather barren, bordering closely on the *mauvais terre*. We had entirely lost sight of the Black Hills, which showed that we had traveled a long way since the previous night. It was a little after 9 o'clock when we turned the rocky angle alluded to before and came in sight of Red Cloud agency, with its combination of Indian tepees, wooden houses, and cavalry encampments. A crowd of soldiers standing around the saw-mills saw us enter. None of the party looked like officers, and a boy in blue, looking straight at Crook, shouted: "Hallo, boys, where the devil have *you* been? One of the staff answered laconically, but sharply, "In hell, of course," and the soldier, recognizing a "shoulder strap" under all that dust and dirt, disappeared in double-quick time. The poor fellow was not to blame if he mistook us for mule-whackers.

The peace commissioners and the Indian chiefs were having a big "powwow" when we got in. Mr. [John W.] Dear, the post-trader, treated us very hospitably, and nothing could be kinder than the manner in which we were received by the hospitable and courteous officers of the 4th and 5th cavalry (two companies of the latter regiment being stationed at the agency) and the 4th artillery. Your correspondent was the guest of Capt. [John M.] Hamilton and Lieut. [Edwin P.] Andrus, of H company of the 5th cavalry, both of whom possess the soldierly virtues in a very high degree. Gen. Crook remained only an hour and went over to Fort Laramie, escorted by a small squad of the 4th cavalry, by ambulance. The infantry officers accompanied him.

After a day's rest at Red Cloud, Randall and Libby [*sic* Sibley] having come up, we set out for Fort Laramie, passing through the peaceful villages of the agencies of the Sioux, Cheyennes, and Arapahoes. I am certain that many of the stalwart warriors who frowned upon us as we passed them were engaged in the summer fights against us. Old Red Cloud, the bosom friend of the redoubtable "Sitting Bull of the North,"—the northern Osceola—is now a magnificent ruin—very different from the towering chief whose plumed war-bonnet swept the ground that bloody December day in the defiles before Fort Phil Kearny when Fetterman and his fated comrades died on "Massacre Hill." His features, now in their decay, preserve an air of savage haughtiness and his expression is that of a baffled devil wishing to injure but impotent for evil.[19]

Spotted Tail has the same wonderfully Caucasian face which appeared in Washington not many years ago, and which truly indicates a great intellect—the greatest possessed by any sage of the existing generation. He is a natural orator, a shrewd plainsman, and, for a Sioux, a man of his word. Spotted Tail, it is acknowledged on all hands, is opposed to the war and would, if he were permitted, always live amicably with the whites. "Blue Teeth" is an average-looking "brave," rather old and considerably wrinkled. "Sitting Bull of the South" (Grant's pet) is a fine-looking Indian, about 35 years old, tall, muscular, and of martial bearing. Rumor has it that he will go north and join the great namesake before spring opens. "Red Dog" and "Young-Man-Afraid-of-His-Horses" are very intelligent warriors, and, evidently, have some influence with the more restless spirits of their tribes.

Three easy marches brought us to Fort Laramie, which we reached on Sunday, Sept. 24. Halfway to that place we met Gen. McKenzie [*sic* Ranald Mackenzie] and a part of his regiment (the 4th cavalry) returning to Red Cloud. I had heard much of this officer and was gratified to find him the *beau ideal* of his profession in physique—tall, square-shouldered, and of handsome, manly features. Two fingers of his right hand have been left on some bloody field as a tribute to "the gods of battles."

I met Gen. Crook and he was confident of making a campaign against the Sioux this winter. About November the climate of the Black Hills, and all that latitude, must be akin to the Siberian. Even this early in the fall it needs a great amount of covering to keep a man moderately warm at night. "Jack Frost" is a worse enemy to encounter than the Sioux. The greatest of all soldiers found him a conqueror after Europe had become the footstool of that one audacious and immortal despot. Crook's brigade dread Boreas more than Sitting Bull.

I left Fort Laramie on the 26th, riding in the stage coach, which was uncomfortably full, and reached this place that same night. It seems strange to see a railroad once more, but it is comfortable to know that a fellow can travel like the wind without any exertion on his part. So, this afternoon, I will say to the west, *vale*.[20]

J. F. F.

CHICAGO, Oct. 6, 1876. Since my return I have had to endure the usual boredom shoved upon an ephemeral human curiosity. One fellow says, "You're fat." The next man, "You're thin." Another fellow assures you that "You're not changing except for the better." An observing party discovers that your face, and especially your nose, is "awfully red." The constitutional, inevitable, universal "damphool" has asked me a dozen times: "You weren't in earnest when you said you lived on horse meat? Didn't you make that up?" This species of biped jackass flourishes in every community, and can hardly be expected to be absent from Chicago.

In concluding the series of letters which I have written for THE TIMES, in connection with the Sioux expedition, from May 6 to date, I have only to say that I have endeavored "naught to extenuate and naught to set down in malice." I despise the meanness of professional exaggeration, and, in the campaign just closed, there was nothing to exaggerate, the reality being of a character sufficiently sensational to satisfy the most morbid of imaginations. Whatever the future of Indian warfare may disclose, I feel convinced that hardly anything more exciting or more distressing can occur that than which the summer and fall of the centennial year have witnessed from the lower Big Horn to the Belle Fourche.

JOHN F. FINERTY

APPENDIX

Finerty's Sioux War Dispatches Published in the Chicago Times

"Frontier Fighters," May 15, 1876 (Special Correspondence) — Chapter 2

"Gold and Gore," May 18, 1876 (Special Telegram) — Chapter 2

"Facing the Foe," May 20, 1876 (Special Telegram) — Chapter 2

"Crook on the War-Path," May 22, 1876 (Special Telegram) — Chapter 2

"Fighting Folks," May 24, 1876 (Special Telegram) — Chapter 2

"Crook's Campaigners," May 28, 1876 (Special Telegram) — Chapter 2

"Bound for Blood," May 31, 1876 (Special Correspondence) — Chapter 2

"Old Crow," June 21, 1876 (Special Telegram) — Chapter 3

"A Bull Fight," June 24, 1876 (From Our Own Reporter) — Chapter 4

"Uncle Sam's Crook," July 1, 1876 (From Our Own Correspondent) — Chapter 3

"Braving the Braves," July 5, 1876 (From Our Own Reporter) — Chapter 4

"Sound on the Goose," July 12, 1876 (From Our Own Reporter) — Chapter 5

"Crook Safe," July 16, 1876 (Special Telegram) — Chapter 5

"Booked for Blood" July 23, 1876 (From Our Own Reporter) — Chapter 5

"In a Horn," July 26, 1876 (From Our Own Reporter) — Chapter 5

"The Door of Death," July 27, 1876 (From Our Own Reporter) — Chapter 5

"'Lo' Game" August 1, 1876 (From Our Own Reporter) — Chapter 5

"In at the Death," August 9, 1876 (From Our Own Reporter) — Chapter 6

"The Hunt for Hair," August 19, 1876 (From Our Own Reporter) — Chapter 6

"Skedaddle or Starve" September 9, 1876 (From Our Own Reporter) — Chapter 7

"Squaw Scalps," September 17, 1876 (From Our Own Reporter) — Chapter 7

"Mule-Masticators," September 21, 1876 (From Our Own Reporter) — Chapter 7

"The Ways of War," September 22, 1876 (From Our Own Reporter) — Chapter 6

"The Boys in Blankets," September 23, 1876 (From Our Own Reporter) — Chapter 8

"After the Sioux," September 25, 1876 (Special Telegram) — Chapter 8

"The Hungry Heroes," September 30, 1876 (From Our Own Reporter) — Chapter 7

"The Last of Lo," October 7, 1876 (From Our Own Reporter) — Chapter 8

Notes

Chapter 1. Finerty's World

1. *War-Path and Bivouac* is known in no less than six distinctive editions and thirteen printings, and remains in print today. O'Keefe, *Custer, The Seventh Cavalry, and the Little Big Horn: A Bibliography*, 180–81.

2. Ffrench, "John F. Finerty," 27; Catherine Finerty to Oliver Knight, April 4, 1967, Timmons Papers, University of Texas at El Paso (hereafter cited as UTEP); "Passing of a Noted Irishman," *Omaha Daily Bee*, June 11, 1908; Diehl, *The Staff Correspondent*, 71–72 (quotation).

3. Catherine Finerty to Oliver Knight, April 4, 1967, Timmons Papers, UTEP; Ffrench, "John F. Finerty," 27–28; R. V. Comerford, "Fenian Movement and the Irish Republican Brotherhood," Encyclopedia.com, https://www.encyclopedia.com/international/encyclopedias-almanacs-transcripts-and-maps/fenian-movement-and-irish-republican-brotherhood, accessed November 4, 2019.

4. "John F. Finerty," National Park Service: The Civil War, https://www.nps.gov/civilwar/search-soldiers.htm#q=finerty,+John+f, accessed October 23, 2018; Ffrench, "John F. Finerty," 28 (quotation); "99th Regiment New York State Militia," New York State Military Museum and Veterans Research Center, http://dmna.ny.gov/historic/reghist/civil/infantry/99thInfNYSM/99thInfNYSMMain.htm, accessed February 5, 2019; "Elmira Prison," Wikipedia, https://en.wikipedia.org/wiki/Elmira_Prison, accessed October 27, 2019.

5. Ffrench, "John F. Finerty," 28; Flinn, "John F. Finerty," 151–52; Walsh, *To Print the News and Raise Hell*, 4, 206, 217.

6. "Chicago Times," Wikipedia, https://en.wikipedia.org/wiki/Chicago_Times, accessed March 9, 2019; Diehl, The Staff Correspondent, 53; Walsh, *To Print the News and Raise Hell*, 237; Wilkie, *Personal Reminiscences*, 100, 303 (quotations).

7. Finerty, *War-Path and Bivouac*, 25 (first quotation), 26 (second quotation), 27 (third quotation).

8. Barnard, *I Go with Custer*, 105, 109; Reilly, *Bound to Have Blood*, 42–43; Diehl, *The Staff Correspondent*, 53–55, 84. Of the many newsmen and correspondents with Crook, Finerty and Reuben Davenport reported the campaign for their respective newspapers alone, although several of their stories were cribbed in other papers.

Diehl's interesting coverage of Terry's summer operation, post the Little Big Horn debacle, is reproduced in full. See Diehl, "Terry's Tribulations."

9. Diehl, *The Staff Correspondent*, 15; Wilkie, *Personal Reminiscences*, 177, 178 (quotation).

10. "The Last of Lo," *Chicago Times*, October 7, 1876; Finerty, *War-Path and Bivouac*, 292 (quotation).

11. John Finerty, Jr., to Elmo Watson, October 17, 1941, Watson Papers, Newberry Library. Watson had pressed the son on the whereabouts of papers and memorabilia and John Jr. allowed that what little he had was lost some years ago while being transported from Saint Paul to Washington; Letter, Finerty, Jr., to Watson, May 21, 1941, Watson Papers.

12. Ffrench, "John F. Finerty," 30; "Francis T. Nicholls," Wikipedia, https://en.wikipedia.org/wiki/Francis_T._Nicholls, accessed September 24, 2019; "Pittsburgh Railroad Strike of 1877," Wikipedia, https://en.wikipedia.org/wiki/Pittsburgh_railroad_strike_of_1877, accessed August 9, 2019.

13. Ffrench, "John F. Finerty," 30; Timmons, *John F. Finerty Reports Porfirian Mexico*, vi, xiv, 39.

14. Timmons, *John F. Finerty Reports Porfirian Mexico*, vi–vii, 94 (quotation), 112–13, 117–18. The members of the deputation are named on 68–71.

15. Timmons, *John F. Finerty Reports Porfirian Mexico*, vii (quotation), viii, 314, 326. Timmons reproduced all twenty-seven *Times* articles penned by Finerty in 1877 and 1879, beginning with "Lone Star Twinklings," on August 25, 1877, and ending with "The Lawless Land," appearing on May 3, 1879. The collected reworked essays comprised a book manuscript that Finerty labored on in 1904. He titled his manuscript "Mexican Flash Lights: A Narrative of Travel, Adventure, and Observation in Mexico, Old and New."

16. Timmons, *John F. Finerty Reports Porfirian Mexico*, 295–96.

17. Finerty, *War-Path and Bivouac*, 311–12; Hedren, *After Custer*, 160–62.

18. Finerty, *War-Path and Bivouac*, 313, 321–22, 323 (quotation), 328–29.

19. Finerty, *War-Path and Bivouac*, 348 (quotation), 349.

20. Finerty, *War-Path and Bivouac*, 353 (quotation), 354, 364.

21. Finerty, *War-Path and Bivouac*, 364, 365 (first quotation), 366 (second quotation); Hedren, *After Custer*, 154. The distinctive stone heaps were a phenomenon of the prairie. Boundary surveyors marking the international line heaped five- to eight-foot-high stone cairns of glacial till or earth mounds every three miles across the plains, some 388 in all, and the Sioux quickly realized that that line, the Medicine Line, represented a territorial and social divide between the Americans to the south and the British to the north. See LaDow, *The Medicine Line*, 10–11; McGrady, *Living with Strangers*, 51; and Lass, "The North Dakota-Canada Boundary," xx.

22. Finerty, *War-Path and Bivouac*, 372, 377. In his book at 376 Finerty quietly fumed over his failure to interview the chief, especially in light of another reporter's success in doing so just weeks ahead of this visit. That that interview appeared

in the competitive *Chicago Daily Tribune* also stung. Finerty certainly knew the individual—Stanley Huntley—but he went nameless here. For details see Saum, "Stanley Huntley Interviews Sitting Bull."

23. Finerty, *War-Path and Bivouac*, 400, 401 (first and second quotations); Bourke, *Diaries*, 3:333 (third quotation); Knight, *Following the Indian Wars*, 302 (fourth quotation). Finerty's principal dispatches from Ute Country have been reproduced. See Finerty, "With Merritt's Command."

24. Flinn, "John F. Finerty," 152; Bourke, *Diaries*, 4:168 (first quotation), 274 (second quotation); Bourke, *Diaries*, 5:104.

25. Knight, *Following the Indian Wars*, 306 (quotation); Collins, "On the March with Major Tupper's Command," 237–38, 246. Collins's essay reproduced most of Finerty's dispatches from Arizona. See also Finerty, "On Campaign after Cibicue [sic] Creek," reproducing the same sheaf of letters plus several others apparently ignored by Collins.

26. Flinn, "John F. Finerty," 152; Ffrench, "John F. Finerty," 31; "Alice R. Finerty," Find A Grave, https://www.findagrave.com, accessed November 14, 2019.

27. Flinn, "John F. Finerty," 152; Ffrench, "John F. Finerty," 31–32; Diehl, *The Staff Correspondent*, 95, 96 (quotation).

28. Flinn, "John F. Finerty," 152; Ffrench, "John F. Finerty," 33; Barry, "The Late Col. John F. Finerty," 438; "1884 United States Presidential Election," Wikipedia, https://en.wikipedia.org/wiki/United_States_presidential_election,_1884, updated November 9, 2019.

29. Flinn, "John F. Finerty," 152; Ffrench, "John F. Finerty," 34; Barry, "The Late Col. John F. Finerty," 439; Quaife, "Historical Introduction," xliv; Finerty, "Oration by Col. Finerty."

30. Finerty's books included *War-Path and Bivouac, Or, The Conquest of the Sioux* (1890); *Ireland in Pictures: A Grand Collection of Over 400 Magnificent Photographs of the Beauties of the Green Isle, with Historical and Descriptive Sketches* (1898); *Ireland: The People's History of Ireland*, 2 vols. (1904); and, posthumously, "Mexican Flash Lights: A Narrative of Travel, Adventure, and Observation in Mexico, Old and New," published as Timmons, *John F. Finerty Reports Porfirian Mexico, 1879* (1974). "Braving the Braves," *Chicago Times*, July 5, 1876 (quotation).

31. Bourke, *Diaries*, 4:168.

32. Collins, "On the March with Major Tupper's Command," 245–46.

33. King, *Indian Campaigns*, 73.

34. King, *Campaigning with Crook and Stories of Army Life*, 116 (first quotation), 130 (second quotation), 153 (third quotation).

35. King, "Address by General Charles King," 41.

36. Timmons, *John F. Finerty Reports Porfirian Mexico*, 314, 315 (quotation).

37. Robert E. Strahorn, "Ninety Years of Boyhood," College of Idaho, Strahorn Library, 177 (second quotation), 178 (first quotation), 192 (third quotation); Carrie Adell Strahorn, *Fifteen Thousand Miles by Stage*, 97 (fourth quotation).

38. "Braving the Braves," *Chicago Times*, July 5, 1876 (quotations); Finerty, *War-Path and Bivouac*, 106–7, with subtle word changes, e.g., squaws "greasy" instead of "filthy" (106).

39. Collins, "On the March with Major Tupper's Command," 238; Walsh, *To Print the News and Raise Hell*, 62–64. The concept of total war, implying among other things the victimization of women and children, was an old one in America. For a discussion see Hedren, *Great Sioux War Orders of Battle*, 38–39. Storey's enlightenment had its limits, however, and his open-mindedness toward Indians did not extend to the nation's blacks, upon whom he heaped in his newspapers a steady stream of abuse and ridicule.

40. Finerty, *War-Path and Bivouac*, 373.

41. "The Ways of War," *Chicago Times*, September 22, 1876; Knightley, *The First Casualty*, 4–5, 10, 17.

42. Knightley, *The First Casualty*, 20, 34–36; Perry, *A Bohemian Brigade*, 7–8, 18, 29 (quotation); Walsh, *To Print the News and Raise Hell*, 142.

43. Carlson, *Junius and Albert's Adventures in the Confederacy*, 27; Knightley, *The First Casualty*, 21 (first quotation); Perry, *A Bohemian Brigade*, 110 (second quotation); Mueller, *Shooting Arrows & Slinging Mud*, 4 (third quotation).

44. Knightley, *The First Casualty*, 23, 31–32.

45. Carlson, *Junius and Albert's Adventures in the Confederacy*, 5 (quotation), 35, 217, 244; Perry, *A Bohemian Brigade*, 40, 78–79, 156, 173, 228–29; Browne, *Four Years in Secessia*.

46. Knight, *Following the Indian Wars*, 31, 32ff., 57ff., 69ff., 108ff., 171–72; McDermott, *Red Cloud's War*, 1:99–100, 138; Krause and Olson, *Prelude to Glory*, 9, 39, 79–80, 97, 147, 187; King, *Campaigning with Crook*, 130.

47. Catherine Finerty to Wilbert Timmons, April 23, 1969, Timmons Papers, UTEP; "Passing of a Noted Irishman," *Omaha Daily Bee*, June 11, 1908; "John F. Finerty," *New York Tribune*, June 11, 1908, in Abrams, *Sioux War Dispatches*, 335; Quaife, "Historical Introduction," xlv; Barry, "The Late Col. John F. Finerty," 439 (quotation). Finerty was buried in Calvary Cemetery, Evanston, Illinois. "John Frederick Finerty," www.findagrave.com, accessed November 14, 2019.

Chapter 2. Preparing for War

1. Catherine Finerty to Wilbert Timmons, August 9, 1970, Timmons Papers, UTEP; Robert E. Strahorn, "Brave Boys Are They," 262. This same story is partly excerpted in Knight, Introduction, xiv, with an added line important to Finerty's physical description.

2. These matters of local geography are discussed in Hedren, *Fort Laramie in 1876*, 25–28.

3. Reneau, *The Adventures of Moccasin Joe*, 54.

4. The assassination story is told in full in Hedren, *Rosebud*, 33–35.

Notes to Chapter 2

5. Captain James "Teddy" Egan, Company K, Second Cavalry. Finerty wrote "Egann" here, though Egan later.

6. Foremost here, Finerty describes the recent Big Horn Expedition and its central battle on the Powder River on March 17, 1876. The battle and campaign were deemed a failure by Crook, most everyone else in the military hierarchy, and the press. For particulars, see Hedren, *Powder River*. For the story from Crook's perspective, see Magid, *The Gray Fox*, ch. 16. Finerty here and elsewhere commonly mentions other worldwide military campaigns. Marshal of the Empire Michel Ney was a French military commander during the Napoleonic Wars. "Michel Ney," Wikipedia, https://en.wikipedia.org/wiki/Michel_Ney, updated October 22, 2019.

7. Finerty refers to Long John Wentworth, one-time mayor of Chicago, who in the mid-nineteenth century eliminated a criminal ward of gambling dens and brothels known as The Sands, located where the Chicago Tribune and Wrigley buildings stand today. "Chicago Crime Scenes Project: The Sands," *The Chicago Crime Scenes Project*, http://chicagocrimescenes.blogspot.com/2008/12/sands.html, accessed April 27, 2018.

8. Charlie Clark, the Fort Laramie–Camp Robinson mail carrier, killed while driving a wagon and team alone along the White River. Hedren, *Rosebud*, 34.

9. The killing by Indians of the Black Hillers W. C. Shaw and James C. Sanders near Custer City was fresh news in Cheyenne during Finerty's pause. "Reported Murder of Three Men," *Cheyenne Daily Leader*, May 18, 1876; "Notices," *Laramie Daily Sentinel*, May 18, 1876.

10. In fact, on the Powder River battlefield Reynolds did abandon a living soldier to the enemy and unceremoniously abandoned his other fatalities on the field, matters of great consternation to the troops engaged then and subsequently. See Hedren, *Powder River*, ch. 8, "Abandoning Private Ayers."

11. Finerty's letters are filled with literary, courtly, and historical side notes. Scipio was a Roman general best remembered for defeating Hannibal at the final battle of Zama in 202 B.C. "Scipio Africanus," Wikipedia, https://en.wikipedia.org/wiki/Scipio_Africanus, updated November 2, 2019.

12. The Indian raid on the Hunton Ranch, and the killing of young James Hunton on May 5, caused widespread alarm among the denizens of southeastern Wyoming, the episode occurring well south of the supposed protection provided by Fort Laramie. Hedren, *Fort Laramie in 1876*, 83–85.

13. Charles Lever and Thomas Mayne Reid were Irish-born novelists popular in the mid-nineteenth century. From time to time both wrote military themed stories, and each was praised for his readable, unpretentious literary style. "Charles Lever," Wikipedia, https://en.wikipedia.org/wiki/Charles_Lever, updated October 5, 2019; "Thomas Mayne Reid," Wikipedia, https://en.wikipedia.org/wiki/Thomas_Mayne_Reid, accessed November 14, 2019.

14. The land north of the North Platte River was commonly referred to as Indian Country, a notion dating to the time of the 1868 Fort Laramie Treaty with the Sioux stipulating that the country north of the North Platte and east of the summits of

the Big Horn Mountains was unceded Indian territory, fit only for hunting buffalo and where no whites could settle. Kappler, "Treaty with the Sioux," *Indian Treaties*, 1002–3.

15. At this early stage of the movement, Finerty must be forgiven for his confusion over names and associations. Here spellings and assignments have not been corrected, if only to show this bewilderment. In subsequent telegrams and letters this became less of an issue, although when writing in haste Finerty's misspellings still abound. See Hedren, *Rosebud*, Appendix A, Big Horn and Yellowstone Expedition Order of Battle.

16. Louis Richard, a mixed-blood interpreter long associated with Fort Laramie and Red Cloud Agency and a participant in the Big Horn Expedition in March.

17. Finerty's initial understandings of northern plains landmarks and geography could not be fuzzier. The Blue Stone mentioned here is almost certainly the well-drained high country in southeastern Montana between the Powder and Little Missouri rivers. Others knew this locale as the Blue Mountains, a well-forested feature having the Chalk Buttes on its western margins. Indeed, Sitting Bull had camped there that spring.

Chapter 3. Life on the Trail

1. "Uncle Sam's Crook/Beaver Creek," *Chicago Times*, July 1, 1876. For a careful examination of this notion of Crook somehow being lost, see Hedren, *Rosebud*, 85–86.
2. "Uncle Sam's Crook/On the March," *Chicago Times*, July 1, 1876.
3. "Uncle Sam's Crook/The Junction," *Chicago Times*, July 1, 1876.
4. "Uncle Sam's Crook/Clear Creek," *Chicago Times*, July 1, 1876.
5. "Uncle Sam's Crook/Lo's First Appearance," *Chicago Times*, July 1, 1876.
6. Finerty inexplicably identified Andrew W. Evans here as Maj. Graves, after having repeatedly appropriately introducing the officer in earlier communications. Confusing the point, a miner names Graves appeared on the scene about now.
7. *Sic*. The Third Cavalry, fielding ten companies, not forty, was divided into two battalions of four companies each plus a two-company squadron.
8. Finerty's preferred spelling was Kearney, a common contemporary misnomer corrected here and throughout. That post was named for Phil Kearny, killed at Chantilly, Virginia, in 1862. McDermott, *Red Cloud's War*, 1:90.
9. The loss of these cattle was crippling to the Big Horn Expedition. See Hedren, *Powder River*, 102–3.
10. The column this day had crossed the several branches of the Cheyenne River and camped for the evening in its waterless, open headlands. Stanton, "Annual Report," 707.
11. Finerty compares this episode to an imagined parallel in the Battle of Balaclava during the Crimean War. "Balaklava," Wikipedia, https://en.wikipedia.org/wiki/Balaklava, accessed October 9, 2019.

12. Private Francis A. Tierney of Company B, Third Cavalry, accidently shot himself when throwing his holstered revolver to the ground on the afternoon of May 30. Doctor Albert Hartsuff was summoned, but the wound proved fatal seven days later. Tierney was originally interred at the mouth of Prairie Dog Creek but is now buried in the Custer National Cemetery at Little Bighorn Battlefield National Monument, near Crow Agency, Montana.

13. Indians fired upon the troops of the Big Horn Expedition twice while on their march north, once at their first night's camp when the cattle herd was run off, and again at Fort Reno on the evening of March 5. This playful episode likely occurred then, but on the Powder River, not the Crazy Woman's Fork. Hedren, *Powder River*, 106.

14. Finerty refers here to Second Lieutenant Frederick Schwatka, Company M, Third Cavalry, and Captain Alexander Sutorius, Company E, Third Cavalry. At this point, Sutorius and Finerty were messmates on the campaign and the captain figures commonly in the reporter's stories. Schwatka's story about the Pawnee picket and watch reads apocryphally as no Pawnees accompanied the campaign in March, and neither did that officer.

15. The casualties referred to are consequences of continuous bloodshed along the Bozeman Trail in the weeks and months following the Fetterman disaster at Fort Phil Kearny in December 1866. See McDermott, *Red Cloud's War*, 2:328–29.

16. Montana miners, whether en route to the Black Hills or exiting therefrom, become an interesting sidenote on this campaign. Several of the characters mentioned here are discussed in Hedren, *Rosebud*, 79.

17. Here, Finerty has the names correct—Grouard, Richard, and Pourier, though he often corrupted their spellings in coming letters. He confuses blooded heritage, however. Richard was a mixed blood of French and Sioux parentage. Pourier was a Missouri Frenchman married into the sprawling Richard clan and Louis Richard's brother-in-law. Grouard was a mixed blood of Anglo and native Hawaiian stock. For particulars on these individuals see Hedren, *Powder River*, 88–90; and Glass, *Reshaw*, 262, 264.

18. By one account, the name derives from a Crow legend hundreds of years old in which an apparitional white woman, speaking through the Great Spirit, implores the Crows to make peace with the Sioux. For a while, apparently, that may have been possible, but peace did not endure. The effort was remembered, however, in an image of a white woman hovering over the mountains at Crazy Woman's Fork. Tuttle, *Three Years on the Plains*, 147–49.

19. These widely presumed Indian signal fires dominated the conversation on June 4. As was learned later, however, this was smoke from a prairie fire accidently ignited by outward-bound Black Hills miners who soon appeared in Crook's column. Hedren, *Rosebud*, 83–84.

20. Captain William J. Fetterman, Captain Frederick H. Brown, and Second Lieutenant George W. Grummond. In the *Times* letter the name Drummond appears,

an error perchance attributable to a typesetter. Finerty has it as Grummond in *War-Path and Bivouac*, 84.

21. Bugler Adolph Metzger, not Metzker as Finerty noted it. See McDermott, *Red Cloud's War*, 1:256–57.

22. Finerty refers to Fort William Henry, a British fortification at the southern end of Lake George, near Albany, New York. In a prolonged siege in 1757, British troops surrendered to French and Heron forces and were subjected to notorious atrocities by the Indians, episodes subsequently immortalized in James Fenimore Cooper's novel *The Last of the Mohicans*. "Fort William Henry," Wikipedia, https://en.wikipedia.org/wiki/Fort_William_Henry, accessed September 19, 2019.

23. André Masséna, prominent in the French Revolutionary and Napoleonic wars, was one of Napoleon's original eighteen Marshals of the Empire. Torres Vedras was an impenetrable salient protecting Lisbon, Portugal. Challenged there by the lack of food and forage in a mid-winter campaign, Masséna could only retreat at great cost to his forces. en.wikipedia.org/wiki/André_Masséna. Accessed November 14, 2019.

24. Finerty quotes from Charles Wolfe's "The Burial of Sir John Moore after Corunna," Bartleby.com, https://www.bartleby.com/101/603.html, accessed November 4, 2019.

25. Ben Arnold, one of the expedition's couriers, was a native Ohioan, not a local mixed-blood, although his roughshod character and familiarity with the Sioux and other northern plains tribal dialects easily suggested as much.

26. Ernest Hornberger and others identify this miner as Sylvester Reese. Hedren, *Rosebud*, 47, 76, 318.

27. The notion of gold somehow being panned with a hooped blanket is preposterous. Perhaps the miner was describing some variation of a sluice, but even so its derivative pay dirt still required panning.

28. Edmo LeClair, a Shoshone mixed blood.

29. The term "roystering devils" was common in early America, appearing in the works of Washington Irving, Hudson River travel guides, and elsewhere, and sometimes referring to Indians and as often to river ruffians.

30. *Vae victis*, Latin for "woe to the vanquished."

31. Two Stantons were associated with the Big Horn and Yellowstone Expedition but not concurrently. Marching north with Crook on May 29 was Captain William S. Stanton, Corps of Engineers and chief engineer for the Department of the Platte. By June 21 Captain Stanton's varied duties were essentially complete and he departed the expedition when Rosebud's wounded soldiers were evacuated to Fort Fetterman. The Stanton mentioned here was Major Thaddeus H. Stanton, Pay Department and a Department of the Platte paymaster based in Cheyenne. Major Stanton arrived with Colonel Wesley Merritt and the Fifth Cavalry, which at the moment was operating on the Fort Laramie–Custer City Road.

Chapter 4. The Rosebud Battle

1. "Braving the Braves," *Chicago Times,* July 5, 1876.
2. Davenport's and Strahorn's campaign and battle reports, plus those of Thomas MacMillan, writing for the *Chicago Inter-Ocean,* and Joe Wasson, writing principally for the San Francisco *Alta California,* have been transcribed and published. See Abrams, *Newspaper Chronicle of the Indian Wars,* Vols. 5–7; and Legoski, *General George Crook's Campaign of 1876.* Both volumes also recognize the work of sketch artist Charles St. George Stanley, employed by *Frank Leslie's Illustrated Newspaper,* as well as several of the independent correspondents who accompanied the column. In the Stanley instance, see also Hedren, "Charles St. George Stanley."
3. Hedren, *Rosebud,* 305.
4. In fact, the entire five-company infantry battalion accompanied the movement, all mounted.
5. For an accounting of these men, names fully given and properly spelled, and the nature of their wounds, see Hedren, *Rosebud,* App. B.
6. Patrice de MacMahon was an officer and squadron chief in a succession of French infantry and cavalry units, including the Second Regiment of the French Foreign Legion. He distinguished himself in action across the tribal occupied plains of northern Africa in the 1830s and 1840s, and served as President of France in the 1870s. The Chasseurs d'Afrique were a light cavalry corps in the French Armée d'Afrique. "Patrice de MacMahon," Wikipedia, https://en.wikipedia.org/wiki/Patrice_de_MacMahon,_Duke_of_Magenta, accessed August 25, 2019.
7. Captain Avery B. Cain, Company D, Fourth Infantry. Finerty identified him as Kane.
8. Here Finerty again identified Evans as Graves.
9. Captain Guy V. Henry, commanding the Second Battalion, Third Cavalry, who Finerty identified here as Berry. This is almost certainly a compositor's error because elsewhere in this same story the officer is correctly identified.
10. Captain Furey commanded the wagon train on its return to Fort Fetterman. Major Chambers, leading one company of the Fourth Infantry and one of the Ninth Infantry, accompanied as escort, riding in empty wagons. Hedren, *Rosebud,* 316–17.
11. This is the third stanza of a poem published in 1846 titled "Oh! For a Steed," by Thomas Osbourne Davis, an Irish writer and nationalist. "Oh! For a Steed," poetry nook, https://www.poetrynook.com/poem/oh-steed, accessed May 3, 2018.
12. Finerty refers to Second Lieutenant Henry R. Lemly, cavalry brigade adjutant; Second Lieutenant Charles Morton, cavalry brigade acting assistant quartermaster, both serving under Royall; and Second Lieutenant George F. Chase, acting Third Cavalry adjutant, serving under Evans.

Chapter 5. Loafing Hangs Heavily upon Us

1. "'Lo' Game," *Chicago Times*, August 1, 1876 (quotations). To the matter of exterminating the buffalo, see Hedren, *After Custer*, Chapter 5, "The Buffaloes Are Gone."

2. Pourier, "The Sibley Scout," 274.

3. "'Lo' Game," *Chicago Times*, August 1, 1876 (quotations). The extraction issue is thoroughly discussed in Hedren, *Rosebud*, Appendix C.

4. Charley O'Malley was a character in one of Irish writer Charles Lever's popular nineteenth-century novels of the same name. The book's worth in inspiring military careers is neatly explained by Charles Diehl, another Sioux war correspondent writing for the *Chicago Times*, who tells of such mesmerizing campaigning and high adventure and glory in the book as to nearly compel his own career orientation to West Point. Diehl, *The Staff Correspondent*, 14–15.

5. Lines from the poem "The Mountain Top," by Irish physician and poet John Thomas Campion. "Dr. John Thomas Campion," From-Ireland.net, http://www.from-ireland.net/doctor-john-thomas-campion/, accessed August 10, 2018.

6. Ignis fatuus: a nineteenth-century fictional notion of mysterious, secretive places and lures that drew travelers to dangerous marshes, bogs, and quagmires instead of the Land of Eden or the next El Dorado. "Ignis fatuus," The Free Dictionary, https://thefreedictionary.com/ignis+fatuus, accessed November 14, 2019.

7. News of a new treaty commission was making the rounds. The effort was not directed at somehow negotiating an end to this Indian war but instead maneuvering a resolution to the so-called Black Hills crisis. That summer a government commission led by George W. Manypenny, former commissioner of Indian affairs, indeed finessed a wide-ranging agreement with the agency Sioux that stripped the Black Hills from the Great Sioux Reservation, eliminated hunting rights in the Powder River country, allowed wagon roads across the reservation, and raised the prospect of removing the Sioux to the Indian Territory, all in contravention to terms in the 1868 Fort Laramie Treaty. See Hedren, *Fort Laramie in 1876*, 155–56.

8. Finerty imagines an odd lot of calamities. His mention of William Bross was almost surely intended for his senior editor, Wilbur Storey. Bross was a rabble-rousing mid-nineteenth century Chicago newspaperman, a strong supporter of Lincoln and the Republican Party, and an outspoken opponent of slavery. Storey, a crusading Copperhead, held opposite views in almost all respects. Dwight Moody was an evangelizing Chicagoan dubbed by some as "Crazy Moody," and others as "Brother Moody." Moody took his crusade to the British Isles in the early 1870s, where his revivals drew crowds of ten and fifteen thousand. He returned to America in the fall of 1875 and for the next several years drew comparably enormous audiences at rallies in Brooklyn, Philadelphia, New York, Chicago, and elsewhere. Grant was noted in attendance at Moody's Philadelphia event. Walsh, *To Print the News and Raise Hell*, 8; "William Bross," Wikipedia, https://en.wikipedia.org/wiki/William_Bross, accessed April 18, 2019; "Biography of D. L. Moody," believer's web, https://believersweb.org/view.cfm?ID=82, March 13, 2003, accessed May 3, 2018.

9. In Finerty's day Bridgeport was an Irish-American neighborhood on Chicago's Southside. That heritage lingers. "Bridgeport, Chicago," Wikipedia, https://en.wikipedia.org/wiki/Bridgeport,_Chicago, accessed November 4, 2019.

10. Finerty, for the first time in his letters, mentions two other campaign newsmen, Joseph Wasson, representing the San Francisco *Alta California* and *Philadelphia Press*, and Reuben Davenport, representing the *New York Herald*. Robert E. Strahorn, representing the Denver *Rocky Mountain News*, remained in camp and was unnamed. Weeks earlier Thomas MacMillan, of the *Chicago Inter-Ocean*, had departed with the wagon train when Crook's Rosebud wounded were evacuated to Fort Fetterman. So did illustrator Charles St. George Stanley, representing *Frank Leslie's Illustrated Newspaper*. Both are also unnamed.

11. Finerty mentioned Warren, meaning Wasson.

12. John Graves led a party of sixty Montana miners west to prospect the Big Horns, having given up on the Dakota diggings. They joined Crook's column on June 5. These miners mostly tended to themselves, although a few joined the column when it marched to the Rosebud.

13. Referencing Colonel Caleb C. Sibley, USMA 1829, a resident of Chicago until his passing on February 19, 1875. "Col. Caleb C. Sibley," *New York Times*, February 24, 1875.

14. White Antelope was a well-known Northern Cheyenne warrior. He survived this war and was among Cheyenne kinsmen who surrendered at Camp Robinson in 1877, only to be promptly relocated to the Darlington Agency in the Indian Territory. White Antelope and his wife fled Darlington with Little Wolf and Dull Knife in 1878, and both were killed in the breakout from Fort Robinson that winter. Powell, *People of the Sacred Mountain*, 2:1161, 1206–7; Greene, *January Moon*, 102–3, 264n14.

15. Private Valentine Rufus, Company E, Second Cavalry. "Crook Safe," *New York Herald*, July 16, 1876; Mangum, *Battle of the Rosebud*, 114.

16. Sergeant Oscar R. Cornwall, Company D, Second Cavalry; and Private Harry G. Collins. "Crook Safe," *New York Herald*, July 16, 1876. Mangum, *Battle of the Rosebud*, 111, 113, 115. Mangum notes a Private Marvin Collins, Company A, Second Cavalry; and a Private John E. Collins, Company I, Second Cavalry, but no Harry Collins.

17. Washakie, venerable sixty-six-year-old chief of the Shoshone Indians.

18. Rawolle given as Snowell in Finerty's letter, and here referring to Wells and Company E, and Rawolle, Company B, Second Cavalry.

19. This is an accurate estimation of the nation's population at the time.

20. A story told by Hedren in "Three cool, determined men."

21. Finerty's comparison of the Big Horn and Tyrolean landscapes of Montana and the Eastern Alps, respectively, is apt, with both featuring a dominant mountainscape and picturesque rivers and valleys. "Tyrol," Wikipedia, https://en.wikipedia.org/wiki/Tyrol, accessed October 29, 2019.

22. Finerty here compares the rugged snowy passes of the Big Horn Mountains with the better-known Gotthard Pass in the Swiss Alps. "Gotthard Pass," Wikipedia, https://en.wikipedia.org/wiki/Gotthard_Pass, accessed August 13, 2019.

23. Privates William Evans, Benjamin F. Stewart, and James Bell, all of Company E, Seventh Infantry. Hedren, "Three cool, determined men," 15.

24. Finerty mistakenly identifies Captain William H. Powell's Fourth Infantry company as D, when meaning G. Rosebud veteran Captain Avery Cain commanded D. The officers additionally mentioned are Captain James Kennington, Captain Daniel W. Burke, Captain Thomas F. Tobey, and First Lieutenant Frank Taylor.

25. Irishman Finerty's Moorland is likely a reference to the grassy open hill countryside of West England rather than the lands of the Moors on the Iberian Peninsula and islands of the Mediterranean Sea. "Moorland," Wikipedia, https://en.wikipedia.org/wiki/Moorland, accessed November 6, 2019.

26. A reference to Emir Abdelkader, an Algerian religious and military leader who led the struggle against the French colonial invasion of his country in the mid-nineteenth century. "Emir Abdelkader," Wikipedia, https:/en.wikipedia.org/wiki/Emir_Abdelkader, accessed May 24, 2018.

27. Finerty provides here a reasonable transcription of verse 3 of Lord Byron's "Ode on Waterloo" (1815), substituting Custer's name for Murat's. Joachim Murat, a French marshal, was a daring, charismatic cavalry officer in the age of Napoleon. Unlike Custer's death, however, Murat's death was not on a field of battle. After Napoleon's fall, Murat was arrested for treason and sentenced to death by firing squad. Facing his executioners, he stood upright, proud and undaunted, kissed a cameo on which was carved the head of his wife, and gave the word: "Soldiers! Do your duty! Straight to the heart but spare the face. Fire!" "Lord Byron," Wikipedia, https://en.wikipedia.org/wiki/Lord_Byron; Lord Byron, "Ode on Waterloo," Bartleby.com, http://www.bartleby.com/205/32.html; "Joachim Murat," Wikipedia, https://en.wikipedia.org/wiki/Joachim_Murat. Each accessed May 24, 2018.

28. This marrying of lines may principally derive from the time of French Marshal Michel Ney, who Napoleon called "the bravest of the brave." "Michael Ney," Wikipedia, https://en.wikipedia.org/wiki/Michel_Ney, accessed July 13, 2018.

29. Kelley [sic]. The antics of the "half-insane" miner-turned-courier known only as Kelly were noted by many in Crook's camp. As Finerty reports, Kelly made two unsuccessful attempts at carrying messages from Crook to Terry, and was successful on a third try and thereafter dropped from the campaign record. Crawford, *Rekindling Camp Fires*, 256; Bourke, *On the Border with Crook*, 338; Bourke, *Diaries*, 1:374; Willert, *March of the Columns*, 197, 345.

30. The green-eyed monster is commonly interpreted as jealousy personified. The expression is a quotation from Shakespeare's Othello, where Iago warns: "O! beware, my lord, of jealousy; it is the green-eyed monster which doth mock the meat it feeds on." "Green-eyed monster," The Free Dictionary, https://idioms.thefreedictionary.com/green-eyed+monster, accessed May 25, 2018.

31. Finerty is referring to Merritt's detour in mid-July into western Nebraska to intercept a band of Northern Cheyennes bolting Red Cloud Agency, resulting in the memorable clash at Warbonnet Creek on July 17. Sheridan and Sherman endorsed the action, while Crook, unaware, brooded over the delay for weeks. Hedren, *First Scalp for Custer*, 17, 19, 22.

32. The song is a loose rendition of an Irish ballad from 1647 titled "The Green Flag." Around American wartime campfires, such words in the original song as the "green flag," symbolic of Ireland, became the "old flag." "Hibernian Songster," Irish Song Lyrics, http://www.traditionalmusic.co.uk/hibernian-songster/hibernian-songster%20-%200239.htm, accessed May 25, 2018.

Chapter 6. The Trail Leads to Terry

1. The enormity of Terry's steamboat operation is explored carefully by Lass, *Navigating the Missouri*, 304–7; and Clark, *Supplying Custer*, 56–58, 63–67. The story is personalized in the biography of Grant Marsh, famed captain of the sternwheeler *Far West*, in Hanson, *The Conquest of the Missouri*. The lucrative business of sutlering on the Yellowstone in 1876 is explored by Gray, "Sutler on Custer's Last Campaign," and Innis, "Bottoms Up!"

2. By the time the Fifth Cavalry joined Crook, the configuration of the Big Horn and Yellowstone Expedition had expanded dramatically from the days of its start at Fort Fetterman on May 29, 1876. For particulars, see Hedren, *Great Sioux War Orders of Battle*, 113–17.

3. Finerty is referring to a manner of warfare birthed in the days of Quintus Fabius Maximus Verrucosus, a Roman statesman and general in the third century B.C. Fabius Maximus carefully avoided decisive contests and foiled Hannibal by harassing his army by marches, countermarches, and ambuscades, a timeless strategy of delays and cautions reflective in more recent times in the tactics of guerrilla warfare. "Quintus Fabius Maximus Verrucosus," Wikipedia, https://en.wikipedia.org/wiki/Quintus_Fabius_Maximus_Verrucosus, accessed September 10, 2019; "Fabian policy," The Free Dictionary, https://www.thefreedictionary.com/Fabian+policy, accessed August 18, 2018.

4. Finerty's description of Crook's cavalry brigade is confusing. With the arrival of Wesley Merritt and the Fifth Cavalry, the horse component was reorganized. As senior-most cavalry officer with Crook, Colonel Merritt now commanded all mounted troops. Lieutenant Colonel Eugene Carr subsequently led the Fifth Cavalry, which in turn was subdivided into two battalions and comprised the so-called right. Lieutenant Colonel William Royall now commanded elements of the Second and Third Cavalry, which in turn was subdivided into three battalions and comprised the so-called left. Right and left are simple terms used to establish the relative positions of troops facing forward, or toward the enemy. Hedren, *Great Sioux War Orders of Battle*, 114–15.

5. The utterance "Oh, blood and thunder! And oh, blood and wounds! These are but vulgar oaths," is a passage in the Eighth Canto of Byron's epic poem *Don Juan*. "What Does 'Blood and Thunder' Mean?," wiseGEEK, http://www.wisegeek.com/what-does-blood-and-thunder-mean.htm, accessed May 26, 2018.

6. Boreas, the Greek god of the North Wind.

7. Major Thaddeus H. Stanton, Pay Department, not to be confused with Captain William S. Stanton, Corps of Engineers, who departed the expedition on June 21. Major Stanton joined on August 3, arriving with the Fifth Cavalry.

8. By now the myth of a prepared Indian ambush awaiting Crook had he advanced down the Rosebud Narrows on the afternoon of June 17 had full currency. This is countered fully, however, by Indian testimony refuting such a claim, particularly when those weary and hungry warriors only wished to return to their Reno Creek camp. Even today those hillsides abound in downed timber, a natural condition. It was true, however, that the narrowness of the valley would have seriously impeded conventional cavalry maneuvering. For more on these points, see Hedren, *Rosebud*, 292–94.

9. Erebus: the Greek God of deep darkness.

10. A line from Edgar Allen Poe's "Annabel Lee," Wikipedia, https://en.wikipedia.org/wiki/Anabel_Lee, accessed November 6, 2019.

11. An apparent reference to Professor John Tyndall, a pioneering Irish physicist remembered for his studies of radiant energy, glaciology, and other matter. He lectured in America in 1872. The notion of the "missing line" is unclear. "John Tyndall," Wikipedia, https://en.wikipedia.org/wiki/John_Tydall, accessed November 1, 2019.

12. By now John H. Graves, the one-time Black Hills prospector, had been added to the corps of Fort Fetterman couriers. Hedren, *Ho! For the Black Hills*, 201, 209–10.

13. From a 1788 work by Robert Burns, "Of A' The Airts The Wind Can Blaw," www.robertburns.org/works/date, accessed November 7, 2019.

14. Finerty chiefly refers to the six-company battalion of the Twenty-Second Infantry commanded by Lieutenant Colonel Elwell S. Otis, recently arrived from Michigan in the Division of the Atlantic. Hedren, *Great Sioux War Orders of Battle*, 59, 95.

15. A tongue-in-cheek reference to Irish journalist William Howard Russell, war correspondent for *The Times* of London in the mid-1850s and 1860s. Russell's critical coverage of the Battle of Bull Run in July 1861 gained him the enmity of the Lincoln Administration and much of the North, despite his otherwise stalwart embrace of the Union cause. The reference is buried in a discourse on soldiers' travails with lice. Knightley, *The First Casualty*, 34–35; Perry, *A Bohemian Brigade*, 23–29; Boatner, *The Civil War Dictionary*, 714; "Notable Visitors," Mr. Lincoln's White House, http://www.mrlincolnswhitehouse.org/residents-visitors/notable-visitors/notable-visitors-william-howard-russell-1820–1907/, accessed May 29, 2018.

Notes to Chapter 6   245

16. A likely reference to Robert Burns's sonnet, "To a Mouse," Wikipedia, https://en.wikipedia.org/wiki/To_a_Mouse, accessed November 17, 2019, with a nod to Karen L. Raber, Distinguished Professor of English, University of Mississippi, for drawing the connection.

17. Bourke mentions discovering the bodies of two prospectors or trappers on the Tongue River, evidently surprised and killed by the Sioux. Bourke, *Diaries*, 2:60.

18. A reference to Émile Erckmann's and Alexandre Chatrian's jointly written *Waterloo: A Story of the Hundred Days* (1865). "Erckmann Chatrian," Wikipedia, https://en.wikipedia.org/wiki/Erckmann-Chatrian, accessed May 29, 2018.

19. "And found," meaning food and lodging.

20. Finerty confuses a few details, but relates the night of September 8, 1865, when a command of volunteer cavalry commanded by Colonel Nelson D. Cole, operating on the Powder River against the Sioux, was hit by a thirty-six-hour bout of freezing rain and sleet. With no protection for the stock, some 250 horses were found dead on picket lines and another hundred or more were so cold and hungry that they would neither stand nor walk and were destroyed. Wagner, *Powder River Odyssey*, 190–93.

21. A reference to British General Sir Charles James Napier, commander of British Indian infantry in Afghanistan and the North-West Frontier Province in British India (subsequently Pakistan) in the mid-nineteenth century. "Rifles," Wikipedia, https://en.wikipedia.org/wiki/125th_Napier%27s_Rifles, accessed May 29, 2018; "North-West Frontier Province," Wikipedia, https://en.wikipedia.org/wiki/North-West_Frontier_Province, accessed August 20, 2018.

22. Doubtless referring to Napoleon's army in the Battle of Austerlitz. "Battle of Austerlitz," Encyclopedia Britannica, https://www.britannica.com/event/Battle-of-Austerlitz, accessed November 11, 2019.

23. Clark Street was an original north-south avenue in Chicago passing several blocks west of the city center. "Clark Street (Chicago)," Wikipedia, https://en.wikipedia.org/wiki/Clark_Street_(Chicago), accessed May 29, 2018.

24. There is meager collaboration for this side note, and what is known is conflicting. Bourke suggests that the retrieved individual was an orderly in Terry's headquarters detachment, not a cook. Bourke, *Diaries*, 2:63. In *War-Path and Bivouac*, 229, Finerty refers to the man as an officer's cook but not necessarily Terry's, although both Bourke and Finerty acknowledge that Terry was instrumental in retrieving the stricken individual. In one of Terry's letters to his sisters, he acknowledges the services of a personal cook. Willert, *The Terry Letters*, 37. In Willert's *March of the Columns*, 374, he names the wretch, unsourced: Private David N. Eshelman, Company H, Ninth Infantry. But that soldier, a veteran of the recent Rosebud fight, stood deep in Crook's column, making an association with Terry's headquarters contingent rather doubtful. The afflicted character's name remains a mystery.

25. Dexter bank: the right-hand bank.

Chapter 7. Mud, Mules, and Blood

1. "The Hungry Heroes/The March for Life," *Chicago Times*, September 30, 1876.

2. "The Hungry Heroes/The March for Life," *Chicago Times*, September 30, 1876; "The Hungry Heroes/Food for the Famished," *Chicago Times*, September 30, 1876.

3. "The Hungry Heroes/The Battles of the Buttes," *Chicago Times*, September 30, 1876 (quotation); "Official Report of Captain Anson Mills," in Mangum, *Battle of the Rosebud*, 152.

4. Crook's Shoshone scouts departed the Big Horn and Yellowstone Expedition on August 20. The departure was amicable enough but dispiriting. Bourke, *Diaries*, 2:74–75. Finerty suggests that he had written about this previously, but no such dispatch is known. Perhaps the dispatch was lost. Maybe a seemingly parallel circumstance in the story of Jack Crawford's letters from the 1876 campaign to the *Omaha Bee* provides an explanation. In Crawford's case, his editors found the news in one letter so untimely that it was not published, and they told their readers so. Hedren, *Ho! For the Black Hills*, 206–7. Finerty expressed the matter differently in *War-Path and Bivouac*, 236, declaring simply, "The Snake and Crow Indians, appalled by the hardships which they clearly saw in store for them, abandoned the column the moment we faced up the Powder River."

5. Ute John appeared with the Shoshone contingent from Wind River. The individual, a Shoshone or Ute, was quite acculturated, having lived in the Salt Lake Valley for five or six years. He was fluent in English, may have been a baptized Mormon, and aggressively proselytized Indians living near their settlements. Finerty called Ute John's English perfect. Bourke saw it as broken. Ute John befriended Crook, whom he called "Clook," or "Shennel Cluke." Bourke, *Diaries*, 2:48, 69.

6. Blue devils: demons causing depression.

7. Finerty refers obliquely to comments made by Colonel William B. Hazen in a pamphlet, *Our Barren Lands*, disparaging the worth of the lands west of the 100th Meridian. The year before, he and Lieutenant Colonel George Custer openly feuded over the matter in an exchange appearing in the *Minneapolis Tribune* and *New York Tribune*, with Custer openly espousing the worth of those lands and Hazen brazenly criticizing their value *and* Custer. For an exposé, see Stewart, *Penny-an-Acre Empire in the West*.

8. In greater likelihood, Crook's column intersected Terry's and Custer's trail from several months earlier.

9. A line from the 1782 ode "The Solitude of Alexander Selkirk," by William Cowper, a popular English poet. "The Solitude of Alexander Selkirk," Bartleby.com, http://www.bartleby.com/106/160.html, accessed May 31, 2018.

10. Ajax: a Greek mythological hero.

11. Lines from the second verse of Alfred, Lord Tennyson's epic poem, "The Charge of the Light Brigade" (1854). "The Charge of the Light Brigade," Poetry Foundation, https://www.poetryfoundation.org/poems/45319/the-charge-of-the-light-brigade, accessed June 1, 2019.

12. The name Menamed Creek has all but disappeared. Likely Finerty refers to today's Big Nasty Creek, a lesser tributary of the South Fork of the Grand River, as its spatial location relatively conforms to the mentioned mileage. Bourke notes only an evening bivouac on a rivulet of doubtful water, about five miles short of the South Fork of the Grand River, again confirming, if obliquely, today's Big Nasty Creek. Bourke, *Diaries*, 2:105–7.

13. Finerty's word here is "guards."

14. Finerty uses "Kehoe," meaning Captain Myles W. Keogh, Company I, Seventh Cavalry, killed in the Battle of the Little Big Horn.

15. These names, affiliations, and injuries are detailed in Greene, *Slim Buttes*, 127–29.

16. Mont St. Jean: a prominent sector of the Waterloo battlefield, and also the name Napoleon Bonaparte bestowed on that engagement. "Mont-Saint Jean, Belgium," Wikipedia, https://en.wikipedia.org/wiki/Mont-Saint-Jean,_Belgium, accessed June 2, 2018.

17. The run-on mention of sacred edifices, steeples, Brooklyn, Beecher, and "nest-hiding" invites a reflection on the manly world of Indian campaigning in 1876. Finerty plainly refers to the famously adulterous affair occurring in Brooklyn, New York, in 1868–69 between Elizabeth "Libby" Tilton, wife of New York newspaper editor Theodore Tilton, and American preacher-novelist Henry Ward Beecher, who was Tilton's best friend. Despite Beecher's attempts at "nest hiding," word of the affair spread widely. Tilton pressed charges, and the subsequent courtroom drama in 1875 was one of the most widely reported trials of the century. As for Finerty, after three and a half months on the campaign trail the inspiration derived from the dramatic clayey spires of the Slim Buttes can only be imagined. "Henry Ward Beecher," Wikipedia, https://wikipedia.org/wiki/Henry_Ward_Beecher, accessed December 12, 2019.

18. Egyptian darkness: very intense darkness. An expression drawn from the Old Testament, Exodus 10:21–22, "and let darkness, darkness so thick that it can be felt, cover Egypt." "Egyptian darkness," Wiktionary, https://en.wiktionary.org/wiki/Egyptian_darkness, accessed June 4, 2018.

19. Greene, *Slim Buttes*, 127–29.

20. In fact, this was a small mixed camp of Miniconjous, Oglalas, Brulés, and Northern Cheyennes, largely regarded as belonging to American Horse, an Oglala. Roman Nose, a lesser chief, was an Oglala, not a Brulé. Greene, *Slim Buttes*, 49–50.

21. Captains Andrew S. Burt, Daniel W. Burke, Samuel Munson, and Gerhard L. Luhn, the latter given by Finerty as Loon.

22. These additional wounded are detailed in Greene, *Slim Buttes*, 128, with several names corrected here from Finerty's original text.

23. Finerty gives it at the Belle Faurchee River.

24. Finerty's or more likely his typographer's word here was "interesting" rather than "increasing."

25. The unfortunate slaying of Private Cyrus B. Milner, Company A, Fifth Cavalry, called Miller by Finerty, is detailed in King, *Campaigning with Crook*, 142; and Greene, *Slim Buttes*, 103, 173n15.

Chapter 8. Deadwood Gold and the End of the Trail

1. On Deadwood's performers in Finerty's day, see Penn, *Ballads, Banjos & Bullets*, and Cochran, "The Gold Rush Trail," with exposés on Brown, Langrishe, and Garrettson.

2. "The Last of Lo," *Chicago Times*, October 7, 1876.

3. Ethan Bennett Farnum (given by Finerty as Farnham), Joseph Miller, and Andrew Rea Zina Dawson were businessmen in early Deadwood. "E. B. Farnum," Wikipedia, https://en.wikipedia.org/wiki/E._B._Farnum, accessed October 26, 2019; "Andrew Rea Zina Dawson," PhpGedView, http://genealogy.susanvmayer.com/individual.php?pid=127385&ged=FamilyTree, accessed June 12, 2018. See also Parker, Deadwood, 54–55, 178, 216–17.

4. The coming of Regular Army artillerymen was a new feature in the Sioux War story. For details, see Hedren, "The Fourth U.S. Artillery and the Great Sioux War."

5. Among the officers in the contingent, Finerty mentioned Burke, meaning Bourke (there was a Burke with the larger column, but not with this hurried advance), and Clarke, meaning William Philo Clark. Bourke, *Diaries*, 2:130.

6. An unnamed correspondent with the *Chicago Times* was regularly reporting on the Black Hills treaty proceedings, the so-called Manypenny Commission, then underway at Red Cloud Agency. "The Boys in Blankets/The Treaty of Peace," *Chicago Times*, September 23, 1876.

7. Finerty refers to Walter Jenney's then recently published report, *The Mineral Wealth, Climate and Rain-Fall, and Natural Resources of the Black Hills of Dakota*, documenting, in part, the scientific survey of the Black Hills in 1875.

8. An oblique reference to a comment, perhaps apocryphal, made in January 1875 by Chicago Mayor Harvey D. Colvin to King David Kalakaua of the Sandwich Islands on the occasion of his visit to the city. "Chicago Notes," *New York Times*, January 17, 1875.

9. Attorney William R. Keithly (sometimes Keithley), most recently of Salt Lake City, was a frontier gadfly, boasting of roaming the California, Cariboo (British Columbia), and Idaho gold diggings before wending his way to the Black Hills. His reputation as an attorney and judge was suspect. Many in Deadwood remembered him as "Old Necessity," a reflection of his questionable comprehension of the law. Kellar, *Seth Bullock*, 62; Parker, *Deadwood*, 221; "Which Keithley Line?" Relative Storyboards, https://kbea831.wordpress.com/2011/01/22/which-keithley-line/, accessed January 22, 2011.

10. In all probability, Keithly is referring to Whitewood, not Whitehead, Creek, a point easily confused by Finerty in a line that also mentioned J. R. Whitehead.

Judge James R. Whitehead departed Cheyenne for Deadwood in mid-July. "Personal Paragraphs," *Cheyenne Daily Leader*, July 16, 1876.

11. The Wheeler Brothers gold haul alluded to by Finerty and Keithly was the richest placer recovery in the history of the gulch. Early in the northern rush, William P. Wheeler and a handful of close associates (collectively referred to as the Brothers) acquired Claim Number 2 below Discovery on Deadwood Creek. Over a fifty-day period in the spring and summer of 1876, working two sluice boxes day and night, the partners recovered $43,000 worth of gold. In four months the accumulation exceeded $150,000, which at the Treasury's fixed price of $20.67 per troy ounce amounted to more than 7,250 troy ounces, with a value today of nearly $9 million. Mitchell, *Nuggets to Neutrinos*, 108–9; "Almost a Ton of Gold," *Cheyenne Weekly Leader*, September 21, 1876; "The Black Hills," *Chicago Tribune*, September 13, 1876; "Mr. Wheeler's Story," *Black Hills Weekly Times*, May 6, 1877; Hedren, *Ho! For the Black Hills*, 23, 252.

12. Finerty has it as Monto Cristo, a reference to The Count of Monte Cristo, a popular adventure novel by Alexandre Dumas. "Count of Monte Cristo," Wikipedia, https://en.wikipedia.org/wiki/The_Count_of_Monte_Cristo, accessed November 11, 2019.

13. Mickey Free was the name of the comic servant in Charles Lever's 1841 novel, Charles O'Malley. In Western American circles, the name was also common during Crook's time in Arizona, where a worldly Frank Grouard-type character, Mickey Free, birth name Felix Telles, interpreted and scouted for the army during the Apache wars. "Free, Major Mickey," Northern Illinois University Libraries, https://www.ulib.niu.edu/badndp/free_mickey.html, accessed July 13, 2018; "Mickey Free," Wikipedia, https://en.wikipedia.org/wiki/Mickey_Free, accessed September 26, 2019; Hutton, *The Apache Wars*, 1–2.

14. Finerty's new informant, William H. Parenteau of Central City, Colorado, age twenty-seven, was an individual of visible good standing and education in the mining community who later served as a Colorado state mine inspector. "William H. Parenteau," www.findagrave.com, accessed October 18, 2018.

15. Finerty's aside on the Fenian invasion refers to discord in the late-1860s along the eastern American-Canadian border between Irish nationalists—the Fenian Brotherhood—and British troops, aimed at pressuring Britain to withdraw from Ireland. President Andrew Johnson intervened and enforced American neutrality laws. U.S. troops seized Fenian weapons and munitions and stemmed further border transgressions. A chief Fenian rabble-rouser, John O'Neill, relocated to Nebraska and next ballyhooed the invasion of the Black Hills after Custer's gold discovery there in 1874. "Fenian raids," Wikipedia, https://en.wikipedia.org/wiki/Fenian_raids, accessed May 31, 2018; Parker, *Gold in the Black Hills*, 30–31.

16. Finerty's embrace of the bards of his homeland continues, here mentioning Thomas Moore, an Irish poet and songwriter, and Robert Burns, a Scottish poet and lyricist. The melody is drawn from Moore's "As Slow Our Ship," sung to the air

"The Girl I Left Behind Me." "Thomas Moore," Wikipedia, https://en.wikipedia.org/wiki/Thomas_Moore, accessed September 8, 2019.

17. Referring to a 1770 poem by Oliver Goldsmith, "The Deserted Village," with an opening line, "Sweet Auburn! loveliest village of the plain." "The Deserted Village," Wikipedia, https://en.wikipedia.org/wiki/The_Deserted_Village, accessed November 16, 2019.

18. Finerty refers to an eminence known then as Red Cloud Buttes, and today as Crawford Buttes, a towering white monolith that from the north serves as an obvious orientation to Red Cloud Agency and Camp Robinson, each located south and slightly west of the landmark.

19. At age fifty-five, Red Cloud, patriarch of the Oglala Sioux, was hardly "a magnificent ruin," as Finerty characterized him, but an influential chief in full stride. For an insightful look at the chief in these tumultuous times, see Larson, *Red Cloud*, ch. 7.

20. Might Finerty be expressing in Spanish "worth it" (vale la pena) or "worth my while?"

Bibliography

Manuscript Materials and Collections

College of Idaho, Strahorn Library, Caldwell, Idaho
  Robert E. Strahorn, "Ninety Years of Boyhood, 1942," TMS
Newberry Library, Chicago, Illinois
  Elmo Scott Watson Papers
University of Texas at El Paso, El Paso, Texas
  Wilbert H. Timmons Papers, MS041

Books and Articles

Abrams, Marc H., ed. *Newspaper Chronicle of the Indian Wars, Vol. 5, Jan. 1, 1876–Jul. 12, 1876*. Brooklyn, N.Y.: Abrams Publications, 2010.
———. *Newspaper Chronicle of the Indian Wars, Vol. 6, Jul. 13, 1876–Aug. 24, 1876*. Brooklyn, N.Y.: Abrams Publications, 2010.
———. *Newspaper Chronicle of the Indian Wars, Vol. 7, Aug. 26, 1876–Dec. 31, 1876*. Brooklyn, N.Y.: Abrams Publications, 2010.
———. *Sioux War Dispatches: Reports from the Field, 1876–1877*. Yardley, Pa.: Westholme Publishing, 2012
Barnard, Sandy. *I Go with Custer: The Life and Death of Reporter Mark Kellogg*. Bismarck, N.Dak.: Bismarck Tribune, 1996.
Barry, P. T. "The Late Col. John F. Finerty." In *Journal of the American Irish Historical Society, Vol. IX*, ed. Thomas Z. Lee, 438–40. Providence, R.I.: The Society, 1910.
Boatner III, Mark Mayo. *The Civil War Dictionary*. New York: David McKay Company, 1987.
Bourke, John G. *The Diaries of John Gregory Bourke, Volume One, November 20, 1872–July 28, 1876*, ed. Charles M. Robinson III. Denton: University of North Texas Press, 2003.
———. *The Diaries of John Gregory Bourke, Volume Two, July 29, 1876–April 7, 1878*, ed. Charles M. Robinson III. Denton: University of North Texas Press, 2005.

———. *The Diaries of John Gregory Bourke, Volume Three, June 1, 1878–June 22, 1880*, ed. Charles M. Robinson III. Denton: University of North Texas Press, 2007.

———. *The Diaries of John Gregory Bourke, Volume Four, July 3, 1880–May 22, 1881*, ed. Charles M. Robinson III. Denton: University of North Texas Press, 2009.

———. *The Diaries of John Gregory Bourke, Volume Five, May 23, 1881–August 26, 1881*, ed. Charles M. Robinson III. Denton: University of North Texas Press, 2013.

———. *On the Border with Crook*. New York: Charles Scribner's Sons, 1891.

Browne, Junius Henri. *Four Years in Secessia: Adventures within and beyond the Union Lines*. Chicago: Geo. & C. W. Sherwood, 1865.

Carlson, Peter. *Junius and Albert's Adventures in the Confederacy: A Civil War Odyssey*. New York: MJF Books, 2013.

Clark, Gerald R. *Supplying Custer: The Powder River Supply Depot, 1876*. Salt Lake City: University of Utah Press, 2014.

Cochran, Alice. "The Gold Rush Trail: Jack Langrishe's Mining Town Theaters." *Montana The Magazine of Western History* 20 (Spring 1970): 58–69.

Collins, Charles, ed. "On the March with Major Tupper's Command: John F. Finerty Reports the Cibecue Campaign of 1881." *Journal of Arizona History* 40 (Autumn 1999): 233–66.

Crawford, Lewis F. *Rekindling Camp Fires: The Exploits of Ben Arnold (Connor)*. Bismarck, N.Dak.: Capital Book Co., 1926.

Diehl, Charles S. *The Staff Correspondent*. San Antonio, Tex.: Clegg Company, 1931.

———. "Terry's Tribulations." In *Eyewitnesses to the Indian Wars, 1865–1890, Vol. 4, The Long War for the Northern Plains*, ed. Peter Cozzens, 391–412. Mechanicsburg, Pa.: Stackpole Books, 2004.

Ffrench, Charles, ed. "John F. Finerty." In *Biographical History of the American Irish in Chicago*. Chicago: American Biographical Publishing Co., 1897.

Finerty, Catherine P. *In a Village Far from Home: My Years among the Cora Indians of the Sierra Madre*. Tucson: University of Arizona Press, 2000.

Finerty, John F. *Ireland: The Peoples History of Ireland*. 2 vols. New York: Co-operative Publication Society/P. F. Collier & Son, 1904.

———. *Ireland in Pictures: A Grand Collection of Over 400 Magnificent Photographs of the Beauties of the Green Isle, with Historical and Descriptive Sketches*. Chicago: J. S. Hyland & Co., 1898.

———. "On Campaign after Cibicue Creek." In *Eyewitnesses to the Indian Wars, 1865–1890, Vol. 1, The Struggle for Apacheria*, ed. Peter Cozzens, 236–61. Mechanicsburg, Pa.: Stackpole Books, 2001.

———. "Oration by Col. Finerty." In *Contributions to the Historical Society of Montana, Vol. VI*. Helena: Historical Society of Montana, 1907; reprint, Boston: J. S. Tanner and Company, 1966.

———. *War-Path and Bivouac, Or, The Conquest of the Sioux*. Chicago: Donohue & Henneberry, 1890.

———. "With Merritt's Command." In *Eyewitnesses to the Indian Wars, 1865–1890, Vol. 3, Conquering the Southern Plains*, ed. Peter Cozzens, 642–58. Mechanicsburg, Pa.: Stackpole Books, 2003.

Flinn, John J., ed. "John F. Finerty." In *Hand-Book of Chicago Biography*. Chicago: Standard Guide Company, 1893.

Glass, Jefferson. *Reshaw: The Life and Times of John Baptiste Richard*. Glendo, Wyo.: High Plains Press, 2014.

Gray, John S. "Sutler on Custer's Last Campaign." *North Dakota History* 43 (Summer 1976): 14–21.

Greene, Jerome A. *January Moon: The Northern Cheyenne Breakout from Fort Robinson, 1878–1879*. Norman: University of Oklahoma Press, 2020.

———. *Slim Buttes, 1876: An Episode of the Great Sioux War*. Norman: University of Oklahoma Press, 1982.

Hanson, Joseph Mills. *The Conquest of the Missouri: Being the Story of the Life and Exploits of Captain Grant Marsh*. Chicago: A. C. McClurg & Co., 1909.

Hedren, Paul L. *After Custer: Loss and Transformation in Sioux Country*. Norman: University of Oklahoma Press, 2011.

———. "Charles St. George Stanley, *Frank Leslie's Illustrated Newspaper*, and the Rosebud Campaign." *Greasy Grass* 35 (May 2019): 1–13.

———. *First Scalp for Custer: The Skirmish at Warbonnet Creek, Nebraska, July 17, 1876*. Glendale, Calif.: Arthur H. Clark Company, 1980; reprint, Lincoln: Nebraska State Historical Society, 2005.

———. *Fort Laramie in 1876: Chronicle of a Frontier Post at War*. Lincoln: University of Nebraska Press, 1988.

———. *Great Sioux War Orders of Battle: How the United States Army Waged War on the Northern Plains, 1876–1877*. Norman, Okla.: Arthur H. Clark Company, 2011.

———. *Powder River: Disastrous Opening of the Great Sioux War*. Norman: University of Oklahoma Press, 2016.

———. *Rosebud, June 17, 1876: Prelude to the Little Big Horn*. Norman: University of Oklahoma Press, 2019.

———. "'Three cool, determined men': The Sioux War Heroism of Privates Evans, Stewart, and Bell." *Montana The Magazine of Western History* 41 (Winter 1991): 14–27.

Hedren, Paul L., ed. "The Fourth U.S. Artillery and the Great Sioux War." In *The Frontier Army: Selected Essays from Dakota and the West*, ed. R. Eli Paul, 24–45. Pierre: South Dakota State Historical Society Press, 2019.

———, ed. *Ho! For the Black Hills: Captain Jack Crawford Reports the Black Hills Gold Rush and Great Sioux War.* Pierre: South Dakota State Historical Society Press, 2012.

Hutton, Paul Andrew. *The Apache Wars: The Hunt for Geronimo, the Apache Kid, and the Captive Boy Who Started the Longest War in American History.* New York: Crown, 2016.

Innis, Ben. "Bottoms Up! The Smith and Leighton Yellowstone Store Ledger of 1876." *North Dakota History* 51 (Summer 1984): 24–38.

Jenney, Walter P. *The Mineral Wealth, Climate and Rain-Fall, and Natural Resources of the Black Hills of Dakota.* Washington, D.C.: Government Printing Office, 1876.

Kappler, Charles J. *Indian Treaties, 1778–1883.* Mattituck, N.Y.: Amereon House, 1972.

Kellar, Kenneth C. *Seth Bullock, Frontier Marshall.* Aberdeen, S.Dak.: North Plains Press, 1972.

King, Charles. "Address by General Charles King." In *The Papers of the Order of Indian Wars*, ed. John M. Carroll, 37–47. Fort Collins, Colo.: Old Army Press, 1975.

———. *Campaigning with Crook and Stories of Army Life.* New York: Harper & Brothers, 1890.

———. *Indian Campaigns: Sketches of Cavalry Service in Arizona and on the Northern Plains.* Fort Collins, Colo.: Old Army Press, 1984.

Knight, Oliver. *Following the Indian Wars: The Story of the Newspaper Correspondents among the Indian Campaigners.* Norman: University of Oklahoma Press, 1960.

———. Introduction to *War-Path and Bivouac, Or, The Conquest of the Sioux*, by John F. Finerty. Norman: University of Oklahoma Press, 1961.

Knightley, Phillip. *The First Casualty, From the Crimea to Vietnam: The War Correspondent as Hero, Propagandist, and Myth Maker.* New York: Harcourt Brace Jovanovich, 1975.

Krause, Herbert, and Gary D. Olson. *Prelude to Glory: A Newspaper Accounting of Custer's 1874 Expedition to the Black Hills.* Sioux Falls, S.Dak.: Brevet Press, 1974.

LaDow, Beth. *The Medicine Line: Life and Death on a Northern American Borderland.* New York: Routledge, 2001.

Larson, Robert W. *Red Cloud: Warrior-Statesman of the Lakota Sioux.* Norman: University of Oklahoma Press, 1997.

Lass, William E. *Navigating the Missouri: Steamboating on Nature's Highway, 1819–1935.* Norman, Okla.: Arthur H. Clark Company, 2008.

———. "The North Dakota–Canada Boundary." *North Dakota History* 63 (No. 4, 1996): 2–23.

Legoski, Robert J. *General George Crook's Campaign of 1876, June 5 through August 3: Newspaper Accounts of the Day.* Sheridan, Wyo.: By the author, 2000.
Magid, Paul. *The Gray Fox: George Crook and the Indian Wars.* Norman: University of Oklahoma Press, 2015.
Mangum, Neil C. *Battle of the Rosebud: Prelude to the Little Bighorn.* El Segundo, Calif.: Upton & Sons, 1987.
McCrady, David G. *Living with Strangers: The Nineteenth-Century Sioux and the Canadian-American Borderlands.* Lincoln: University of Nebraska Press, 2006.
McDermott, John D. *Red Cloud's War: The Bozeman Trail, 1866–1868.* 2 vols. Norman, Okla.: Arthur H. Clark Company, 2010.
Mills, Anson. *My Story.* Washington, D.C.: By the author, 1918.
———. "Official Report of Captain Anson Mills." In *Battle of the Rosebud: Prelude to the Little Bighorn,* by Neil C. Mangum, 150–52. El Segundo, Calif.: Upton & Sons, 1987.
Mitchell, Steven T. *Nuggets to Neutrinos: The Homestake Story.* Np.: By the author, 2009.
Mueller, James E. *Shooting Arrows & Slinging Mud: Custer, the Press, and the Little Bighorn.* Norman: University of Oklahoma Press, 2013.
O'Keefe, Michael, ed. *Custer, The Seventh Cavalry, and the Little Big Horn: A Bibliography.* 2 vols. Norman, Okla.: Arthur H. Clark Company, 2012.
Parker, Watson. *Deadwood: The Golden Years.* Lincoln: University of Nebraska Press, 1981.
———. *Gold in the Black Hills.* Norman: University of Oklahoma Press, 1966.
Penn, Chris. *Ballads, Banjos & Bullets: Trailing the Tangled Lives of Ira "Dick" Brown & Fannie Garretson.* London: English Westerners' Society, 2018.
Perry, James M. *A Bohemian Brigade: The Civil War Correspondents—Mostly Rough, Sometimes Ready.* New York: John Wiley & Sons, 2000.
Pourier, Baptiste. "The Sibley Scout." In *Voices of the American West, Vol. 2, The Settler and Soldier Interviews of Eli S. Ricker, 1903–1919,* ed. Richard E. Jensen, 272–82. Lincoln: University of Nebraska Press, 2005.
Powell, Peter J. *People of the Sacred Mountain: A History of the Northern Cheyenne Chiefs and Warrior Societies, 1830–1879, With an Epilogue 1969–1974.* 2 vols. San Francisco: Harper and Row Publishers, 1981.
Quaife, Milo Milton. Historical Introduction to *War-Path and Bivouac: The Big Horn and Yellowstone Expedition,* by John F. Finerty. Chicago: R. R. Donnelley & Sons Company, 1955.
Reilly, Hugh J. *Bound to Have Blood: Frontier Newspapers and the Plains Indian Wars.* Lincoln: University of Nebraska Press, 2011.
Reneau, Susan C. *The Adventures of Moccasin Joe: The True Life Story of Sgt. George S. Howard.* Missoula, Mont.: Blue Mountain Publishing, 1994.

Saum, Lewis O. "Stanley Huntley Interviews Sitting Bull: Event, Pseudo-Event or Fabrication?" *Montana The Magazine of Western History* 32 (Spring 1982): 2–15.

Stanton, William S. "Annual Report of Captain W. S. Stanton, Corps of Engineers, for the Fiscal Year Ending June 30, 1876." In *Report of the Chief of Engineers, 1876*, Part III, 704–18. Washington, D.C.: Government Printing Office, 1876.

Stewart, Edgar I., ed. *Penny-an-Acre Empire in the West*. Norman: University of Oklahoma Press, 1968.

Strahorn, Carrie Adell. *Fifteen Thousand Miles by Stage*. New York: G. P. Putnam's Sons, 1911.

Strahorn, Robert E. "Brave Boys Are They: Newspaper Correspondents with Crook's Army." In *Eyewitnesses to the Indian Wars, 1865–1890, Vol. 4, The Long War for the Northern Plains*, ed. Peter Cozzens, 261–64. Mechanicsburg, Pa.: Stackpole Books, 2004.

Timmons, Wilbert H. *John F. Finerty Reports Porfirian Mexico, 1879*. El Paso: Texas Western Press, University of Texas at El Paso, 1974.

Tuttle, Edmund B. *Three Years on the Plains: Observations of Indians, 1867–1870*. Norman: University of Oklahoma Press, 2002.

Wagner, David E. *Powder River Odyssey: Nelson Cole's Western Campaign of 1865, The Journals of Lyman G. Bennett and Other Eyewitness Accounts*. Norman, Okla.: Arthur H. Clark Company, 2009.

Walsh, Justin E. *To Print the News and Raise Hell: A Biography of Wilbur F. Storey*. Chapel Hill: University of North Carolina Press, 1968.

Wilkie, Franc B. *Personal Reminiscences of Thirty-five Years of Journalism*. Chicago: F. J. Schulte & Company, 1891.

Willert, James. *March of the Columns: A Chronicle of the 1876 Indian War, June 27–September 16*. El Segundo, Calif.: Upton and Sons, 1994.

———, ed. *The Terry Letters: The Letters of General Alfred Howe Terry to His Sisters during the Indian War of 1876*. La Mirada, Calif.: By the editor, 1980.

Index

Allen, William, 88
American Horse, 183, 184, 247n20; dies, 188, 196; meets Crook, 185; surrenders, 195
American Industrial Deputation, 7
Andrews, William, 42; and Rosebud battle, 87; and Tongue River Heights fight, 70
Andrews Creek, 173
Andrus, Edwin, 225
Apache Indians, 12
Arapaho Indians, 143, 225
Arikara scouts, 157
Arnold, Ben, 67, 105, 238n23; and Crow scouts, 74
Ash Creek, 134
Atwell, H. Wallace, 44

Bannock Indians, 124
Barry, Patrick, 24
Bear Creek, 128
Bear Spring, 37, 38
Beaver Creek, 64, 65, 89, 170, 172, 173, 191
Becker, John, 115, 118
Bell, James, 127, 242n23
Belle Fourche River, 5, 178, 189, 196, 197, 198, 203, 206, 208, 227
Big Goose Creek, 116, 122
Big Horn and Yellowstone (BH&Y) Expedition, xiii, 4, 49, 97, 128, 142, 148, 149, 161, 164, 169; medical staff of, 41; Merritt assumes command, 206; and miners, 60, 61, 67–68; morale of, 139; organization of, 41–42, 48–49, 58, 146, 243n4; and summer malaise, 100
Big Horn Expedition, 45, 51, 237n13
Big Horn Mountains, 5, 17, 43, 51, 55, 58, 89, 100, 101, 134, 146; and Fort Phil Kearny, 61; and gold prospects, 50, 66, 68, 98, 108, 110, 111, 113, 114, 125, 139; grandeur extolled, 59; and Sioux camp abandoned, 152
Big Horn River, 69, 74, 111, 113, 125, 127, 227
Big Horn Valley, 125, 148
Big Horn–Yellowstone confluence, 130
Big Nasty Creek, 247n22
Bismarck, N.Dak., 8, 143, 147
Bismarck Tribune, 4, 22
Black Hills, 23, 51, 164, 165, 176, 191, 192; and Custer exploration, 22; and Dodge exploration, 23; gold prospects of, 39, 200, 208, 211; and gold rush, x, xi; grandeur extolled, 206–7; and mail service, 17; and miners, 45, 210; and mines, 198, 215; and water issues, 208–9, 213
Black Hills Commission, 105, 240n7
Black Hills Pioneer, 201, 220
Black Hills Road, 26; Indian troubles on, 38–39, 199, 213–14
Black Tail Creek, 215
Blue Stone, 43, 236n17
Blue Teeth, 226

Bohemian Brigade, 20–21; and
  Finerty, 47; and Indian wars, 22
Bourke, John, 2, 34, 41, 53–54, 98, 204,
  223; and Crook, 110; and Finerty, 11,
  12, 14; and *On the Border with Crook*,
  1; and Rosebud battle, 85, 95; and
  Slim Buttes battle, 194
Box Elder Creek, 204, 220
Bozeman, Mont., 17
Bozeman Trail, 22, 45, 46, 50
Bridger Trail, 65
Brown, Dick, 201
Brown, Frederick, 61
Browne, Junius, xviii, 21, 47
Bubb, John, 149, 178, 181, 189, 197
Buffalo Gap, 200, 223
Burke, Daniel, 128, 182, 195
Burrowes, Samuel, 23
Burt, Andrew, 42, 204, 223; and Crow
  scouts, 74; and Slim Buttes battle,
  195; and Tongue River Heights
  fight, 72

Cabin Creek, 171, 191
Cain, Avery, 94
Camp Cloud Peak, 100, 103, 104, 110,
  116, 122, 125, 127, 128, 129, 131. *See also*
  Goose Creek camp
Camp Hancock, 143
Camp Robinson, 17, 26, 28, 197, 200,
  204, 241n14, 250n18
Canadian Pacific Railroad, 11
Canby, Edward, 22
Captain St. John's party, 56
Carpenter, William, 42, 110
Carr, Eugene, 105, 145, 146, 150, 243n4;
  and Cody, 108; and Finerty, 12, 14;
  and Slim Buttes battle, 186
Carr, John, 43
Carrington, Henry, 61, 62, 63
Carrington, Margaret, 63–64
Castle Creek, 28, 221, 222
Castleton, 221
Central City, Colo., 201, 219

Chambers, Alexander, 48, 62, 124,
  138, 146, 204, 223, 239n10; and
  astonishing infantry, 150, 159, 161;
  and Rosebud wounded, 97; and
  Slim Buttes battle, 186, 195
Chase, George, 42, 189, 197, 239n12;
  and Rosebud battle, 99
Cheyenne, Wyo., x, 34, 35, 37, 16, 206,
  216; and Black Hills gold rush,
  25–26, 30, 32–33; and Black Hills
  prospectors, 28, 200; and Finerty,
  xi, 25–26; and Indian raiding, 28;
  and telegraph, 16
Cheyenne Indians, 126, 144, 150.
  See also Northern Cheyenne Indians
Cheyenne River, 128, 204, 223, 224
Chicago, 23, 24, 201
Chicago Evening Post, 3
Chicago Inter-Ocean, 3, 22–23
Chicago Press Club, 13
Chicago Republican, 3, 21–22
Chicago Times, 3, 14, 83; and Civil
  War, 3, 20; and Diehl, 240n4; and
  Finerty, ix, x, 1, 2, 4; and Lincoln,
  3; and London bureau, 4; and Sioux
  war, 4, 16; and telegraph tolls,
  3–4; telegrams vs. letters, xiv; and
  Wilkie, 4
Chicago Tribune, 3, 233n22
Chugwater Creek, 26, 36, 37
Chugwater Valley, 37, 38, 41
Citizen, The, 13
Civil War, and battlefield journalism,
  19–20
Clark, Charlie, 34, 235n8
Clark, William, 204, 223; in
  Deadwood, 220; and Slim Buttes
  battle, 182, 194
Clay Ridge Creek, 179, 189
Clear Creek, 47, 60, 68
Cloud Peak, 58, 111
Cloutier, George, 196
Cody, William F., 108, 145; and Jack
  Crawford, 154; and Crook, 156, 170;

Index

and Grouard, 150; and Terry, 147, 155–56; and White, 194
Cole, Nelson, 159, 245n20
Collins, John, 72
Conner Campaign, 159
Cosgrove, Tom, 76, 78, 93
Crawford, Emmett, 42, 44, 48, 55, 178, 180; and Slim Buttes battle, 181, 193
Crawford, Jack, 143, 246n4; and Slim Buttes battle, 180; as Slim Buttes courier, 189
Crazy Horse, 29, 30, 34, 43, 197, 207, 220; and agency Indians, 69; and Black Hills, 205; and Grouard, 73; and Powder River battle, 107; and Slim Buttes battle, 185, 186, 188, 195
Crazy Woman's Creek (Fork), 48, 53, 58, 68, 78, 114
Crimean War, and battlefield journalism, 19
Crook, George, xi, xii, 1, 4, 29, 33, 41, 43, 53, 58, 80, 96, 115–16, 136, 144, 151, 154, 173, 174, 179, 191, 198, 205, 223, 224–25; and American Horse, 185, 195; assassination attempt, 28–29, 34; and BH&Y Expedition, 48, 50, 99, 105, 206; and Big Horn Expedition, 30–31, 45; and Black Hills, 176–77, 207, 221; and councils of war, 76–77, 78–79; in Deadwood, 201, 202, 203, 209, 210, 217; and Fifth Cavalry, 81, 139; and Finerty, 31–32, 162, 166; and Goose Creek camp, 69, 72; as "Gray Fox," 66; and Grouard, 73; and hunting forays, 62, 110, 112, 114, 123, 125; and Indian scouts, 28, 45, 57, 92; and Merritt, 140, 145, 149, 186; and Mills, 189, 192, 194; personal qualities of, 31, 66, 170–71, 174; and Powder River battle, 107, 235n6; and Prairie Dog Creek route, 46, 236n1; and Rosebud battle, 82, 83, 85, 87, 93, 94, 98, 100–101, 140, 165; and Sheridan, 197, 200, 202, 204, 206; and Sitting Bull, 85, 92, 137, 138, 142–43, 152; and Slim Buttes battle, 10, 165, 182, 183; and Starvation March, 164, 190; and summer campaign, 89, 99, 143, 145; and summer malaise, 100, 148; and Terry, 124, 129, 130, 131, 136, 137, 147, 157, 162; and Tongue River Heights fight, 70; and Wasson, 22; and winter campaign, 205, 226
Crook City, S.Dak., 189, 190, 197, 198, 200, 206, 209, 219; and Crook, 202, 207; described, 207–8; and Mills, 197
Crow Agency, 46, 57
Crow Indians, 44, 55, 66, 69, 73, 78, 84, 90, 156, 157, 160; and Burt, 74; and Crook, 17, 45, 48, 57, 75, 246n4; depart from Crook, 89, 97; depart from Crook again, 170; and Rosebud battle, 85, 87, 96, 97; and Sioux, 76–77, 78, 135; and Terry, 130, 134, 146
Curtis, William, 22–23
Custer, George, 1, 4, 22, 26, 100, 124, 128, 134, 135, 137, 139, 142, 148, 155, 179, 194; and Crook, 138; and Hazen, 172, 246n7; and Little Big Horn disaster, 123, 127, 129, 131, 133; and newspapermen, 20
Custer City, S.Dak., 16, 29, 34, 39, 177, 200, 202, 204, 209, 220, 222; and City Hotel, 222; and Finerty, xi; and water issues, 223
Custer City Road, 26
Custer trail, 173
cutoff route, 26, 37

Davenport, Reuben, 83, 204, 231n8, 239n2, 241n10; Big Horns, exploration of, 112; and Black Hills, 23; criticizes Crook, 137, 166; and Rosebud battle, 21, 166; and Royall, 82, 166; and Slim Buttes battle, 166, 181

Dawson, Andrew, xi, 202, 206, 210; and Finerty interview, 208–9
Deadwood, S.Dak., x, 16, 164, 177, 190, 191, 192, 200, 201, 202, 205, 206, 219, 221, 223; bathhouse in, 211; citizens characterized, 210; and Crook, 202, 203, 210; described, 216; and Finerty, xi, 28; gaming in, 218; and gold prospects, 204, 218–19; and Grand Central Hotel, 202, 210; named, 211; and variety performers, 220; and women, 218
Deadwood Creek, 28; gold yields from, 209; placer mining on, 212; and Wheeler Brothers, 215, 249n11
Dear, John, 225
Department of Dakota, 165
Department of the Platte, 4, 165
Dewees, Thomas, 42, 68, 122
Diaz, Porfirio, 7, 10
Diehl, Charles, 5, 232n8, 240n4
Division of the Missouri, 144
Dodge, Richard, 23
Donaldson, Aris, 22

Egan, James, 29, 204, 222; and Egan's grays, 224; remounts Crook party, 205, 223
Eighteenth Infantry, 56, 63
Elmira Military Depot, 3
Evans, Andrew, 33, 37, 42, 43, 99, 138; characterized, 48; and Rosebud battle, 94
Evans, William, 242n23

Farnum, Ethan, 202, 210
Far West (steamboat), 161
Feather Head, 75, 78
Fenian Brotherhood, 2–3, 220–21, 249n15; and Finerty, 23
Fetterman, William, 61, 63, 64, 225
Fifth Cavalry, 15, 69, 105, 128, 129, 139, 198, 205; and BH&Y Expedition, 145, 146, 150, 159, 243n4; and Carr, 12; chases Cheyennes, 140, 142, 150; at Fort Laramie, 81; at Red Cloud Agency, 225; and Slim Buttes battle, 179, 186–87, 188, 194, 195, 196; and Slim Buttes casualties, 182, 194, 196; and Thaddeus Stanton, 244n7
Finerty, Catherine, xv
Finerty, John: and American Industrial Deputation, 7; and Apache campaign, 12, 18; and battlefield journalism, 19, 22; and Big Horn gold, 98; Big Horns, exploration of, 112–14, 125; and Black Hills gold, 28, 200, 201, 208–9, 216–17; Black Hills mines, exploration of, 211; and *Black Hills Pioneer*, 201, 220; and Black Hills prospectors, 200, 219–20; and Bohemian Brigade, 47; books by, 233n30; and Bourke, 12; and Browne, 21; and buffalo extermination, 101; and Canadian Indians, 18; and carbine extraction issues, xi, 102–3; characteristics of, 25; and Cheyenne, Wyo., 25–26, 30, 32, 32–33; Chicago asides, 52, 56, 108, 109–10, 153, 159, 162, 177, 211, 218, 235n7; and Chicago newspapers, 3; and Chicago Press Club, 13; and *Chicago Republican*, 21–22; and *Chicago Times*, ix, 1, 2, 12, 231n8; and *Chicago Times* letters, 45–47; and *Chicago Times* story types, 16; childhood, 2; children, xv, 5; and *The Citizen*, 13; and Civil War, 3, 21–22; classical asides, 152, 175; as congressman, 13; criticizes army, xii; Crook, interview of, 162, 176–77, 198; Crook, meeting of, 30–32; and Crook's dilemma, 176–77; and Crook's third campaign, 202; and Custer, 4; and Davenport, 23; Dawson, interview of, 208–9; and Deadwood, 28, 201; death of, 23; Diaz, interview of, 7, 10; and Diehl, 5;

education of, 2; 1877 railroad strike, reporting of, 6; eulogizes the dead, 47, 60–61; and Fort Laramie, 26; funeral of, 23; geographical asides, 73, 111, 125, 131, 154; and Grouard, 102; headline news, xi; and Henry, 11; historical asides, 30, 36, 52, 64, 65, 75, 88, 90, 104, 132, 140, 157, 158, 159, 168, 173–74, 174–75, 187, 189, 191–92, 220–21, 235n6; horseflesh, savoring of, 165, 189–90; hunting with Crook, 110, 113–14; as Irishman, x, 13, 14; Keithly, interview of, 211–15; and Lawson, xii; lineage of, 2; literary asides, 32, 40, 57, 103, 104, 105, 148, 216, 218; and MacMillan, 23; marriages of, 12, 13; and Meagher, 14; and Merritt, 142; and "Mexican Flash Lights," 232n15; Mexico, exploration of, 6, 7; and Miles, ix, 9; and Mills, 82, 165, 166; natural world asides, 77, 103, 108, 149, 189; and Nicholls-Packard dispute, 6; and Ojibwa Indians, 11; Parenteau, interview of, 219; poetic asides, 98, 104, 133–34, 138, 140–41, 153, 154, 157, 173, 176, 221–22; and post–Sioux war assignments, 6, 8; and racial fury, 17–19, 24, 91–92, 98, 101, 105–6, 132; and railway tours, 11; and reaping the whirlwind, 107; and Rosebud battle, xii, 1, 83ff; and Rosebud reports, 82–84, 92–93; and Seventh Cavalry, 143; and Sheridan, xii, 31, 144; and Sibley scout, 15, 101–2, 116–23, 125–26; and Sioux war, 1, 4, 14; and Sitting Bull, 8, 9–10, 18, 232n22; and Slim Buttes battle, 1, 165, 180; and Storey, 4, 5, 6, 11, 12, 22, 25; and Strahorn, 7, 15; and Sutorius, xii, 237n14; and Terry, 143; and Terry's cook, 160, 245n24; and Third Cavalry, xii; and Tongue River Heights fight, 47;

and Ute campaign, 11; and Walsh, 9, 10; and *War-Path and Bivouac*, ix, 1, 2, 14; in Washington, D.C., 11–12; and Wasson, 23; and Wilkie, 5; and winter campaign, 226; on worthiness of American officers, 175; on worthiness of American soldiers, 174–76

Finerty, John, Jr., xv, 5, 23, 232n11

Finerty, Michael, 2

Finerty, Sadie, 23

Finerty, Vera, 23

Flynn, Margaret, 2

Fort Abraham Lincoln, 16, 17, 143, 164, 165, 176, 191, 192

Fort Apache, 12

Fort Buford, 9

Fort Caspar, 63

Fort C. F. Smith, 48, 55, 78, 89

Fort C. F. Smith Road, 46, 62, 116

Fort D. A. Russell, 26, 33, 35, 36, 50, 99

Fort Donelson, 21

Fort Ellis, 56

Fort Fetterman, x, xi, 30, 33, 35, 36, 40, 41, 42, 48, 49–50, 51, 69, 78, 89, 92, 105, 123, 127, 128, 129, 134, 139, 143, 144, 200, 200, 205, 241n10; and BH&Y Expedition, 41–42, 43; and couriers, 69, 84, 99, 137, 154; and cutoff route, 26, 37; and postal service, 17; and Rosebud wounded, 97; and telegraph, 16

Fort Keogh, 9

Fort Laramie, xi, 26, 29, 33, 40, 48, 81, 165, 192, 202, 204, 222, 223, 225, 226; and Black Hills gold rush, 28, 41, 200; and Indian raiding, 28, 39–40; and North Platte bridge, 26; and postal service, 17, 34; and Sheridan's visits, 197, 198, 205, 206; and telegraph, 16, 26

Fort Laramie Road, 26, 238n31

Fort Peck, 8, 9

Fort Phil Kearny, 22, 46, 50, 55, 61, 63, 64, 69, 73, 74, 123, 127, 134, 225; and cemetery, 62
Fort Reno, 43, 44, 51, 55–56, 59, 69, 73, 128, 237n13; and cemetery, 47, 56, 61; Crook dispatches Grouard, 46
Fort Reno Road, 48
Fort Robinson, 241n14. *See also* Camp Robinson
Fort Thomas, 12
Foster, James, 42, 70
Fourteenth Infantry, 128, 159
Fourth Artillery, 204, 220, 225
Fourth Cavalry, 202, 205, 225, 226
Fourth Infantry, 42, 159, 239n10; and Rosebud battle, 94; and Rosebud casualties, 88, 97; and Ute campaign, 11
Four Years in Secessia (Browne), 21
Fox, Edward, 22
French, Chase, Gardner & Co., 215
French Creek, 28
Frenchman's Creek, 9
Furey, John, 41, 49, 77, 80, 84, 97, 149, 150, 239n10

Garrettson, Fannie, 201
Gibbon, John, 59, 77, 80, 99, 124, 127, 128, 159, 174
Glass, Edward, 181, 194
Glendive Creek, 172
Glover, Ridgeway, 22
Golden Gate, 213
Good Heart, 75, 78
Goose Creek, 14, 46, 62, 64, 72, 74, 84, 111, 137, 138, 142, 145, 147, 148, 162, 200; fishing on, 100, 108
Goose Creek camp, xii, 17, 73, 78, 83, 88, 89, 149. *See also* Camp Cloud Peak
Grand River, 179, 192
Grand River South Fork, 247n12
Grant, Ulysses, 6, 157; and newspapermen, 20; and Peace Policy, 18

Graves, John: Big Horns, prospecting in, 114–15, 125, 241n12; as courier, 154, 244n12
Gray Bull River, 113
Great Sioux War, 1, 14; and battlefield journalism, 19; and *Chicago Times*, xiii; and weapons issue, xi
Grouard, Frank, 44, 46, 57, 69, 93, 119, 237n17; background of, 73; and Cody, 150; and Crow scouts, 73, 74, 78, 85; explores deserted Big Horn village, 145; and Rosebud Narrows, 96; and Sibley scout, 101, 115–23, 125–26, 127; and Slim Buttes battle, 180, 182–83, 189, 193
Grummond, Frances, 63–64
Grummond, George, 61, 63

Hamilton, John, 225
Harney Peak, 221
Hartsuff, Albert, 41, 223, 237n12
Hat Creek, 200, 224
Hat Creek Breaks, 26
Hazen, William, 172, 246n7
Heart River, 173, 176, 178, 191, 192, 199
Helena, Mont., 14
Hennessey, Sadie, 13
Henry, Guy, 41, 48, 52–53; and Finerty, 11; and Rosebud battle, 11, 86, 95, 96; and Ute campaign, 11; wounded at Rosebud, 87, 88, 96
Hermann, George, 179
Hill City, S.Dak., 222
Homestake Mine, 201
Hornberger, Ernest, 68
Huntley, Stanley, 233n22
Hunton, James, 28, 38, 235n12
Hunton Ranch, 26, 28, 36, 37, 41, 235n12

Indian Country, 40, 235n14
Irish Confederation, 2
Irish National Land League, 13

Index 263

Jenney, Walter, 207
Julesburg, Colo., 32

Keim, Debenneville, 22
Keithly, William, xi, 201, 217, 219,
  248n9; and Chief of the Hills mine,
  215; Finerty, interview of, 211–15
Kellogg, Mark, 4
Kelly, Richard, 136–37, 144, 242n29
Kennedy, Edward, 182, 194, 196
Kenyon, John, 2
Keogh, Myles, 181, 195
King, Charles, 15, 23
Knappen, Nathan, 22
Knight, Oliver, xv

Lake DeSmet, 62
Langrishe, Jack, 201
Laramie Peak, 51
Laramie Plains, 198
Laramie River, 26, 37, 40, 42
Lawson, Joseph, 41, 169; and Finerty,
  xii; and Tongue River Heights
  fight, 70
Lemly, Henry, 42, 99, 110, 112, 114,
  239n12
Little Big Horn battle, 4, 124, 194–95
Little Big Horn River, 101, 127, 133,
  134, 142, 143; deserted village on,
  145; headwaters of, 148; and Indian
  trail, 152; and Sibley scout, 116, 125
Little Goose Creek, 122
Little Missouri River, 145, 161, 162,
  164, 171, 176, 191, 205, 206; and
  Indian trail, 169, 173
Little Powder River, 105, 128
Lodgepole Creek, 35, 36
Lower Deadwood, 210
Luhn, Gerhard, 195

Mackenzie, Ranald, 202;
  characterized, 226
MacMillan, Thomas, 239n2, 241n10;
  and Black Hills exploration, 23

McGillycuddy, Valentine, 188
Meagher, Thomas, 14
Medicine Bow, 33, 37
Medicine Crow, 75, 78
Medicine Line, 10, 232n21
Meeker, Nathan, 11
Meinhold, Charles, 42, 50, 53, 129, 169;
  and Tierney's death, 66–67
Menamed Creek, 178, 247n12
Merritt, Wesley, 128, 129, 140, 144, 148,
  205, 206; and BH&Y Expedition,
  146, 202, 204, 206, 243n4; and
  Crook, 142, 145, 149; and Northern
  Cheyennes, 243n31; and Slim Buttes
  battle, 186; and Thaddeus Stanton,
  238n31
Metzger, Adolph, 62, 238n21
Miles, Nelson, ix, 147; and Finerty, 9;
  and Sitting Bull, 9
Miller, Joseph, 202
Mills, Anson, 42, 47, 129, 138, 151; and
  BH&Y Expedition, 48; Big Horns,
  exploration of, 110, 112–14, 125;
  and Crook City, 197; and Finerty,
  82, 166, 167; and *My Story*, 167;
  and Powder River battle, 166; and
  race for rations, 189, 190, 192; and
  Rosebud battle, 21, 83, 86–87, 95, 96,
  165, 166–67; and Slim Buttes battle,
  165, 166, 179, 180, 181, 182, 192, 193,
  194, 195; and Tongue River Heights
  fight, 70
Milner, Cyrus, 198, 248n45
Milwaukee Sentinel, 15
Missouri River, 16, 106, 107, 143
Modoc War, and battlefield
  journalism, 22
Montana City, 210
Montana miners, 56–57, 59, 60
Montana Road, 50, 55, 63
Montgomery, Robert, 188
Moore, Thomas, 41, 49, 178, 181; and
  dead mule, 182, 184
Morton, Charles, 99, 239n12

Munson, Samuel, 42, 182, 194, 195
Mushroom Creek, 10, 18
My Story (Mills), 167

National Brotherhood of St. Patrick, 2
Nawkee, 76
New York Herald, 20, 21, 22, 23, 82, 137, 166
New York Times, 20
New York Tribune, 20, 21, 23
New York World, 21, 23
Nickerson, Azor, 41, 62, 97; and Rosebud battle, 87, 96; and Ute scouts, 129
Ninety-Ninth New York Infantry, 3
Ninth Infantry, 42, 48, 72, 80, 85, 97, 128, 159, 196, 239n10
Northern Cheyenne Indians, 124; and Merritt, 140, 142, 243n31; and Red Cloud Agency, 225; and Sibley scout, 101, 126
Northern Pacific Railroad, 11, 143
North Platte River, 26, 37, 42, 43, 44, 48; and Indian Country, 40, 235n14
North Tongue River, 132, 137
North-West Mounted Police, 9
Noyes, Henry, 42, 48, 129, 138, 179; and Rosebud Narrows, 83, 96; and Slim Buttes battle, 186

O'Fallon Creek, 171, 191
Ojibwa Indians, 18
Old Crow, 75, 76, 78
Old Woman's Park, 43
Omaha, Nebr., 16, 25, 31, 180
Order of Indian Wars, 15
Otis, Elwell, 244n14
Owl Creek, 189

Parenteau, William, xi, 201, 249n14; and Finerty interview, 219
Patzki, Julius, 41
Paul, Augustus, 42, 70
Pawnee Indians, 54–55

Peace Commission, 225
Philadelphia Inquirer, and battlefield journalism, 20
Philadelphia Photographer, 22
Philadelphia Press, 22
Pine Ridge, 26
Piney Creek, 61, 64
Platte bridge, 63
Pole Creek, 35, 36
Pourier, Baptiste, 46, 57, 195, 237n17; and Crow scouts, 74; and Finerty, 101; and Sibley scout, 101, 115, 116–17, 125, 127; and Slim Buttes battle, 182–83, 194
Powder River, 44, 45, 55, 57, 58, 59, 60, 160, 144, 159, 161, 167, 169, 171, 172, 191, 198, 201, 203, 211; and Cole Expedition, 245n20; Indian trail on, 147; and Sioux, 107, 142
Powder River battle, 30–31, 235n6, 235n10; backlash from, 35, 107; wounded, 35
Powder River country, 240n7
Powder River depot, 205
Powder River Dry Fork, 52, 56
Powder River trail, 81
Powder River valley, 52, 160
Powder-Yellowstone confluence, 160, 161
Powell, William, 128, 204, 223
Power, James, 22
Prairie Dog Creek, 46, 47, 65, 150, 154; Tierney burial, 47, 237n12
Pumpkin Buttes, 51
Pumpkin Creek, 148, 159

Quaife, Milo, xv

Radin, Alice, 12
Randall, George, 41, 76, 204, 223; and Indian scouts, 80, 85; and Rosebud battle, 95; and Washakie, 150
Rapid Creek, 28
Rawlins, Wyo., 11

Index

Rawolle, William, 41, 122, 123; and Tongue River Heights fight, 72
Red Cañon, 26, 29, 200, 223
Red Cloud, 62, 225, 250n18
Red Cloud Agency, 26, 34, 35, 42, 62, 105, 144, 179, 197, 200, 204, 220, 223, 224, 225, 226, 250n18; and Crook, 106; and Indian departures, 69; and Northern Cheyennes, 142, 243n31; and Powder River battle, 28
Red Cloud Agency Road, 26
Red Cloud Buttes, 250n18
Red Dog, 226
Reese, Sylvester, 68
Reno, Marcus, 135, 156
Reynolds, Bainbridge, 42, 87
Reynolds, Joseph, 30–31, 235n10; abandons soldier, 35
Richard, Louis, 42–43, 46, 57, 74, 237n17; as courier, 84, 123; and Crow scouts, 73, 76; and deserted Big Horn village, 144
Richardson, Albert, 21
Rocky Mountain News, 15, 83
Rogers, Calbraith, 182, 194
Roman Nose, 194, 247n12
Rosebud Creek, 89, 131, 138, 147, 160, 162; and BH&Y Expedition, 151; and Sioux, 77, 142, 155; and Terry-Crook encampment, 147
Rosebud Creek battle, x, xi, xii, 11, 15, 29, 84, 85, 94, 100–101, 137, 200; carbine extraction issues, xi, 102, 136; and casualties, 87, 88; and Crook's Hill, 82, 83; and Gap, 21; and Kollmar Creek, 21, 83; munitions expended, 88, 97; and Narrows episode, 83, 85, 86, 95, 100; reports of, 16, 17, 82; Sheridan's reaction, 124; and Sitting Bull's village, 152; sprawling landscape, 82
Rosebud Narrows, 151, 244n8
Rosebud Valley: as Indian paradise, 151; and scorched prairie and woods, 154

Royall, William, 26, 33, 36, 37, 43, 44, 49, 69, 93, 138; and BH&Y Expedition, 48, 50, 58, 99, 146, 150, 243n4; and Black Hills miners, 38–39; and Cody, 155–56; and Davenport, 82, 83; and deserters, 35; and Rosebud battle, 21, 86, 94; and Sibley scout, 123; and Slim Buttes battle, 186, 194
Rufus, Valentine 119
Russell, Charles, 41
Russell, William, 157, 244n15; pioneer war reporter, 19

Sacramento Record, 22
Sage Creek, 48, 53
Saint Louis *Missouri Democrat*, 22
Saint Paul Daily Pioneer, 22
Saint Paul Daily Press, 22
San Carlos Reservation, 22
Sand Creek, 34
Sanders, James, 34, 235n9
Salt Creek, 50
Salt Lake City, 128, 201
Schuyler, Walter, 105, 204, 223; hunts with Crook, 110, 112
Schwatka, Frederick, 42, 54, 57, 178; and Slim Buttes battle, 180, 193; and Tongue River Heights fight, 70
Second Cavalry, 9, 36, 68, 129, 205; and BH&Y Expedition, 41–42, 48, 146, 150, 159, 243n8; and desertions, 35; and Egan's grays, 224; and Montana component, 156; and Rosebud battle, 87, 94, 96, 151; and Rosebud casualties, 88, 87; and Sibley scout, 102, 115, 125, 127; and Slim Buttes battle, 179, 186, 194; and Slim Buttes casualties, 182, 194; and Tongue River Heights fight, 70–71, 72
Seventh Cavalry, 123, 139, 143; and relics in deserted Big Horn village, 145; and relics in Slim Buttes village, 181; on Rosebud Creek, 156

Shaw, W. C., 34, 235n9
Sheridan, Philip, 22, 30, 69, 105, 177, 203; and Custer, 133; and Crook, 124, 142, 223; Crook, summons, 198, 200, 204, 206; and Fifth Cavalry, 140; and Finerty, 144; at Fort Laramie, 81, 197, 202; and Merritt, 142; and Rosebud battle, 93, 124; and Sioux war, xii, 131, 138
Sheridan Butte, 52
Sherman, William, 131; and newspapermen, 20; and Sioux war, 138
Shoshone scouts, 69, 74, 78, 80, 84, 90, 129, 130, 132, 145, 149, 150, 156, 157; and Crook, 17, 45–46, 75–76, 123, 127–28, 246n4; Crook, abandon, 89, 111; Crook, abandon again, 170, 246n4; and deserted Big Horn village, 145; and Rosebud battle, 85, 87, 94, 95; and Rosebud casualties, 88, 97; and Sioux, 146; and Terry's column, 155
Sibley, Caleb, 116, 126, 241n13
Sibley, Frederick, 41, 204, 223, 225; escorts Crook, 206
Sibley scout, x xii, 1, 6, 15, 101, 102, 115–23, 125–26, 127, 130, 145
Sidney, Nebr., 17, 36
Silver City *Owyhee Avalanche*, 22
Sioux Indians: and Big Horn Mountains, 111; and buffalo, 135, 144; burn countryside, 124, 145; and Canada, 148; Chugwater Valley, raid of, 38; and Crook, 45; Crook's camp, harassment of, 123, 128; dread infantry, 136; and Fort Laramie Treaty, 48, 55; harass Gibbon, 77; and hunting grounds, 107; and Red Cloud Agency, 225; and reservation, 107; and Rosebud battle, 85, 106, 151; and Rosebud casualties, 87, 97, 97; on Rosebud Creek, 77, 80; and scorched prairie, 146, 147, 151, 153–54; and Sibley scout, 101, 126; and Slim Buttes battle, 165, 180–81, 193; and Slim Buttes casualties, 196; and trail after Little Big Horn battle, 130, 147, 149, 152, 191
Sitting Bull, 8, 30, 43, 52, 85, 99, 105, 106, 129, 130, 146, 148, 197, 202, 207, 225; and buffalo, 101, 134; in Canada, 9; Crook, stymying of, 100, 138, 142–43; and Crows, 69; and Finerty, 18; and Gibbon, 142; and Metis traders, 206; and Rosebud battle, 85, 86, 87, 95, 96, 137; and scorched earth, 132; and Sibley scout, 101, 117, 125–26; and Sioux war, 138; Terry and Crook, eluding of, 142, 157, 162; trail of, 142, 145, 161
Sitting Bull of the South, 226
Sixth Cavalry, 12
Slim Buttes, 185–86, 189, 192
Slim Buttes battle, x, xi, 1, 6, 10, 12, 15, 21, 165, 179, 199, 200, 203; afternoon fight, 186, 195; and burials, 185; evening fight, 186–87, 195–96; Indian casualties, 18, 183–84, 188, 196; rearguard fight, 188, 196; reports of, 16; and Sioux captives, 194, 197; soldier casualties, 188, 196, 198; and two hundred dogs, 193
Snowden, Clinton, 4
Smith, Frank, 204, 220
Snake Indians. *See* Shoshone scouts
South Cheyenne River, 51, 66
Spearfish Creek, 208
Spotted Tail, 107, 123, 225–26
Spotted Tail Agency, 26, 28, 35, 69, 179, 194
Spring Creek, 28
Springfield breech-loaders, 102–3, 135–36
Stanley, Charles, ix, 239n2, 241n10
Stanley, Henry, 22

Index

Stanton, Thaddeus, 81, 150, 191, 223, 244n7
Stanton, William, 41, 238n31, 244n7
Starvation March, 15, 164, 198
Stevenson, John, 184, 194, 196
Stewart, Benjamin, 127, 242n23
Storey, Wilbur, xviii, 3, 6, 11, 12, 15, 24; on Crook, 4; and Custer, 4; and Diehl, 5; and epigrammatic headlines, xiv; and Finerty, 4, 5, 11, 12, 16, 22, 25, 83; and Indians, 18, 234n39; and Kellogg, 4; and racial attitudes, 18, 234n39; and telegraph, 3–4, 16, 83; and wartime reporting, 4, 5, 20; and Wilkie, 5
Strahorn, Carrie, 15–16
Strahorn, Robert, 204, 239n2, 241n10; and Finerty, 7, 15; and Rosebud battle, 83; and Slim Buttes battle, 181
Sutorius, Alexander, 42, 54; and Finerty, xii, 237n14; and Rosebud battle, 86, 95; and Tongue River Heights fight, 70
Sully, Alfred, 173
Sully trail, 172
Sumner, Samuel, 145, 188; and Slim Buttes rearguard fight, 196
Sweetwater Valley, 69, 74

Terry, Alfred, 4, 34, 80, 99, 105, 129, 131, 148, 191, 203; commands combined force, 157, 162; cook episode, 160, 245n24; and Crook, 124, 127, 130, 134, 136, 144, 147, 156, 157, 169; and Crow scouts, 146; and Dakota column, 143, 156; on Rosebud Creek, 156; and supply operations, 147, 167, 174
Third Cavalry, xi, 36, 44, 129, 162, 197, 205; and BH&Y Expedition, 41–42, 48, 146, 150, 159, 243n4; and desertions, 35; and Finerty, xii, 11; and race for rations, 178, 192; and Rosebud battle, 83, 86, 87, 94, 95–96, 151; and Rosebud casualties, 88, 97; and Royall, 166; and Slim Buttes battle, 165, 166, 186–87, 194, 195; and Slim Buttes casualties, 184, 194; and Tierney's death, 66; and Tongue River Heights casualties, 72; and Ute campaign, 11
Thornburgh, Thomas, 11
Tierney, Francis, 47, 53, 237n12; burial, 66–67
Times, The (London), 19
Timmons, Wilbert, xv
Tobey, Thomas, 128
Tongue River, 46, 54, 57, 65, 66, 69, 71, 72, 80, 90, 111, 114, 118, 120, 121, 129, 131, 134, 144, 146, 148, 150, 151, 159, 161; buffalo on, 52; and Crow scout episode, 74; Indian trail on, 147, 155, 158; and Sioux, 107, 134, 128; and Tierney burial, 47
Tongue River Cañon, 150–51, 155
Tongue River Heights fight, x, 15, 29, 47, 69–72, 150; casualties, 72
Tony Pastor's Opera Troupe, 57
Tupper, Tullius, 12
Twenty-Second Infantry, 156, 244n14

Union Pacific Railroad, 32
Upham, John, 145, 198
Utah Clair, 76
Ute Indians, 11, 124, 128, 129
Ute John, 170, 185, 246n5; and Slim Buttes battle, 184

Van Vliet, Frederick, 42, 44, 48, 55, 56, 57, 129; and Rosebud battle, 86, 95
Vicksburg, Miss., 21
Von Luettwtiz, Adolphus, 42, 162, 178; background of, 180–81; leg amputated, 196; wounded at Slim Buttes, 180, 193, 194
Vroom, Peter, 42, 50, 53; and Rosebud battle, 87, 96

Walsh, James, 9, 10
Warbonnet Creek skirmish, 140, 243n21
Warfield, John, 72
War-Path and Bivouac, ix, x, xii, xiii, 1, 4, 14, 19, 231n1; and Merritt, 142; and reprint editions, xv; and Rosebud, 84
Washakie, 76, 150, 241n17; joins Crook, 123, 127
Wasson, Joe, 114, 204, 239n2, 241n10; and Crook, 22; explores Big Horns, 112
Waukee, 80
Wells, Elijah, 41, 123
Wentworth, John, 33, 235n7
Wenzel, John, 181, 184, 194
Wesha, 76, 80
Wheeler Brothers, 215, 249n11
White, Charlie, 182, 184–85, 194
White Antelope, 118, 120, 126, 241n14
Whitehead, James, 215, 216
White River, 28
Whitewood Creek, 15, 28, 56, 202, 203, 206, 208, 211; placer mining on, 209, 212
Whitewood Creek Hydraulic Mining Co., 215
Wilkie, Franc, 4, 5
Willow Creek, 189, 198
Wind River, 51, 52, 113, 125
Wind River Country, 45
Wind River valley, 76, 78, 111, 115, 144
Wing, Henry, 21
Wood Mountain, 10, 18
Wyant, William, 67–68

Yarnell, Nelson, 76
Yellowstone River, 5, 43, 77, 80, 90, 106, 113, 142, 144, 146, 155, 156, 159, 162, 170, 200; buffalo on, 52; and Sioux, 107, 149, 152; and steamboats, 143; and Terry, 127, 129; troop movements on, 99, 124
Young Ireland Movement, 2
Young Man Afraid of His Horses, 226

Also by Paul L. Hedren

First Scalp for Custer: The Skirmish at Warbonnet Creek, July 17, 1876 (Glendale, Calif., 1980; revised, Lincoln, Nebr., 2005)

With Crook in the Black Hills: Stanley J. Morrow's 1876 Photographic Legacy (Boulder, Colo., 1985)

Fort Laramie in 1876: Chronicle of a Frontier Post at War (Lincoln, Nebr., 1988); reprinted as *Fort Laramie and the Great Sioux War* (Norman, Okla., 1998)

(ed.) *The Great Sioux War, 1876–77: The Best from* Montana The Magazine of Western History (Helena, Mont., 1991)

(ed.) *Campaigning with King: Charles King, Chronicler of the Old Army* (Lincoln, Nebr., 1991)

Traveler's Guide to the Great Sioux War (Helena, Mont., 1996; revised, 2008)

We Trailed the Sioux: Enlisted Men Speak on Custer, Crook, and the Great Sioux War (Mechanicsburg, Penn., 2003)

Great Sioux War Orders of Battle: How the United States Army Waged War on the Northern Plains, 1876–1877 (Norman, Okla., 2011)

After Custer: Loss and Transformation in Sioux Country (Norman, Okla., 2011)

(ed.) *Ho! For the Black Hills: Captain Jack Crawford Reports the Black Hills Gold Rush and Great Sioux* War (Pierre, S. Dak., 2012)

Powder River: Disastrous Opening of the Great Sioux War (Norman, Okla., 2016)

Rosebud, June 17, 1876: Prelude to the Little Big Horn (Norman, Okla., 2019)

www.ingramcontent.com/pod-product-compliance
Lightning Source LLC
Chambersburg PA
CBHW031431160426
43195CB00010BB/692